MATH
By All Means®

AREA AND PERIMETER
Grades 5–6

by Cheryl Rectanus

A MARILYN BURNS REPLACEMENT UNIT

MATH SOLUTIONS PUBLICATIONS

Editorial direction: Toby Gordon
Copyediting and production coordination: Alan Huisman
Book design: Aileen Friedman
Typesetting, page makeup, and illustrations: David Healy, First Image
Cover and border designs: Jenny Greenleaf
Author photo: Mary Price

Marilyn Burns Education Associates is dedicated to improving mathematics education. For information about Math Solutions courses, resource materials, and other services, write or call:

Marilyn Burns Education Associates
150 Gate 5 Road, Suite 101
Sausalito, CA 94965
Telephone (415) 332-4181
Fax (415) 331-1931

The "blob" assessments are adapted from "Use a Cake Pan and Leave Out the Pi" (*Arithmetic Teacher,* May 1986, pp. 12-16), by Walter Szetela and Douglas T. Owens.

Printed in the United States of America
02 01 00 99 98   2 3 4 5 6 7 8 9

ISBN 0-941355-18-7

This book is printed on recycled paper.

A MESSAGE FROM MARILYN BURNS

This book is part of a larger effort by Marilyn Burns Education Associates to publish teacher resources and provide inservice courses and workshops. In 1984, we began offering **Math Solutions** five-day courses and one-day workshops nationwide, now attended by more than 60,000 teachers and administrators in 34 states. Our goal, then and now, has been to help teachers improve how they teach mathematics to students in kindergarten through grade 8. Since 1987, we have also published books as a way to support and extend the experiences provided at our courses and workshops.

Following are brief descriptions of the various **Math Solutions** courses, workshops, and publications currently available. Books may be obtained through educational catalogs or at your local teacher bookstore. For further information about inservice programs and to learn how MBEA works in partnership with school districts, regional consortia, and state education departments to improve mathematics instruction, please call us at **(800) 868-9092.** Or visit our Web site: **http://www.mathsolutions.com**

MATH SOLUTIONS INSERVICE COURSES AND WORKSHOPS

Five-Day Summer Courses

Teachers are the key to improving classroom mathematics instruction. Math Solutions intensive, week-long staff development courses help teachers develop new classroom outlooks and skills.

- **Math Solutions, Level 1 (K–8)** presents practical and proven ways to help teachers implement the NCTM standards.

- **Math Solutions, Level 2 (K–8)** is a continuation of Level 1 with an emphasis on making assessment and student writing integral to math instruction.

- **Math Solutions, Level 3 (K–8)** provides an extended look at the challenges of teaching mathematics. Participants learn how to organize instruction into curriculum units. Two versions are available:

  Learning More Mathematics. This course offers an in-depth investigation of the mathematics in the lessons teachers teach to their students.

  Preparing Teacher Leaders. This course is for school districts that want to increase their capacity to support the improvement of classroom math teaching.

One-Day Workshops

These workshops build teachers' interest in improving their mathematics teaching and provide follow-up support for teachers who have attended inservice programs. They are tailored specifically to the particular needs of schools and districts.

- **Introducing Problem Solving**
  The Way to Math Solutions (K–8)
  Math for Middle School (Grades 6–8)
  Developing Number Sense (Grades 3–8)

- **Integrating Math and Language Arts**
  Math and Literature (K–3, 4–6, or K–6)
  Writing in Math Class (Grades 2–8)

- **Teaching with Manipulative Materials**
  For any materials and any K–6 grade range

- **Teaching with Replacement Units**
  Money (Grades 1–2)
  Place Value (Grades 1–2)
  Multiplication (Grades 2–4)
  Division (Grades 3–4)
  Geometry (Grades 1–2, 3–4, or 1–4)
  Probability (Grades 1–2, 3–5, or 1–5)

- **Working with District Math Teams**
  Preparing Teacher Leaders (K–8)
  Math Solutions for School-Based Change (K–8)
  Conference for Administrators (K–8)

(over, please)

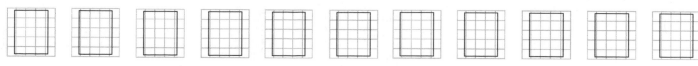

MATH SOLUTIONS PUBLICATIONS

General Interest

Here are three excellent ways for educators to communicate with parents about math education issues.

- **Getting Your Math Message Out to Parents: A K–6 Resource** by Nancy Litton
- **Math: Facing an American Phobia** by Marilyn Burns
- **Mathematics: What Are You Teaching My Child?**, a videotape with Marilyn Burns

Resource Books for Problem Solving

These books bring to teachers a vision of teaching mathematics through problem solving. They set the standard for professional teaching resources by stimulating, inspiring, and supporting teachers to translate the NCTM standards into actual classroom instruction.

- **About Teaching Mathematics** by Marilyn Burns
- **50 Problem-Solving Lessons: The Best from 10 Years of Math Solutions Newsletters** by Marilyn Burns
- **A Collection of Math Lessons from Grades 1 through 3** by Marilyn Burns and Bonnie Tank
- **A Collection of Math Lessons from Grades 3 through 6** by Marilyn Burns
- **A Collection of Math Lessons from Grades 6 through 8** by Marilyn Burns and Cathy Humphreys

Linking Mathematics and Language Arts

The first book in the list below explains why students should write in math class, describes different types of writing assignments, and offers teaching tips and suggestions. The other three books show teachers how to use children's literature to introduce important math ideas to elementary students.

- **Writing in Math Class: A Resource for Grades 2–8** by Marilyn Burns
- **Math and Literature (K–3), Book One** by Marilyn Burns
- **Math and Literature (K–3), Book Two** by Stephanie Sheffield
- **Math and Literature (Grades 4–6)** by Rusty Bresser

Math Replacement Units

Designed as an alternative to textbook instruction, each *Math By All Means* Replacement Unit presents a cohesive plan for five to six weeks of classroom instruction. The units focus on thinking and reasoning, incorporate the use of manipulative materials, and provide opportunities for students to communicate about their learning.

- **Math By All Means: Money, Grades 1–2** by Jane Crawford
- **Math By All Means: Place Value, Grades 1–2** by Marilyn Burns
- **Math By All Means: Geometry, Grades 1–2** by Chris Confer
- **Math By All Means: Probability, Grades 1–2** by Bonnie Tank
- **Math By All Means: Multiplication, Grade 3** by Marilyn Burns
- **Math By All Means: Division, Grades 3–4** by Susan Ohanian and Marilyn Burns
- **Math By All Means: Geometry, Grades 3–4** by Cheryl Rectanus
- **Math By All Means: Probability, Grades 3–4** by Marilyn Burns
- **Math By All Means: Area and Perimeter, Grades 5–6** by Cheryl Rectanus

Books for Children

For more than 20 years, I've brought my math message directly to children, beginning with *The I Hate Mathematics! Book,* first published in 1974. In 1994, I launched the Marilyn Burns Brainy Day Books series.

- **Amanda Bean's Amazing Dream** by Cindy Neuschwander
- **Spaghetti and Meatballs for All!** by Marilyn Burns
- **The Greedy Triangle** by Marilyn Burns
- **The King's Commissioners** by Aileen Friedman
- **A Cloak for the Dreamer** by Aileen Friedman
- **The $1.00 Word Riddle Book** by Marilyn Burns
- **The I Hate Mathematics! Book** by Marilyn Burns
- **The Book of Think** by Marilyn Burns
- **Math for Smarty Pants** by Marilyn Burns

PREFACE

In a workshop I attended more than 25 years ago, I remember doing an investigation like the *Foot Stuff* lesson in this unit. I had traced my foot on squared paper and figured out its area. Then I had carefully placed a string around the outline of my foot and cut it so it was the same length as the perimeter of my foot. I taped the string into a square on the squared paper and figured out its area. Whoops, I thought, something is wrong. The area of the square was much more than the area of my foot.

I didn't expect the area measurements of the foot and the square to be exactly the same, since I knew that measurement is never exact. But I was surprised by the discrepancy. If two shapes have the same perimeter, it seemed to me that their areas should be the same, too. I don't know how I had come to construct this idea for myself, but I remember that most of the others in the workshop had the same notion. They also had similar discrepancies in their area measures. Although we all knew about area and perimeter and were familiar with formulas for figuring them on common shapes, none of us had had any experience comparing the areas and perimeters of shapes.

I rechecked my measurements with care, but I couldn't deny the evidence. I had to face the concrete reality that my foot tracing and string squares had different areas. This experience threw me into what Piaget calls *disequilibrium*, the state that results when something you think you are sure about in the world is all at once proved to be false. Piaget also said that the greatest potential for learning exists when we're in the state of disequilibrium, because we naturally seek to restore order when we're in mental chaos.

So, I said to myself, this means that shapes with the same perimeters don't necessarily have to have the same areas. But I still didn't understand why the two areas were different. And I wondered if different shapes with the same perimeter *could* have the same area.

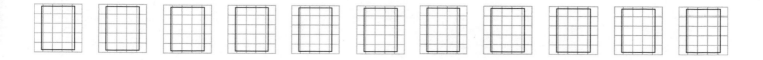

The very heart of learning is the act of going from disequilibrium to equilibrium, and that calls for reconsidering and reorganizing what we thought in order to come to new understanding. Piaget coined a name for this process: *equilibration*. Experiences with physical objects and interaction with others are two ingredients that help equilibration to occur. (For young children, a third ingredient, additional maturation, might also be necessary before they can reorganize their mental constructions and learn something new.)

I did a good deal more fiddling around with my perimeter string and a lot of talking with the other participants. I found that if I shaped my string into a rectangle that was closer to the shape of my foot, then the area of the rectangle was closer to the area of my foot. I checked with others, and they had found the same to be true. I also found that when I shaped the string into a very skinny rectangle, even though the rectangle was longer than either the square or the footlike rectangle, its area decreased. I saw that I could make the rectangle very, very skinny, with hardly any space inside. Someone suggested that doing this was like squeezing the area right out of the rectangle so that there was just a sliver of space. After hearing that, I realized that as I slowly widened the rectangle again, the space inside would grow again. Aha! Of course shapes with the same perimeter can have different areas! After all, my foot isn't shaped like a square, so why should it have the same area as a square?

The "aha" of a moment, however, doesn't guarantee complete understanding. I felt as if my understanding were riding on the tip of a tuning fork that had just been twanged and was still vibrating, not yet quieted. I needed more time before I became settled, intellectually, before my learning was cemented and my understanding was firm. I finally came to a state of understanding after additional experiences about how the area and perimeter of shapes relate, both concrete experiences with physical materials and social experiences in which I talked with others about these ideas.

My learning about all of this spanned quite a bit of time, considering that I probably first encountered ideas about area and perimeter when I was in fifth grade or so. But I no longer expect that two shapes with the same perimeter will have the same area. I now have well-developed mathematical intuition about the areas of shapes with different perimeters and the perimeters of shapes with different areas. My understanding is no longer fragile, but quite robust, and I'm a better teacher for it. When teaching students about these ideas, I have the mathematical intuition and resources to understand what children are thinking. And I have the teaching experience to push and prod them to construct understanding for themselves.

In this book, Cheryl Rectanus shares her experience teaching a unit about area and perimeter that was aimed at helping students look at the two ideas in relationship to each other. The unit not only is a carefully planned teaching guide, it also provides the opportunity for teachers to think more about these ideas.

I know that we can't teach well what we don't understand and, therefore, that it's important that we all increase our own mathematical understanding. I also know that one of the wonderful things about teaching is that we have many opportunities to learn along with, and from, our students. All we need is curiosity, a bit of mathematical courage, and a unit like this. Enjoy.

Marilyn Burns
July 1997

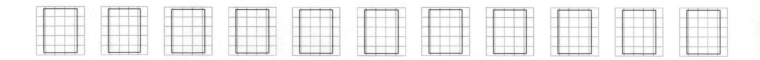

Acknowledgments

I want first to say thank you to the students at Irvington School in Portland, Oregon. I deeply appreciate their enthusiasm, persistence, and willingness to engage with the ideas in this unit.

I'm grateful as well to the parents, colleagues, and administrators with whom I've worked, for sharing their insights and experiences.

While I taught the unit, Iphigenia Johnson took copious notes as part of her teacher education program at Lewis and Clark College in Portland. I appreciate Jenny's thoughtful questions, observations, and continued friendship.

Marilyn Burns provided invaluable suggestions and encouragement as she pushed me for clarity in my writing. Toby Gordon and Alan Huisman contributed skillful editorial help and guidance.

Barbara and Karl Liechty encouraged me as only parents can.

Most of all, I'm grateful to Fred Rectanus, for sustaining me with his love and support.

CONTENTS

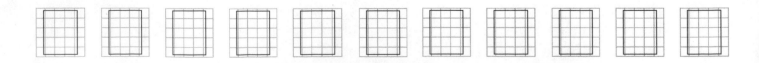

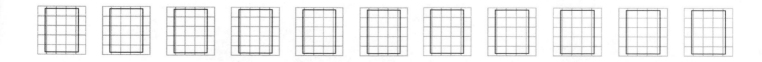

INTRODUCTION

Area and perimeter are standard topics in fifth- and sixth-grade math instruction. Traditionally, students learn what each measurement is, learn formulas for finding the area and perimeter of certain shapes, and practice finding areas and perimeters.

This unit is a classroom-tested plan that offers a broader view. In addition to introducing the ideas of area and perimeter and ways to measure them, the unit also helps children think about the area and perimeter of irregular shapes and encourages them to look at area and perimeter in relationship to each other.

While area and perimeter are its focus, the unit also integrates ideas from several other areas of the mathematics curriculum. First, the activities draw heavily on measurement and geometry, natural tie-ins. In addition, estimating and measuring areas and perimeters provide a context for whole-number computation and for thinking about fractions, decimals, and ratio and proportion. Looking for patterns and applying logical reasoning are also recurrent themes.

Goals for Area and Perimeter Instruction

Several important ideas about area and perimeter emerge from the activities in this unit:

1. **The perimeter of a shape is the total length of its boundary.** Perimeter is measured in units of length. We use a variety of units of length to measure how long things are, picking units that are appropriate to what we are measuring—ribbon in inches or yards, the distance between cities in miles or kilometers, and so on. Length is a one-dimensional measure; common to all measurements of length is that they tell how far something stretches.

2. **The area of a shape is how much surface it takes up.** When measuring how much surface a shape takes up, we need to measure space in two dimensions, not just length. We typically measure area in square units, with one square unit being the region inside a square with sides each one unit of length. As with measuring length, we choose units for measuring area that are appropriate to the situation—square inches for ceramic tile, square feet for countertops, square yards for carpet, acres for farmland, square miles for large land regions, and so on.

It's easy to see how squares and rectangles can be divided into square units to determine their areas. However, other shapes—triangles, circles, octagons, and irregular shapes—are not so easily divided into square units. Curves and corners make for bits and pieces of squares. However, using square units provides a consistent way to talk about the areas of all shapes.

3. **Shapes with the same-length perimeter can have different areas.** One way to think about this idea is to imagine a loop made from a 1-foot-long piece of string. Also imagine holding the loop in between your thumbs and forefingers, stretching the loop into a four-sided figure.

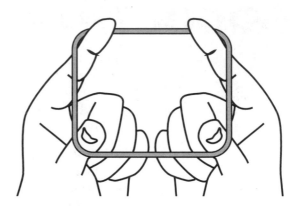

When your fingers are about the same distance apart, the shape will resemble a square.

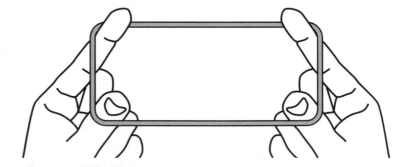

As you slide each forefinger and thumb closer together, however, the shape changes into a longer and thinner rectangle. As you slide your fingers to make the shape longer and thinner, you are decreasing its area; it's as if you are squeezing the area out of the shape.

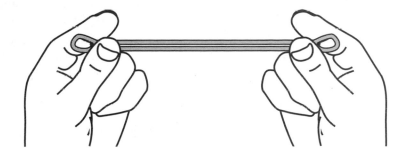

When the string no longer looks like a loop, but more like a doubled length of string, there's no area inside. This shows that when a perimeter remains constant, the area of shapes with that length perimeter can increase and decrease. (You might make a loop of string and demonstrate this for yourself. There's no substitute for firsthand learning.) For rectangles with the same perimeter, the closer the rectangle is to a square, the larger its area. The shape that has the maximum area for any given perimeter is the circle.

4. **Shapes with the same area can have different-length perimeters.** This is the flip side of the previous idea. The unit helps students think about this idea in several ways, one being in the context of seating people at rectangular banquet tables. If you have six square tables to arrange into one larger rectangular table, there are two possible rectangles to build—a 1-by-6 table or a 2-by-3 table.

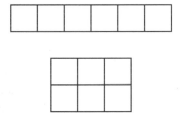

If you think about seating people around these tables, the longer, skinnier table seats more people, because its perimeter is longer. If one person is allotted a side of each smaller square table, the 1-by-6 table seats 14 people, six on each side and one at each end. The 2-by-3 table, however, seats only 10 people, three on each longer side and two at each shorter side.

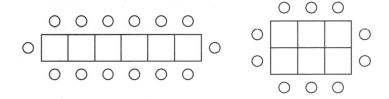

Both tables have the same area of 6 square units, but their perimeters are different lengths. For rectangles with the same area, the closer the rectangle is to a square, the shorter its perimeter. The shape that has the shortest perimeter for a given area is the circle.

5. **There are different ways to measure the area and perimeter of shapes.** Methods for measuring area and perimeter include using measurement tools such as rulers, counting squares inside shapes, and applying formulas. Irregular shapes typically call for different ways to measure than do regular shapes.

6. **Measurement is never exact.** All measurements are approximations. Some tools and methods are more accurate than others. The degree of accuracy necessary for any measurement depends on its purpose.

7. **Area and perimeter have a variety of real-life applications.** Knowing about area and perimeter and how to find and manipulate them is necessary in the construction trades, architecture, painting, carpet laying, roofing, farming, fence building, sewing, wrapping packages, docking ships, and parking airplanes, to name just a few occupations and activities.

What's in the Unit?

In this five-week unit, fifth- and sixth-grade students explore activities that focus on measuring the area and perimeter of regular and irregular shapes in a variety of contexts. The activities are structured so that they can be successfully performed by children with limited experience and ability and still challenge more capable and experienced learners.

Students work with a number of materials: Cuisenaire rods, inch-square Color Tiles, string, paper shapes. These materials pique children's interest and help them think about the concepts in various ways.

During the unit, children participate in whole class lessons, work cooperatively in pairs and groups, and complete activities individually. Throughout they are encouraged to explain their thinking, orally and in writing; writing is an integral part of the instructional approach. Homework assignments further students' classroom experiences and provide ongoing communication with parents about their children's learning.

The Structure of This Book

The directions for implementing the unit are organized into four components: *Whole Class Lessons, Menu Activities, Assessments,* and *Homework.* Blackline masters needed for the activities are also included.

Whole Class Lessons

Three whole class lessons, each requiring one or two class periods, introduce students to the basic ideas relative to area and perimeter and give them a common set of experiences on which to build their later, independent learning.

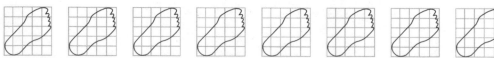

The instructional directions for each whole class lesson are presented in four sections:

Overview gives a brief description of the lesson.

Before the lesson outlines the preparation needed before teaching the lesson.

Teaching directions is a set of step-by-step instructions for presenting the lesson.

From the Classroom describes what happened when the lesson was taught to one class of fifth graders. Each vignette helps bring alive the instructional guidelines by giving an over-the-shoulder look into a classroom, telling how lessons were organized, how students reacted, and how the teacher responded. These vignettes are not standards of what "should" happen but records of what did happen with one class of 27 children.

Menu Activities

The "menu" is a collection of activities that children do independently, either individually, in pairs, or as a small group. The tasks on the menu pose problems, set up situations, and raise questions that give students various experiences with area and perimeter.

There are six menu activities. Two require students to work with a partner or with a group, one is a group activity, one is an individual activity, and two can be done by individuals, partners, or groups.

The instructional directions for each menu activity are presented in four sections:

Overview gives a brief description of the activity.

Before the lesson outlines the preparation needed before introducing the activity.

Getting started provides instructions for introducing the activity.

From the Classroom describes what happened when the activity was introduced to one class of fifth graders. As with the whole class lessons, each vignette is a look into an actual classroom, describing how the teacher gave directions and how the students responded. Class discussions of the activity are included.

For information about how to use a menu in the classroom, see the introduction to the Menu Activities section, page 75.

Assessments

The unit contains five assessments. Although they are grouped as a unit in the table of contents, each assessment is placed near the activity or activities from which it evolves. Assessments are distinguished from the other elements in the book by gray bars in the margins.

For specific information about assessing understanding, see the introduction to the Assessments section on page 15.

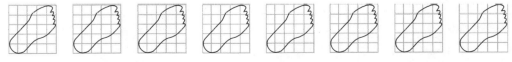

Homework

The unit contains five homework assignments. Homework assignments have three purposes: they extend the work children are doing in class, they inform parents about the instruction their child is receiving, and they help the teacher understand a child's thinking. Homework assignments also stimulate and provide data for classroom instruction. Each homework assignment includes a suggested letter to parents.

Notes About Classroom Organization

Setting the Stage for Cooperation

Throughout much of the unit, students are asked to work cooperatively, sometimes with a partner and sometimes in small groups. Interaction—with one another as well as with adults—is an important ingredient in children's intellectual development.

There are various systems for organizing children to work cooperatively. Some teachers put pairs of numbers in a bag and have students draw to choose partners. Some assign partners. Some ask seatmates to work together. Others allow children to pick their own partners.

Some teachers have students work with the same partner for an entire unit. Some have children choose partners for each activity, allowing them either to change partners or to stay with the same person, or requiring that students choose a different partner each time. And some teachers don't have children work with specific partners but instead with whoever else has chosen the same activity.

The system for organizing students matters less than the underlying classroom attitude. What's important is that children are encouraged to work together, listen to one another's ideas, and help their classmates. Students should see their classroom as a place where cooperation and collaboration are valued and expected. This does not mean, of course, that children never work individually. However, it does respect the principle that interaction fosters learning and, therefore, that collaboration is basic to the culture of the classroom.

A System for the Menu Activities

Again, there are several ways to use the written directions for menu activities. Some teachers make 11-by-17-inch versions of the menu tasks using the enlarging feature of their photocopier, mount the enlargements on construction paper or tagboard, and post them. That way, after the teacher has introduced the activity by reading the directions to the class, individual students can later refer to the posted directions for clarification. (You can buy a prepackaged set of menu-activity posters from Cuisenaire Company of America.) Other teachers duplicate multiple copies of each blackline master for students to take to their seats. (Mounting the copies on tagboard makes them more durable.) Still others copy the directions by hand onto the chalkboard or chart paper.

The materials used in the activities also need to be available. A common classroom practice is for children to take materials from a general supply and then return them when they finish their work or at the end of class.

Whatever system you use, it should be one that encourages students to be independent and responsible for their learning. Children should be able to spend the time they need on any one task and should be allowed to make their own choices about the sequence in which they work on tasks.

How Children Record Their Learning

Teachers use various procedures to organize the way students record and keep track of their learning. Some have each student keep a file similar to a portfolio; they either fold 12-by-18-inch sheets of construction paper in half or use commercial folders. Some require that each child record individually, even when he or she works cooperatively; others allow partners and groups to record collaboratively.

Some teachers have students hand in their finished work each time, placing it in designated baskets, folders, or other containers. Some teachers have students copy the list of menu activities and put a check by activities they complete. Other teachers give each student his or her own copy of the blackline master on page 186.

There are advantages and disadvantages to any recording system. Whatever system you use, it needs to be clear to the class and it needs to help you keep track of students' progress. I find that when I have students place their work in a folder designated for a particular activity, I get a good picture of how the class generally is responding. However, to have a sense of a particular child's thinking I then need to go through each activity folder or basket and pull out that child's work.

The opposite is also true. When I have children keep their work in their own individual folders, I have a better sense of how a given child is thinking. But then, to get a big picture of the class, I need to hunt through every student's folder for his or her work on a particular activity.

It's important to read and respond to students' work often so that you can make instructional decisions while the unit is in progress. If children are keeping their menu work in a folder, I look through five or six children's folders each day and attach sticky notes to particular pieces with my comments.

The first time I tried having students keep their work in folders, I didn't check them regularly and faced a huge stack of folders at the end of the unit. I discovered that some children had been less than careful about keeping work; others had misconceptions that could and should have been addressed in the context of the unit.

About Discussions in Math Class

It is vital to provide regular opportunities for children to share their thinking and hear others' ideas after they have done an activity. By participating in discussions, students cement their own thinking or change it based on new information. Discussions help you learn what and how children are thinking and, when held before a writing assignment, give students ideas about what they might write.

Sometimes teachers rush through a discussion because they are running out of time. When you realize time is short, rather than rush, it's better to wait until the next day: students will be able to look at their work with a fresh eye, and you'll be able to give the discussion the time it deserves. Also, scheduling a discussion for the next day allows you to take home the class set of papers and review them in preparation.

About Writing in Math Class

In many of these activities, particularly the assessments (but not only the assessments), you will rely on children's writing to learn about their thinking. Writing helps children bring meaning to mathematical ideas and skills and helps them understand concepts. When they write, children are actively thinking about math. Writing helps students engage with ideas and reflect on and clarify their thoughts.

The NCTM's *Curricular and Evaluation Standards for School Mathematics* (March 1989) emphasizes the importance of discussion and writing in mathematics:

> Opportunities to explain, conjecture, and defend one's ideas orally and in writing can stimulate deeper understandings of concepts and principles.... Writing and talking about their ideas clarifies students' ideas and gives the teacher valuable information from which to make instructional decisions. (p. 78)

Helping students learn to describe their reasoning processes and to become comfortable doing so is extremely important and requires planning and attention. Experience and encouragement are two major ingredients.

Implementing writing in my math class felt uncomfortable at first for both the children and me. Yet over time and with the experience that comes from making mistakes and discoveries, I am convinced about the value of writing for students. What's most important for me now are the benefits to students from the process of thinking about mathematical ideas and what I can learn about a child's thinking.

Teachers use writing in math class in various ways. Some ask students to write daily about what they did and their reactions to the activities; others have children write only occasionally. Some have students keep math journals or logs; others prefer to have children write on single sheets of paper and to collect all the papers after each activity. Some teachers give students free rein about what they write; others structure the writing by raising questions or providing prompts; still others use a combination of ways to initiate writing assignments.

Children need to know that their writing is important, that it helps you as their teacher learn what and how they are thinking. You need to reinforce over and over again that your students need to provide enough details to make their thinking and reasoning processes clear.

When I taught this particular unit, the children knew that I was planning to write a book about our experiences, and their initial attention to their written work was impressive. They read and revised with little prompting from me. After the first week or so, however, their rigor relaxed and they required the usual amount of prodding.

Some students have difficulty writing and benefit from seeing writing modeled by you or by their peers. When I notice children looking discouraged, not working, or doing something other than math, I check with them to see what's wrong. Often the reason for their behavior can be traced to their having trouble writing. I sit down with them and ask them to tell me what they're trying to communicate. I might say something like, *Sometimes when I get stuck trying to explain something in writing, I pretend I'm telling someone about it instead of writing it. Then I write down what I've said. I do this sentence by sentence, saying it and writing it down. I keep going until I've said and written everything I think I need to.*

I might also ask them to tell me something about the topic of the paper they are trying to write. I check to be sure I understand their thinking. Sometimes children just need help getting started; other times, I need to work with them throughout more or all of the process.

When I have the time and what's going on in the classroom allows me to, I read students' papers for clarity as they hand them in. Sometimes I accept their work; other times I ask a question or make a suggestion to clarify their thinking or ask for more detail and send them back to revise. At times I also pay attention to spelling, punctuation, and grammatical errors; at other times I let these things go. I tailor my decisions to the individual child and to the assignment.

Sometimes I collect children's work, respond to it later (usually on a sticky note), and return the papers a day or two later. Typical responses are, *Your sketch makes it easy for me to follow your reasoning,* or, *It looks like you've done a lot of work, but I'm confused by a few things. Let's talk during menu time.*

I struggle with whether to keep children's work or send it home for students to discuss with parents, especially as portfolio assessment becomes a more common part of many children's education. Photocopying allows me to do both, so I do that when the work reveals a child's thinking; that way, I have a record to refer to and the parents receive information about their child's learning.

Despite the problems involved in asking children to write, I am convinced about the value of doing so. The benefits of having students write are substantial, both for their learning and for my assessments.

Managing Materials and Supplies

When teaching this unit, you may want to allow time at the beginning of the year for students to explore the materials they'll be using. Once their curiosity is satisfied, it's easier for them to focus on specific tasks. Also, be sure to establish guidelines for the care and storage of materials.

Materials

The following materials are needed for this unit, assuming a class of 30:
■ Six trays of Cuisenaire rods
■ Approximately 400 inch-square Color Tiles
■ *Spaghetti and Meatballs for All!*, written by Marilyn Burns and illustrated by Debbie Tilley (Scholastic, 1997)

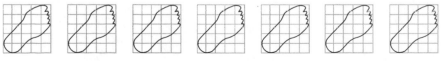

Optional Materials

■ Overhead projector
■ One set of overhead projector Cuisenaire rods
■ One set of overhead projector Color Tiles

General Classroom Supplies

■ An ample supply of paper, including 8½-by-11-inch sheets, 18-by-24-inch sheets, chart paper, centimeter-squared paper, and inch-squared paper
■ Approximately 50 5-by-8-inch index cards, lined or unlined
■ At least one pair of scissors for every two children
■ Glue
■ Tape (clear or masking)
■ A large spindle (or five or six balls) of white string
■ Rulers
■ Calculators
■ Circular objects, at least one for every child (tape loops, cups, garbage cans, bowls or other containers, soda cans, etc.)
■ Post-It™ Notes or other sticky-type paper for responding to student work

Centimeter-squared and inch-squared sheets are included in the Blackline Masters section. Most teachers choose to have supplies of each sheet available for students to take as needed.

A Comment About Calculators

It's assumed that during this unit and throughout the year, calculators are as available in the classroom as pencils, paper, rulers, and other general classroom supplies. You may occasionally ask students not to use calculators if you want to find out about their ability to deal with numbers on their own. However, these times should be the exception rather than the rule. Children should be taught that calculators are tools to be used when doing mathematics.

A Suggested Daily Schedule

You will no doubt want to think through the entire unit and prepare an overall teaching plan in advance. However, it isn't possible to predict how a class will respond as the unit progresses, and you will most likely end up making adjustments and changes to this plan. Below is a suggested day-to-day schedule for five weeks of daily instruction that interweaves whole class lessons, independent work on menu activities, and homework assignments.

Class discussions of menu activities are also included, typically several days or more after the menu activity is introduced. That way children will have had time to experience the activity before they are asked to share their thoughts and ideas about it. The positioning of discussions in the schedule is only a suggestion. Use your judgment about when it's best to have them. You may occasionally want to tell your students that they will discuss a particular activity the next day and that they should be sure to work on the task

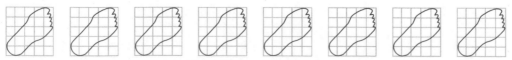

so they can contribute to the discussion. Since students will be working on menu activities at their own pace and completing them at different times, it's also important to check with students individually about their progress.

For general information about the importance of class discussions, see the introduction to Menu Activities, page 75. For suggestions about how to conduct specific discussions, check the "From the Classroom" section in each menu activity.

Day 1   Assessment: What Are Area and Perimeter?

Discuss with the children what they know about area and perimeter. Then introduce the assessment and have students write about their ideas. Start an area and perimeter word list.

Day 2   Whole Class Lesson: The Area Stays the Same

Introduce *The Area Stays the Same*. Students cut the shapes, tape them to a group chart, discuss what they notice, and record their findings.

Day 3   Whole Class Lesson: The Area Stays the Same (continued)

Students post their charts, discuss how they worked together, and present their group's results. Challenge the class to find a way to cut a shape to make an unusually long perimeter.

Day 4   Assessment: The Blob

Present *The Blob* assessment. Read students' work as they finish, and have children revise for examples or clarity.

Day 5   Introduce Menu Activity: The Perimeter Stays the Same, Part 1

Present the directions for the menu activity *The Perimeter Stays the Same, Part 1*. Students work on the activity.

Day 6   Whole Class Lesson: Foot Stuff

Demonstrate for children what they are to do in this lesson—trace their foot on squared-centimeter paper, approximate its area, cut a string as long as the perimeter of their foot, shape the string into a square, and find its area. Children then compare the area of their foot with that of the square, discuss how they figured the areas and why the results differed, and then write about their ideas.

Day 7   Introduce Menu Activity: Round Things

Present the directions for the menu activity *Round Things*. Students choose and work on menu activities.

Day 8   Whole Class Lesson: Spaghetti and Meatballs for All

Read and discuss the picture book *Spaghetti and Meatballs for All!* Students use inch-square tiles to arrange different tables to seat 32 people.

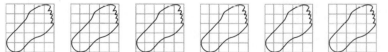

Day 9 Whole Class Lesson: Spaghetti and Meatballs for All (continued)

Students continue to solve the problem or work on an extension and then discuss their results. Give homework assignment: *Hand Measurement.*

Day 10 Introduce Menu Activity: The Banquet Table Problem

Discuss *Hand Measurement* homework. Present the directions for the menu activity *The Banquet Table Problem.* Students work on menu activities. Remind children to be sure to complete the menu activity *Round Things* so they can participate in a class discussion tomorrow.

Day 11 Menu

Children discuss their results from *Round Things.* Students then choose and work on activities from the menu.

Day 12 Introduce Menu Activity: Double the Circumference

Present the directions for the menu activity *Double the Circumference.* Students choose menu activities to work on for the remainder of class.

Day 13 Assessment: The Garden Problem

Present *The Garden Problem* assessment. When children complete the assessment, they choose menu activities to work on for the remainder of the class. Remind children who haven't done the menu activity *The Banquet Table Problem* to complete it so they can participate in a class discussion tomorrow.

Day 14 Menu

Students discuss their findings from *The Banquet Table Problem* and write about what they learned. Students then choose menu activities to work on for the remainder of the class. Give homework assignment: *The Cost of Banquet Tables.*

Day 15 Menu

Collect *The Cost of Banquet Tables* homework to read. Students work on menu activities. Remind children to be sure to complete the menu activity *Double the Circumference* so they can participate in a class discussion tomorrow.

Day 16 Introduce Menu Activity: The Perimeter Stays the Same, Part 2

Children discuss their results from *Double the Circumference.* Present the directions for the menu activity *The Perimeter Stays the Same, Part 2.* Students work on menu activities. Give homework assignment: *Results from Double the Circumference.*

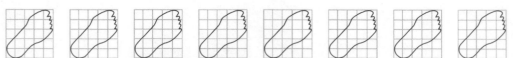

Day 17 **Introduce Menu Activity: Perimeter with Cuisenaire Rods**

Discuss *Results from Double the Circumference* homework. Present the directions for the menu activity *Perimeter with Cuisenaire Rods.* Students then choose and work on activities from the menu.

Day 18 **Menu**

Students work on menu activities. Remind children who haven't done the menu activity *The Perimeter Stays the Same, Part 2* to complete it so they can participate in a class discussion tomorrow.

Day 19 **Menu**

Discuss results from *The Perimeter Stays the Same, Part 2.* Children look at the class charts and discuss what they notice. Students work on menu activities for the remaining time.

Day 20 **Menu**

Students choose and work on menu activities. Give homework assignment: *Half the Square.*

Day 21 **Menu**

Collect *Half the Square* homework to read later. Students work on menu activities. Remind children who haven't done the menu activity *Perimeter with Cuisenaire Rods* to complete it so they can participate in a class discussion tomorrow.

Day 22 **Menu**

Students present and discuss their findings from *Perimeter with Cuisenaire Rods.* Then they choose and work on activities from the menu. Give homework assignment: *Double the Perimeter.*

Day 23 **Assessment: The Blob, Revisited**

Students discuss their *Double the Perimeter* homework. Then pass back children's initial *The Blob* assessment and present *The Blob, Revisited* assessment. Students continue work on menu activities when they are finished.

Day 24 **Menu**

Students choose and work on menu activities.

Day 25 **Assessment: Area and Perimeter, Final Assessment**

Students discuss what they learned during the unit. Then present *Area and Perimeter, Final Assessment.*

A Final Comment

The decisions teachers make every day in the classroom are the heart of teaching. This book attempts to provide clear and detailed information about presenting lessons and activities, organizing the classroom, grouping children, communicating with parents, and dealing with the needs of individual children. Keep in mind that there is no "best" or "right" way to teach the unit. The aim is for students to engage in mathematical investigations, be inspired to think and reason, and enjoy learning.

A Letter to Parents

Although parents will learn about their child's experiences from homework assignments and papers sent home, it's a good idea to give them general information about the unit at the outset. The following sample letter informs parents about the goals of the unit and introduces them to some of the activities their child will be doing.

Dear Parent,

We are about to begin work on a math measurement unit that focuses on area and perimeter. Children need many experiences to learn about these ideas and understand how they relate to each other.

In this unit, children work with a variety of concrete materials. They measure the areas and perimeters of regular figures, such as squares, rectangles, and circles, as well as approximate the areas and perimeters of irregular figures. They learn that there are various ways to measure the area and perimeter of both regular and irregular shapes.

Throughout the unit, children are introduced to the appropriate vocabulary: *area, perimeter, square units, circumference, radius, diameter,* and more.

In completing the activities and investigations in the unit, students will also estimate; manipulate whole numbers, fractions, and decimals; and use ideas from the areas of geometry, patterns, statistics, and logic.

Independent activities extend students' experiences in whole class instruction, and regular assessments provide a way to track children's learning. Homework assignments will give you firsthand experience with the unit.

If you have any questions, please do not hesitate to call.

Sincerely,

CONTENTS

ASSESSMENTS

Assessing children's understanding is an ongoing process. In the classroom, teachers learn about what their students know by listening to what they say during class discussions, observing and listening as they work on independent activities, talking with individual students, and reading their written work. By observing and interacting with children over time, teachers gain insights into their students' thinking and reasoning processes and learn about their mathematical interests and abilities.

It's important to assess children in several different ways rather than rely on one particular encounter or assignment to evaluate their understanding. Ideally, assessment is an ongoing part of instruction that uncovers and evaluates students' emerging understanding. Teachers must make time during regular classroom instruction to pose questions that stimulate children's thinking, to listen to their ideas, and to prod them to explain, clarify, and justify their reasoning.

The topics of area and perimeter typically are part of the curriculum of the upper elementary and middle school grades. However, children's experiences are often limited to finding the area and perimeter of shapes drawn on a textbook page, and their learning is focused on using formulas; much-needed attention to conceptual understanding is given short shrift.

Concentrating on teaching students formulas is a narrow approach to instruction because it focuses on having students apply specific formulas rather than think about a variety of approaches and decide which to use in particular situations. Students should explore the areas and perimeters of irregular as well as regular shapes and should have opportunities to consider area and perimeter in relationship to each other. Also, children need to experience problem-solving situations in which they are expected to think and reason.

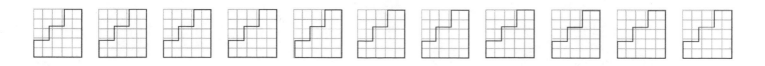

Five assessments are suggested. The unit begins with *What Are Area and Perimeter?*, an assessment that helps identify in general what students know about area and perimeter. *The Blob* focuses on what happens to the area of a figure when its perimeter length is rearranged into the shape of a square. *The Garden Problem* assessment requires children to take what they have learned during the unit so far about relationships between area and perimeter and apply it to a new situation. Given three scenarios for enlarging a garden, students write about which one makes the most sense and explain their reasoning. *The Blob, Revisited* is given near the near of the unit. Children reread their papers from the earlier *Blob* assessment and write about what they think now that they've experienced many activities to help them make sense of relationships between area and perimeter. In *Area and Perimeter, Final Assessment,* students write about all their experiences in the unit.

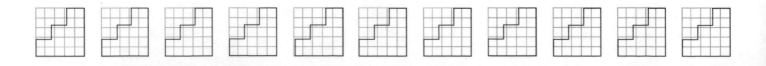

ASSESSMENT   What Are Area and Perimeter?

By the time students reach fifth or sixth grade, they've had classroom instruction in measurement, typically focused on measuring lengths with a variety of units and tools. However, students most likely have not yet been formally introduced to the ideas of area and perimeter, various ways to measure them, how they relate to each other, and how they're encountered and used in real life. Introducing the unit with this assessment is a way to find out what students already know about area and perimeter and their real-life applications.

Begin by posting a sheet of chart paper that you can use to keep track of new vocabulary as it is introduced in the unit. Title it "Area and Perimeter Words." As new vocabulary comes up, record each word and its definition on the chart, including an illustration if possible. The children will be able to use the chart as a reference during the activities and when they're completing their writing assignments.

Tell the students that they are beginning a new unit on measurement and that you'd like to find out what they already know about some of the ideas they'll be studying. Point out the "Area and Perimeter Words" chart and tell them that you'll record all the mathematical vocabulary that comes up in the unit.

Write *area* on the word list and tell them this is one of the two main ideas in the unit. Ask them what they think area is and how it's encountered and used in real life. You may want to ask students to talk first in small groups so that they have a chance to air and compare their ideas. Then let them report what they know during a class discussion. Don't correct erroneous ideas or teach the concept: just listen to their ideas and, if you like, record them on a sheet of chart paper or on an overhead transparency.

Do the same thing for perimeter. Write *perimeter* on the word list and tell students this is the other main idea. Have students talk in small groups about what it means, and then discuss their ideas as a class.

If no students have any ideas about area or perimeter, you may want to use this opportunity to give them some beginning information about these concepts. For example:

Area is what we call the amount of surface a shape takes up. You can think of a shape's area as its footprint.

Perimeter is the distance around a flat shape. You can think of it as a fence surrounding a shape.

We typically measure area in square units, even when a shape isn't square. To measure a handprint, for example, we can divide it into small squares and see how many of these square units there are.

We typically measure perimeter in units of length, choosing a unit that is appropriate. The length of a fence around a yard, for example, would most likely be better measured in feet than in inches.

If you offer explanations like these, do so with a light touch. This kind of information will be more useful after the students have worked on some of the activities in the unit. And remember that if the children do have their own ideas about area and perimeter, now is not the time to impose your ideas—even if their ideas are limited.

FROM THE CLASSROOM

NOTE It's a good idea to have students think about an idea individually before asking them to share their thinking with others, because their own ideas about a question or problem may not surface if they hear others' ideas right away.

Ask each child to write down what he or she knows about area and perimeter. Tell the students that their writing will help you think about what they already know and how the activities you've planned will help them. Also tell them that you will save what they write so that after the unit they can look back and see what they have learned.

If you've recorded (either on a chart or an overhead transparency) the ideas students contributed to the class discussion, save the chart or transparency so that you can repost it at the end of the unit. This will give the students the opportunity later to see what they've learned.

I told the class that we were about to begin a measurement unit, and I pointed to a large sheet of chart paper I had posted headed "Area and Perimeter Words." It was spring, and the children were familiar by now with using word lists for new math vocabulary.

"When I say the word *area,* what comes to mind? What is it and how is it used in real life? Take a minute to think about it by yourself, and then share your ideas with the other students at your table."

The room was quiet for a minute or so, then the children began talking.

"Um … area? I don't know!" Talon giggled to his best friend Marcel, who replied, "Me, neither."

Rifka told her tablemates, "Area is the amount of space something takes up, like a room, and garden, or even a tablecloth."

Erin and Brandon argued. "Area is only found on flat objects," Erin stated.

"No, it's not. You can have it on 3-D objects too. Like how much space is in a cube or a pitcher or something!" Brandon replied.

"But that's not area," Erin quickly retorted. "You're talking about space."

"Oh, yeah," said Brandon, giving in to Erin's insistence.

After a few minutes I called the class to attention. "Since area is one of the main ideas in the unit we're about to study, I'm interested in hearing what you know about area and how it's used in real life," I explained. Several children immediately raised their hand, and I called on David.

"It's the inside of something, like a rectangle," he said. I wrote *Area* on the overhead projector and listed *inside of something* below it.

Eric said, "You find it by taking one side times the other side." I recorded his idea below David's.

Catheryne struggled to find words to explain what she meant. "It's sort of like … the inside area of an object, like Eric said," she offered. Catheryne volunteered only occasionally in class and often had trouble explaining her ideas. I wanted to honor her thinking and wrote *inside area of an object* below Eric's contribution.

Nathan blurted out, "We did this thing last year in math for area where we used centimeter boxes to count to find the area of a square. It's how much room is in the inside of something," he finished.

"What should I write, Nathan?" I asked.

"Just write *count centimeter squares to find the area.* And below that write *it's how much room on the inside,*" he replied. I recorded his ideas.

"Oh, then add *you can measure the inside,*" Kirsten said eagerly.

"And write *space,* since it's how much space something takes up," added Rachel.

NOTE Some children are reluctant to participate in whole class discussions. Asking students to share their ideas with a small group respects their wish for not being singled out, yet provides you with needed information.

NOTE When giving a writing assignment, reinforce for children that you use their papers to think about how better to help all children learn more effectively. What's important is that students write what makes sense to them and that they clearly communicate their thinking.

There were no other comments, but Doug had a question. "What about curved shapes? Can you measure their areas?" he wondered.

"Let's start a second category on the overhead called *Questions* and record your question there. Then we'll remember to investigate it during the unit," I replied, and noted his question.

I was surprised that so few children had volunteered their ideas, since many children usually contributed. Also, I'd heard other students discussing what they knew with the children at their table. JT, for example, had talked about the deck his parents were building. It reminded me that not all children are comfortable speaking in front of their classmates.

I wasn't surprised, though, that students gave few examples of how area is used in real life. Unfortunately, too many children believe that math is something used primarily in school.

"What about *perimeter?*" I asked the class, adding the word to the chart that was to become our area and perimeter word list. "We'll also explore perimeter during this unit. What is perimeter and how is it used in real life? Take a minute or so to think and, again, share your ideas with a neighbor."

The children spent several minutes explaining their ideas to each other in animated conversations. In the meantime, I wrote *Perimeter* on the overhead next to *Area*, and prepared to begin a new list. After the children settled down, I asked them to explain what they knew about perimeter.

"You should write down that it's the length or width around a box or rectangle," Marcus said confidently. It was unusual for him to contribute to a discussion, let alone be so confident about it.

"And it's usually done in feet if you're finding the perimeter of a room," added Ann Maria.

Rifka shared her idea as I wrote down Marcus's and Ann Maria's. "You should write *can be measured and added,* because that's often what carpenters and other people who build things do," she said. I added *can be measured and added* and *carpenters use it* to the list.

Brandon waved his hand insistently. "Write that it can be the length of anything, that it doesn't have to be a rectangle," he said when I called on him.

"Tell us more," I asked, curious about what he meant.

He thought for a moment and replied, "The perimeter goes around the outside of any object. But what I don't get is three-dimensional objects. Can you measure the perimeter of a three-dimensional object? Write that on the question list." I recorded his question and idea and then called on Mike.

"Perimeter is the distance *around* an object," he said.

"But it's only found on two-dimensional objects," interrupted Erin. I wrote down their suggestions and the class fell silent.

Next I asked the children to write individually about what they thought area and perimeter were and how they were used in real life. I told them that their ideas would give me information about what they were thinking, which in turn would help me help them learn new ideas. I also explained that they could include in their writing things we had discussed so far. I wanted students who were unsure to have something to write about.

About half the students explained what area and perimeter were but didn't give any real-life examples.

Luke, for example, wrote: *Area means the amount of two dimensional space something takes up. To find the area of a square multiply its length x its width. If a square is 2 inches x 2 inches it has an area of 4 square inches.*

Perimeter is how far it is around something. If we use the same 2 x 2 square its perimeter is 8 inches because you add up the length of each of the sides.

Volume is the amount of 3 dimensional space something takes up. Volume is found by measuring length x width x depth. If you take the 2 x 2 square and make it 2 inches tall it will have volume. 2 x 2 x 2 = 8 cubic inches.

Erin wrote: *Area and perimeter are both things you would find on a 2 D object. Perimeter is the distance around something, and Area is the area in something.* She included a sketch:

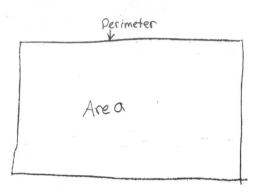

Mike wrote: *Area is the space inside a perimeter. There is area in 3-D objects, but not in 1-D objects. Perimeter is the "fence" around area. Perimeter is just like area, it only exists in 3-D and 2-D.*

About a third of the class included examples of how area and perimeter are used in real life.

Kathleen singled out candy makers and builders as people who work with area and perimeter.

What is Area and Perimeter?

Area is a part or fraction of a whole. For Example:

Perimeter is the outside of a box or circle. Perimeter can be measured. For Example:

People that own candy companies etc. When they box their products they need the perimeter of the boxes to be big or small enough. Also they need the area of the product. How much space is it going to take up.

Builders! They need to know area and perimeter. For the size of the house and bathroom, kitchen etc.

Sharnet, who was typically terse, had a lot to say: *I think area mean like an area in the park. for an example I can say we can have a pinknick at Irvington park because there is a big area there. For another examaple I can say there is a big area in are garage so we can put extra stuff there that we don't need. I also think that area mean something small and big so I think area mean space where you can put things like thuff that your going to sale for a garage sale or something like that. I just think it mean something that have to do with space.*

Several students were confident about area but not perimeter. Alex, for example, wrote: *Area is the surface covered by something. For example, the shaded part of this picture is area.*

The volume of something is how tall it is, the width of something is how wide it is. But I haven't the sligtest what perimater is.

Nathan's paper showed that he was not clear about either area or perimeter.

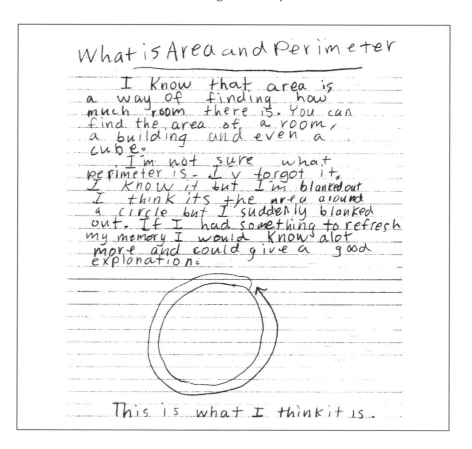

About a fourth of the class were not sure about area and perimeter.

Marcus wrote: *I really don't know much about area and perimeter but I think perimeter is like something around like a block or something that is square or the number of cubes are on the block. thats what I think perimeter is.*

And I think area has something to do with the middle of something with something in the middle.

I worried about Zak's response in particular, since he seemed to make something up simply to please me. Zak frequently seemed disinterested in math, yet he often said that he cared about doing well in school. He seemed to have learned that teachers want students to write a lot on their paper, regardless of what they have to say. He wrote: *This is it but I'm not sure. I think that it means that the area means that it's the area of the number and plus it to the nerest number.*

for exsaple 35 + 34 = 69. I also think that it means that you subtract a number in the othor numbers area.

I'm not that sure about what perlmeter means exsaktly. So I will try.

I think that perlmeter means that: when you need to tell some boddy the perlmeter of somthing.

Typically, some students already knew a lot, while others had a lot to learn. I was eager to get into the unit.

CONTENTS

WHOLE CLASS LESSONS

This unit contains three whole class lessons. Each lesson introduces students to a different way of investigating area and perimeter and prepares them for the independent menu activities that extend their learning.

In the first lesson, *The Area Stays the Same*, children investigate the idea that shapes with the same area can have different perimeters. Working in groups, students compare the perimeters of shapes made from squares that have been cut apart and then pieced together in different ways. They discuss their findings and then investigate ways to cut a shape to make an unusually long perimeter.

In *Foot Stuff*, students investigate the area and perimeter of an irregular shape—one of their feet. First, they figure the area of their foot in square centimeters. Then they take a piece of string equal in length to the perimeter of their foot, arrange it into the shape of a square, and figure the area of this square. Finally, they compare the area of the square with the area of their foot and discuss why the areas are different.

The children's book *Spaghetti and Meatballs for All!*, by Marilyn Burns, provides the context for the third whole class lesson. In the story, Mr. and Mrs. Comfort invite 32 family members and friends over for a reunion and set eight square tables to seat four people at each, one on each side. As more and more people arrive, they rearrange the square tables so that different-size groups can sit together. The story provides a real-world context for area and perimeter as the children investigate how different arrangements of eight square tables can provide seating for different numbers of people.

When you teach the *Area and Perimeter* unit, begin with the whole class lesson *The Area Stays the Same* to introduce the students to investigating and comparing the area and perimeter of various shapes. After that, intersperse whole class lessons with menu activities. Introducing menu activities early in the unit provides students with options during later whole class lessons, when students typically finish work at different times. The Suggested Daily Schedule found on pages 11–13 offers one possible day-by-day plan.

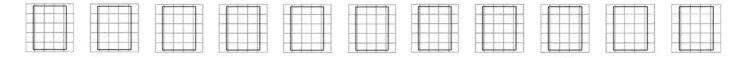

WHOLE CLASS LESSON   The Area Stays the Same

Overview

In this whole class lesson, students encounter the idea that shapes with perimeters of different lengths can have the same area.

Working in groups, the children investigate the perimeters of shapes made from squares that have been cut apart and then pieced together in different ways. They measure and compare the perimeters of the shapes they make. While students typically think that all the shapes will have the same-length perimeter because they all have the same area, they learn that the perimeters can vary quite a bit.

Before the lesson

Gather these materials:
■ 5-by-8-inch index cards, several for each student
■ 18-by-24-inch construction paper, a sheet for each group
■ Centimeter-squared paper, a sheet for each student (see Blackline Masters section, page 193)
■ Ample supplies of scissors, rulers, tape, and string
■ A 5-by-5-centimeter square cut from an index card

Teaching directions

■ Hold up a 5-by-5-centimeter square made from an index card and ask your students how they could explain why the area is 25 square centimeters. Have volunteers describe different ways.
■ Ask the students to suggest ways to cut the square into two or more pieces. Point out that it is okay for them to do so with both straight and curved lines.
■ Explain that each student will cut a 5-centimeter square from an index card, then cut the square into two or more pieces and form a new shape using these pieces. Demonstrate with your square. Point out that one piece may not be placed partially or completely on top of another and that each piece must touch the edge of another piece.
■ Next, ask the students how they might figure out the length of the perimeter of the new shape. One way they can do this is by laying a string along the perimeter, cutting the string at the point it meets itself, and measuring the string.
■ Ask each group of students to prepare a chart documenting their work. It should include the names of the group members, the date, the heading "The Area Stays the Same," each child's shape (either taped to the chart or traced onto it), and a straight line segment equal to the length of that shape's perimeter. Post an example to show them how to organize the chart.

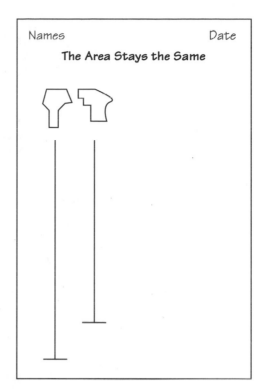

Names   Date
The Area Stays the Same

■ Explain that each group should add a section to their chart discussing what they notice about the shapes and how their perimeters compare.
■ Also, ask each group to repeat the activity with one or more squares, but this time to predict the length of the perimeter before measuring it.
■ If you feel it would be helpful, write the directions on the board for the students to refer to.
■ When all the charts have been posted, hold a discussion with the whole class. You might begin by focusing on group dynamics, asking the students what went well or badly as they worked together. Then have groups present the results of their comparison of perimeters and shapes.
■ Conclude the lesson by asking the students how they would cut apart and rearrange a square to get a really long perimeter. Students' explanations can help you assess their understanding.

FROM THE CLASSROOM

NOTE Asking students how they think you approached a problem and arrived at a solution is a way to find out about their thinking. It also suggests to them that they could use your approach as a model.

"Today you'll work with a group to explore what happens to the perimeters of shapes made from squares that have been cut apart and then pieced together in different ways," I told the class, holding up a 5-by-5-centimeter square that I had cut out from an index card. I also held up a sheet of centimeter-squared paper and placed the square against the centimeter-squared paper to show its size.

"The area of this square is 25 square centimeters," I continued. "How do you think I figured that out?"

"You find the area by multiplying one side by the other, so you just multiply 5 by 5," Doug replied.

"Does someone know a different way to find the area?" I asked.

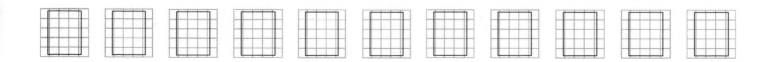

Erin had an idea. "You could draw the square on the piece of graph paper you're holding. Then you could just count the little squares and that would give you the area," she said smugly. Erin often sounded overly confident during class discussions.

"Yes, I could," I agreed. "Does someone have another way?" The class was silent. Then Ann Maria raised her hand.

"You only have to count the top row," she said. "Then you go 5, 10, 15, 20, 25. You count by 5s to see how many squares there are." I nodded.

"How long is the distance around this square?" I asked, running my finger around all four sides. "Talk about this with the others in your group."

In a moment hands from all but one group were raised. I called on Kathleen.

"It's 20," she said. "I went, 5, 10, 15, 20."

Others nodded.

"Twenty what?" I asked. "What's the unit of measurement?"

"Centimeters," several children answered in unison.

"So the perimeter of the square is 20 centimeters," I said, pointing to *perimeter* on the list of words I had started. Then I pointed to my index card square. "How can I cut this square into two or more pieces?"

"You could fold it in half and cut it," Catheryne said.

"Like this?" I asked, running my finger down the middle of the square. Catheryne shook her head yes.

"Or cut it on the diagonal," Brandon added. I ran my finger down the card to show the diagonal. Brandon nodded.

"Let's add the word *diagonal* to our area and perimeter word list," I suggested. I wrote the word and drew a rectangle with a diagonal bisecting it. "While we're at it, let's add two other words we've used this morning, *centimeter* and *square*."

"Does the dividing line have to go straight across?" David asked.

I shook my head no. "You could use straight lines in other ways," I replied, modeling several other possibilities on the board.

"Do you have to use straight lines?" Rifka wanted to know.

Again, I shook my head no.

"Then you could cut it using a curvy line, and put it together in a new way," Rifka suggested, drawing curves in the air with her hand.

Taking a pair of scissors, I cut the square as Rifka had indicated, roughly in an S shape.

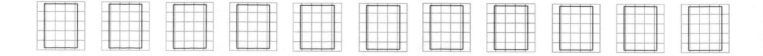

"Like this?" I asked. She nodded.

"Cool idea," Brandon said appreciatively.

I gave my instructions. "Everyone in your group should cut a 5-by-5-centimeter square into two or more pieces and put the pieces together so that they form a new shape. There are two rules you need to follow. First, you can't place one piece partially or completely on top of another. Second, each piece must touch the edge of another piece. That means that having just corners touch isn't okay. Edges have to touch. That way the area of your new shape stays the same as the original 5-by-5-centimeter square." I laid the two S-shape pieces I had just cut on the overhead so edges were touching.

"You can use tape to hold the pieces in place. Just be careful that the tape doesn't hang over the edge," I said as I taped the two pieces together. "Or, to avoid using tape, you can trace the shape onto a new index card and then cut it out." I demonstrated what I meant.

"Next," I continued, "figure out the length of the perimeter of your new shape. How could you determine the length of the perimeter?"

"Measure it?" David offered tentatively.

"How might you do that?" I asked.

"With a ruler?" David wondered.

"How would you use a ruler?" I persisted.

David and the rest of the class were silent. I waited for what seemed an uncomfortably long time. When it was clear that no one had a suggestion, I said, "One way is to lay a piece of string along the perimeter and cut the string at the point where it meets itself." I cut a length of string from a spool so that I could demonstrate.

Luke obviously approved: "Oh, good idea!"

Kirsten was sitting near the overhead, so I asked her to help hold the string as I laid it along the perimeter of my new shape. When we were finished, I cut the string so it was the same length as the perimeter and held it up for the class to see. "Now I can measure the string to find the length of the perimeter," I said.

I then explained how the groups were to organize their work. "Each group will make a chart to display the shapes they've made and their perimeters. That way we can look at our results and talk about them during a class discussion. At the top of a large sheet of construction paper write your names, the date, and the heading "The Area Stays the Same." Tape your group's shapes in a row across the paper and underneath each one use a marker to draw a line segment equal to its perimeter. The marker makes a dark, heavy line, so we'll be able to see each one clearly." I posted an example of a recording sheet.

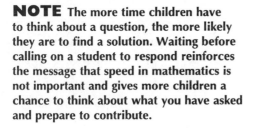

NOTE The more time children have to think about a question, the more likely they are to find a solution. Waiting before calling on a student to respond reinforces the message that speed in mathematics is not important and gives more children a chance to think about what you have asked and prepare to contribute.

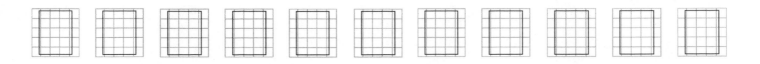

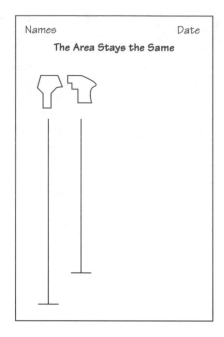

"Be careful to line up your perimeter line segments so that we can compare their lengths," I continued. "Once everyone's shape is on the chart, discuss what you notice about the shapes and how their perimeters compare. Write what you notice on your group's paper. Do you have any questions so far?"

There were none. Because I had given them quite a lot of information, I summed up my expectations. "Let me review what you're to do." I listed the directions on the board, reading the items aloud as I did so.

1. Cut a 5-by-5-centimeter square from an index card.

2. Cut your square into two or more pieces and put the pieces together to create a new shape.

3. Figure out the length of the perimeter of your new shape.

4. Display your group's shapes on a chart, drawing a straight line segment underneath each shape equal to the length of its perimeter.

5. Discuss and write down what you notice.

Then I added two final directions:

6. As a group, repeat this activity with one or more additional squares. This time predict the length of the perimeter before you measure it.

7. Post your group chart when you're done.

"Wait, won't the perimeters all be 20 centimeters?" Brandon asked eagerly.

Nathan echoed, "Yeah, won't the perimeters be 20 centimeters? They should be if their area is 25 square centimeters."

I was about to say, That's exactly the question you'll investigate in this activity, but Rifka spoke up instead. "It's not the area that's changing,

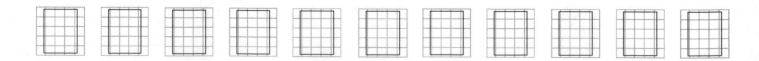

Nathan, it's the perimeter. The perimeter may zig and zag but it's still the same area." Several students nodded in agreement.

"Oh, I get it," said Brandon. "In your example on the overhead, you cut into the space inside of the square but you didn't throw any away. So the area stays the same."

"Huh?" Nathan wasn't convinced.

Luke interrupted, unable to contain himself. "It's like Jell-O. You make it, put it in the pan, and it's done. When you cut it up into different-size pieces, it's still the same amount of Jell-O, even if it's cut up!"

"Oh! I see now," Nathan said, smiling with relief.

I was pleased that the class remained interested in the lively interchange that was taking place. We had worked hard all year on listening to one another's questions and ideas, knowing that it's sometimes hard to follow someone else's reasoning.

I got on my soapbox at this point. Students know that I care passionately about mathematics instruction, and I sometimes share information with them about teaching.

"There was a French psychologist named Jean Piaget who coined the word *disequilibrium*," I said. "It describes the confused feeling we get when something we think we know is proved to be untrue. Piaget said the greatest opportunity for learning occurs when we're in that state, because we want to try to figure out what's really going on. Nathan and Brandon are trying to resolve their disequilibrium and move into equilibration."

I heard Talon mutter under his breath, "I'm still in dis ... dis ... whatever it is. But I'll figure it out."

"Once you each create a new shape from your square and find its perimeter, we'll have a lot of information to examine," I concluded.

Observing the Children

There is usually a flurry of activity as my students get to work, and today was no exception. Earlier in the year, to avoid creating congestion around the shelves of materials, we had set up a routine whereby one person from each group was responsible for getting the supplies the group would need. Today, children got their materials with relatively little trouble.

As I circulated through the room, I noticed that some children were able to rely on my oral instructions, while others needed to consult the directions I had written on the board.

A few groups shared materials and space willingly; others had more difficulty. For example, JT and Zak took some string and were just about to cut a short length when another of their partners, Eric, stopped them.

"Don't cut it if we don't know how long the perimeter will be! That's going to be too short!" he admonished. JT and Zak looked first at each other, then at Eric, and cut the string anyway.

"Oh, brother," said Eric with disgust, and he continued with the task. JT and Zak giggled. This was fairly typical behavior for them.

Catheryne called me over to her table for help before consulting with her group members. "I need help cutting this. It's too hard," she complained. Catheryne often asked for individual help from me before attempting a task herself, and I usually responded as I did now.

"Have you asked a group member to help you yet? Remember our classroom rule." I pointed to the list of rules posted above the board. The

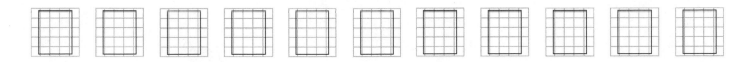

third rule was, *You may ask an adult for help when everyone in your group has the same question.*

"Rifka, help!" pleaded Catheryne.

"Okay, just a sec," replied Rifka, and I moved on.

As I approached Brandon's group, he said excitedly, "Mrs. R, I can make the longest perimeter!"

"How?" I asked.

He drew a snaky line on his index card square.

"Ah, but you've stayed on the lines," I commented, noting that Brandon seemed to have been inspired by the lines printed on the card.

"Oh yeah, I could make my cuts narrower by cutting between the lines. That would give me an even longer perimeter!" Brandon said, smiling. He reached for a new index card square to test his conjecture.

Talon and Alex were quite involved with the task, while their table-mate, Marcus, looked on. Talon was new to our school that year and had been uncomfortable working with others and had had difficulty focusing on work, so I was pleased that he was being successful with both. When he noticed me standing beside their table, Talon said enthusiastically, "Look at the shape I made zig and zag. I didn't want to make a regular shape. Alex said to make it cool! I think it looks like tonsils."

Alex, Marcus, and Talon were surprised that their perimeter strings (not shown completely here) were not all the same length.

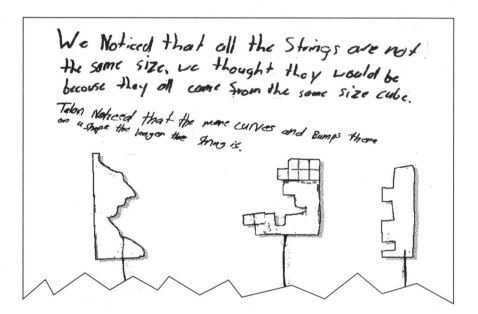

Eric came over to Talon's table to check perimeter lengths. "Oh, good, yours are all different lengths too," he said with a sigh of relief. "I was worried that we were doing it wrong. All of our strings are different lengths, and I thought they should be the same."

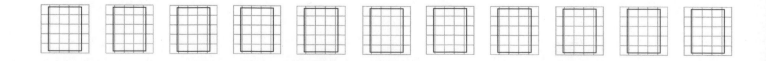

Overhearing Eric, Ann Maria said, "I thought they should be the same, too. But the perimeter doesn't have to stay the same. Look, I made a shape and found the perimeter. Then I rearranged that shape and got a different perimeter. So the area stays the same, but the perimeters don't." Satisfied, Eric returned to his group and rearranged their perimeter strings so they were evenly spaced and ordered by length on the paper.

Several groups taped their shapes next to the corresponding perimeter lines, put their names on the chart, and told me they were finished. I had to remind them to record what they noticed about how the perimeters and shapes related to one another.

"It's hard to write it. We know what we mean, but we can't write it," said Marcus.

"Tell me what your group noticed," I suggested.

"Well, we noticed that all the strings are not the same size, and we noticed—"

"Wait," I interrupted. "Before you say the second thing you noticed, let me write down the first thing. Then you can tell me more." I wrote on a sheet of notebook paper: *We noticed that all the strings are not the same size.*

"What else?" I asked.

"Well, we thought they would be the same size because they all came from the same-size cube," Marcus replied.

"Okay, let's record that," I said and wrote after his first sentence: *We thought they would be the same size because they all came from the same-size cube.*

"Tell me more," I said.

"Talon noticed that the more curves and bumps there are on a shape, the longer the perimeter is," Marcus said. I recorded that as well.

That was all Talon's group had noticed, so I asked Marcus to read what I had written to see whether it was what he meant and whether he wanted to add or change anything.

"It's good," said Marcus.

"When you said cube, were you referring to this square?" I asked Marcus, pointing to a 5-centimeter square.

"Uh-huh," he nodded. I explained the difference between a cube and the two-dimensional square, and Marcus corrected the term on the piece of notebook paper.

"Marcus," I said, "Sometimes when I get stuck trying to explain something in writing, I pretend I'm telling someone about it instead of writing it. Then I write down the first thing I say. I continue and say the next sentence. Then I write it down. I keep going like that until I've said and written everything I want to say."

"That's interesting," said Marcus. Then he returned to his group and added the writing to their chart. (I noticed later that Marcus had used the word *cube* on his group's chart. It was another reminder for me that teaching by telling isn't always effective.)

After about 45 minutes all the groups had completed their charts. I had the children post them on the bulletin board, and we stopped work for the day.

A Class Discussion

I began class the next day by asking the students to focus on their group dynamics. "Before we talk about the math ideas in the activity you did

NOTE Helping children learn to write about their mathematical thinking and reasoning takes time and patience. Students benefit from seeing writing modeled by the teacher or other students.

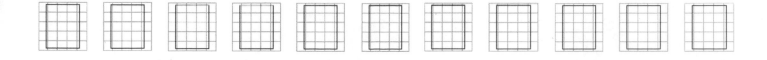

NOTE Working in groups can be difficult at times, and attention needs to be given to the process. Having groups describe how they work together gives other students models for how to handle problems.

yesterday, I'm interested in hearing what went well as you worked with your group. Take a minute to talk it over with those at your table." There was a buzz of conversation.

After getting everyone's attention again, I asked, "What went well?"

Marcus raised his hand, which surprised me. During discussions he mostly deferred to others, rarely offering his opinion.

"Everybody helps each other in my group," he said.

"What do you do to help each other?" I asked, pushing for specifics.

"Well, if someone doesn't know what to do, you just tell them," Marcus replied.

David said, "We're not having troubles in my group, either. Everybody is getting along."

"Why?" I asked.

"We're having fun talking in a good way about stuff like movies and football, but we still get the task done and learn," he responded. I wasn't surprised at the topics of their conversations. David, JT, Eric, and Zak often played football together during recess.

Eric added, "We listened carefully to the directions and knew what to do, so we got right to work."

Rifka said, "We shared materials. Like when someone said they needed the string, it was just handed to them. And we didn't argue about who had what for how long."

"In my group we were yelling in a fun way to remind each other to put everything on the paper the right way," added Luke. "It was fun." The other members of his group nodded in agreement.

I then steered the discussion toward the mathematics of the activity. "I'm interested in hearing about what happened in your group when you compared the perimeters and shapes. Is there a group that would like to come to the board and report on your chart?" I asked. I routinely expect each group to explain their results, and students often are eager to come to the front of the room to present their thinking. To remind the class what I expected of them as an audience, I said, "The rest of you should respond by telling each group what you notice about their results."

Rifka, Catheryne, Nathan, and Anfernee volunteered to go first. "We discovered that even though the area stayed the same, the perimeter changed," said Catheryne, as Rifka and Nathan pointed out the different perimeter line segments.

Rifka, Anfernee, Nathan, and Catheryne explained why they thought the perimeter strings were different lengths.

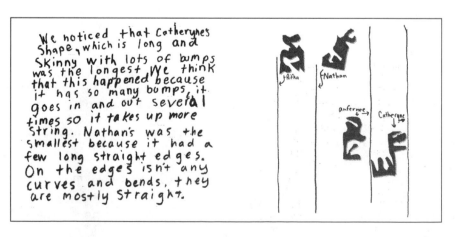

We noticed that Catherynes Shape, which is long and Skinny with lots of bumps was the longest. We think that this happened because it has so many bumps, it goes in and out several times so it takes up more string. Nathan's was the smallest because it had a few long straight edges. On the edges isn't any curves and bends, they are mostly Straight.

"Wow, you had some really interesting shapes!" commented Rachel. Their chart had long, narrow shapes with many appendages.

Ann Maria's group presented next, Ann Maria reading what her group had written. "We noticed that the perimeter changed a lot, but the area stayed the same. This is true because some pieces have twists but others have grooves, making the perimeter longer," she read. The group had included the original square as one of their shapes.

Doug elaborated. "To put it in different words," he said, "Say each shape is a race track. For our curviest shapes, you'd have to do a whole lot of driving to go around the track. But if you were driving around the square you wouldn't have to drive far."

Nathan raised his hand, and Doug called on him.

"You had a lot to say, but your group didn't write a lot. You should write down what you just said, because it was really clear and I learned a lot from it," Nathan said. I thought about reinforcing this comment but kept quiet. Sometimes children listen better to advice from their classmates than to advice given by their teacher.

Doug was somewhat flustered, but he stammered, "Okay, thanks." There were no other comments, so he and his group sat down. (Later I noticed they had not added what Doug said to their paper. It was a reminder to me to push students to revise for completeness and clarity.)

JT, David, Zak, and Eric presented next. "We decided that curvy lines make the most perimeter," said Eric.

Luke immediately said, "It's cool! Look at their paper! As the shapes get skinnier and taller they get more perimeter!"

Nathan added, "I think we noticed that because you guys organized your paper by putting the shortest perimeter shapes on one end and the longest on the other—you went in height order."

I really appreciated having Nathan in class at that moment. I would have asked the class what about Eric's group's paper helped them make that observation if Nathan had not commented on it.

Malkia's group presented their results next. Malkia said, "We think that the more lines and more cracks and holes there are, the longer the lines will be. We think this because the shapes with longer arms and sticky-out things have longer perimeters."

Nathan jumped in again. "None of your shapes have any curves— they're just pretty straight. I think it'd be interesting to make a graph of all the shapes with straight lines, like 20 of them, and figure out which of them have the longest perimeter lines."

I found this suggestion intriguing and in no way anticipated Malkia's reaction. "We didn't want to make shapes with curvy lines, Nathan," she said, "and I think you should just mind your own business." Everyone was momentarily stunned.

Then Brandon, who was Nathan's friend as well as a member of Malkia's group, spoke up: "Malkia, chill out. Nathan wasn't putting us down for having straight lines. He was saying that it'd be cool to see more shapes like our straight ones."

"Yeah, don't worry Malkia," Hilda said gently.

"Oh, I uh …," Malkia smiled with embarrassment. "Sorry Nathan."

"That's okay," Nathan replied.

NOTE Group discussions are important for bringing out mathematical connections and concepts. Sometimes discussions take unexpected twists, especially when a teacher gives more control over to students. But discussions are worth this sort of complication, and it's helpful to have as many students contribute to a discussion as possible.

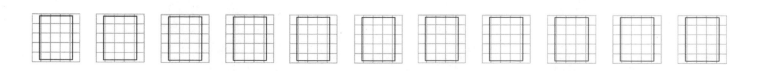

Later I thought about the interchange between Malkia and Nathan. It seemed as though Malkia became defensive about Nathan's suggestion and so wasn't able to hear what he was really saying. The situation could have deteriorated further than it did, and I wondered how I would have handled it if Brandon had not spoken.

Synthesizing the Results

After all the groups had presented their results, I held up a 5-centimeter square and asked the class, "How could I cut this square to get a really long perimeter? Talk with your group about this question and be ready to report back to the whole class."

After a few minutes all of the groups indicated that they had a statement ready. "Even if you agree with something that another group has said, or if they phrase their statement similarly, share yours anyway," I told the class. Then we began.

Rachel's group went first. "The more complicated the shape, like it has many twists and turns, the longer the string … or perimeter, I mean," she said. I recorded her statement on the board as several students applauded.

Kathleen's group offered, "We think the more straight lines you have, the longer the perimeter." I knew that the children were just beginning to construct their ideas about how area and perimeter relate, so I chose not to correct Kathleen's statement.

David, however, questioned it. "I disagree," he said. "The square had straight lines and it wasn't anywhere near the longest perimeter. In fact, it was probably the shortest."

"Oh! We hadn't thought about that," replied Kathleen, and her group members put their heads together and began whispering.

David continued. "Our group said that the curvier the shape the longer the perimeter will be. Write that down." I recorded their idea.

"We agree with David," said Brandon. "If you take a square and cut it back and forth making really curvy cuts, you'll have a long perimeter. Write that down." David, Rachel, and several other students nodded in agreement.

I recorded Brandon's group's statement. "Like this?" I said, drawing a square with short, curved lines along the diagonal. I chose to misconstrue Brandon's statement so that he would have to rethink and clarify his idea.

"No, make the cuts longer," said Brandon.
"Like this?" I asked and drew another square with deeper curves.

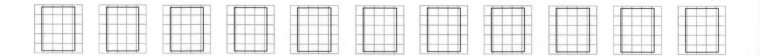

"Yeah, like that!" replied Brandon enthusiastically. "Oh, I guess we need to add the word *long* before the word *curvy* in our statement. I revised his group's statement accordingly.

Nathan spoke for his group. "Cut a square so there are many places for a string to go in and out. That will give you a long perimeter." I recorded his group's statement.

After the remaining groups had offered their statements, I asked the class to look at the charts they had prepared.

"Suppose I had asked you for homework to read all the statements on the charts about what groups noticed. Do you think you'd agree with them all?" I asked.

The students responded immediately, vigorously shaking their heads and calling out no.

"Why not?" I asked.

After a moment I called on Brandon, who said, "Now that we've heard everybody's ideas, I know better what's right and what's wrong. I'd change some things on my chart now."

"How many of you would revise what you wrote?" I wondered. About half the class indicated they would.

During these lessons the students had struggled to make general statements about why different shapes that all had the same area could have different perimeters. Some of the children's ideas were correct and some were incorrect. I was comfortable with this, because I knew they would have opportunities over the next few weeks to investigate the same idea in different ways.

ASSESSMENT   The Blob

In this assessment, students write individually about how the area of an irregular figure compares with the area of a square that has the same-length perimeter. Children think about area and perimeter in relation to each other, a recurring theme in the unit.

Some students have learned that changing the shape of a figure, even when the perimeter is kept constant, can change its area. However, it's common for students (and even adults when they haven't had a great deal of experience thinking about area and perimeter together) to think that different shapes with the same perimeter will have the same area. Often many activities are needed to challenge this misconception or strengthen understanding that is fragile. This assessment gives you insights into what students understand near the beginning of the unit. It can be repeated toward the end of the unit to help you and your students find out how their thinking has changed.

First, draw an irregular figure similar to the one below on the board:

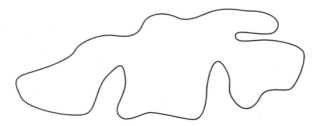

Then present the following problem to the class:

> You want to find the area of this "blob." Your friend has a suggestion: "Lay a piece of string around its perimeter. Arrange the string to form a square and then figure out its area. The area of the square will be just about the same as the area of the blob." Do you agree or disagree with your friend's method? Or are you unsure? Explain your thinking. Use a sketch if it helps explain your ideas.

FROM THE CLASSROOM

I drew an irregular figure on the board (see the example above) and said to the class, "Suppose you need to figure out the area of this blob. Your friend Sally suggests a method. She says you should lay a string around the perimeter of the blob, use the string to form a square, and then figure out the area of the square. Sally thinks that the area of the square will be just about the same as the area of the blob."

Talon raised his hand. "I don't get what you mean by a blob. Why would you need to know the area of a blob?"

I suspected that using the general term *blob* as a context was probably confusing to other children as well. I thought for a moment about how I could make the context more concrete. "Let's imagine that our blob is a new golf course, and Sally wants to find out the area so she knows how much grass to order to cover it."

NOTE Teachers often ask children to write after a discussion that has stimulated ideas and helped them clarify their thinking. However, asking students to work without first hearing others' ideas is another way to assess each child's understanding.

Nathan blurted out, "Would that be grass seed or sod? Because you'd need a lot more sod than you would grass seed to cover the area."

Before I could respond, Sharnet said, "What's sod?" This prompted an enthusiastic and noisy discussion about sod. The class was fascinated by the topic. I, on the other hand, was trying to bring the focus back to the assessment.

After I had regained the students' attention, I said, "Let's think about the problem this way. Pretend that Sally wanted to lay sod on the golf course."

"That makes more sense," Talon said softly.

"Without saying anything out loud," I continued, "spend the next few minutes thinking about whether you agree or disagree with Sally's reasoning. Or are you unsure?"

The class was very quiet. After a few minutes I said, "Without sharing your thinking with anyone else, write about whether you agree with Sally, disagree with her, or are unsure. You may draw a sketch if that helps you explain your ideas."

I walked around the room while the children worked, prompting some to put their name and the date on their paper and reminding others to punctuate their sentences or check their spelling. As children finished writing, I accepted papers that expressed ideas clearly and asked some students to revise their work to make it clearer or include more examples. Their writing showed a range of understanding.

Kirsten understood that the area of the square would be different from that of the blob. She wrote: *I disagree with my friend because this way the perimeter stays the same not the area. The area changes while the perimeter stays the same. For example, if I have a circle, and I squeeze the middle, the perimeter stays the same but the area changes.*

There's less area now. So I'd have to find a different way to figure out how much sod I'd need.

Luke also understood that the areas wouldn't be the same: *I disagree with my friends reasoning because the perimeter stays the same. You can pull out an indentation in the perimeter and make it a bump. The perimeter will stay the same but the area will increase.*

"You obviously have a picture in your mind of what you mean," I said to Luke when he brought me his paper. "Can you sketch something that would help me understand what you're seeing in your mind?"

"Sure," Luke said, "and I just thought of something else I could add." He returned to his seat and added the following illustration:

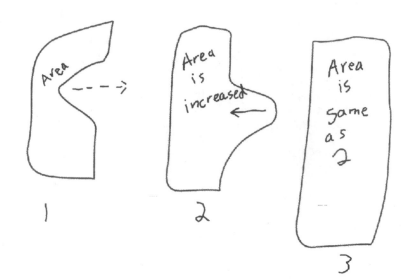

Then he wrote: *If that didn't make any sense here's a new approach. If you draw a square around the golf course it has a larger area than the golf course because of all the squggles. Look at the next diagram. Perimeter is same but area increases on #2.*

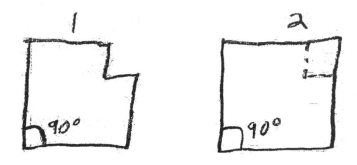

Ann Maria drew from her experience with the activity we had done the day before, *The Area Stays the Same: I disagree with my friend because I remember when we were doing the "area and perimeter shapes" the perimeter changed its lenght, but the area stayed the same because we didn't take any parts away from the square, but if we did take some away then the area would have changed. So that's why, I think because its just like the "area and perimeter shaps.*

While Anfernee disagreed with the method suggested, it wasn't clear why. He wrote: *I do not agree with my friend because by using string it will tell you how much sowed* [sod] *needed but it will not tell you how to do all the eages.* It took Anfernee most of the period to write that. He used his time laboriously looking up the spelling of *using* and *string* in the dictionary, refusing my and other students' offers to help with the spelling. He was clearly spent by his effort when he turned in his paper. I accepted it, knowing that to push Anfernee further that day would have been counterproductive.

NOTE If I had asked the children a multiple-choice question about the problem, Anfernee would have gotten the answer correct. However, his right answer would have hidden his confusion. It's important to remember that correct answers can hide a lack of understanding and that teachers should try to find out as much as possible about what students understand.

NOTE While class discussions are valuable for learning about children's thinking, asking them to write about their experience often provides more information about what students understand—or don't understand.

Talon felt that if he measured carefully, his friend's method would work.

Half of the class agreed with the suggested method. Talon's work was typical. He wrote: *I agree with my friend's reasoning because if you lay the string around the perimeter of the Blob carefully then take it off and make it into the shape of a square, then measure the width and the length you would find out the area.*

I didn't accept Talon's paper when he initially brought it to me. I knew that he loved to draw, so I said, "Talon, would you draw me a picture of what you mean? I think it will help me understand your thinking."

His eyes lit up. "Okay," he said and practically ran back to his seat. He drew a sketch of a blob with the multiplication sentence 7 x 10 = 70 inside it. He also drew a line around the perimeter of the blob and an arrow extending from the line to a square he had drawn in the corner of a rough graph on which both the horizontal and vertical axes were divided into numbered segments. Below the graph Talon had written, 7 x 10 = 70. Talon's drawing did not further explain or defend what he had written but did reinforce that his thinking was unclear.

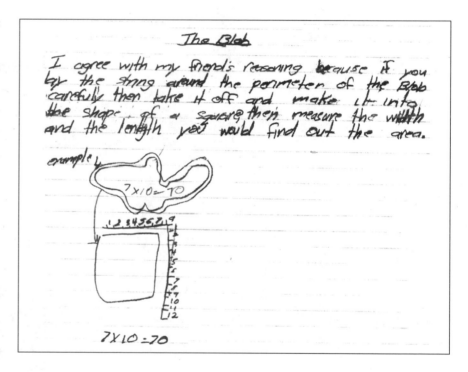

Kathleen's response was similar to Talon's, but she focused on a different aspect: *I agree with my friends reasoning, because the method she used was to measure, and that was a good idea no matter what you do. Laying the string into a square so you can measure is good, but you have to make sure to measure it at the right mark.*

Malkia was her usual forthright self: *I'm not really sure because I don't know about length times width so I don't know if it would work. I'm also not sure because the paper that shows how it is going to look is not the real golf cors so how are you going to know?*

Both Catheryne's and Zak's responses revealed their lack of understanding of area and perimeter. While Catheryne agreed with the method suggested, Zak was not sure.

Catheryne wrote: *I agree with my friend's because if you measure A then B then C then D then E then finally F you will find out how long the sod on the golf course will be.*

Catheryne's explanation reveals a lack of understanding about area and perimeter.

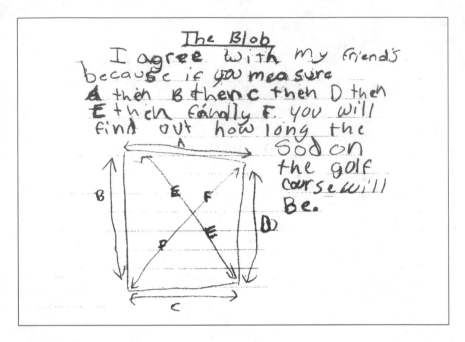

Zak wrote: *I not sure that my friend is right or rong because I think that if this was blob this is how I would do it. My gess would be a 72 ft long corse and 20 ft wid.*

Zak's reasoning was neither confident nor correct.

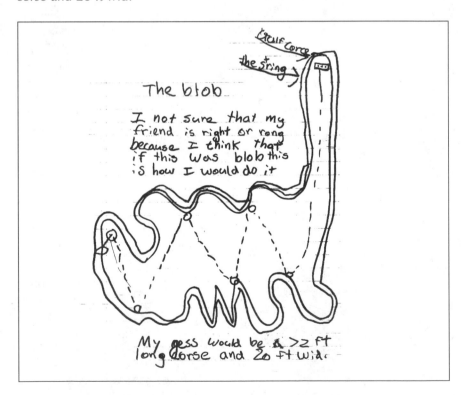

WHOLE CLASS LESSON   Foot Stuff

Overview

This activity provides students an experience with area in a way that is different from the usual focus of applying formulas to regular shapes. *Foot Stuff* also gives children the opportunity to explore the idea that shapes with the same-length perimeters can have different-size areas.

To begin, students figure the area of one of their feet in square centimeters. Then they cut a piece of string equal in length to the perimeter of their foot, arrange this string into the shape of a square, and figure the area of the square. Finally, the children compare the area of the square with the area of their foot. Students typically are surprised that the areas of their foot and the square are not the same, even though they have the same-length perimeter. This activity can help them see that areas of two shapes with the same-length perimeter can be different.

Before the lesson

Gather these materials:

■ An ample supply of centimeter-squared paper (see blackline master, page 195)

■ Ample supplies of scissors, tape, and string.

Write these instructions on the board, make an overhead transparency of them, or distribute individual copies for students to read at their seat as you introduce the activity (see blackline master, page 187):

Foot Stuff

You need: String
         Centimeter-squared paper

1. Trace around your foot (with your shoe off) on a sheet of centimeter-squared paper.

2. Figure the area of your foot in square centimeters and record.

3. Cut a piece of string equal to the length of the perimeter of your foot. Tape your foot string, in the shape of a square, on the sheet of centimeter-squared paper.

4. Figure the area of the square and record the result.

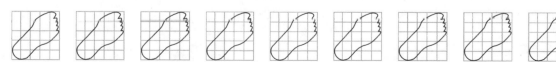

Teaching directions

■ In order to be sure that students are familiar with square centimeters, hold up a sheet of centimeter-squared paper for the class to see. Ask for volunteers to explain why it's called centimeter-squared paper. Clarify that the sides of each square on the paper measure 1 centimeter and that each square is equal to 1 square centimeter.

■ Tell the children that they will take off one of their shoes and draw around their foot on a sheet of centimeter-squared paper. Demonstrate this procedure. Then tell them that they are to figure the area of their foot in square centimeters by finding out how many square centimeters their foot covers. Point out that because a foot is irregularly shaped, they will have to deal with bits and pieces of squares and their answers won't be exact.

■ Show the children the correct mathematical symbolization for square centimeters: *sq cm* or *cm*².

■ Tell the children that after they have found the area of their foot, they are to cut a piece of string that is equal in length to their foot's perimeter. Demonstrate by moving your finger along the outline of your foot tracing. Then they should tape this string, in the shape of a square, to the same sheet of centimeter-squared paper and find the square's area.

■ Direct the students to work on the activity individually, in pairs, or in groups, but make clear that each student is to measure his or her own foot.

■ After the students have found the areas of their foot outlines and string squares, use the following questions to facilitate a class discussion. For each question, you may first have the students talk in small groups and then ask for volunteers to report to the class.

What method did you use to figure the area of your foot?

How did you figure out how to arrange your perimeter string into the shape of a square?

How does the area of your foot compare with the area of the string square? (Students typically are surprised that the areas differ and often think they made a computation error.)

Why do you think it makes sense that the areas of your foot and string square are different?

■ After the discussion, have the children write about why they think the areas of their foot and the square were different. You may want to write the question on the board:

Why do you think the areas of your foot and string square are different?

FROM THE CLASSROOM

"This is a sheet of centimeter-squared paper," I began, holding up a sheet for the class to see. "Why do you think this is called centimeter-squared paper?"

Only five students raised their hand, and I called on Rifka.

"It's called that because each little box is a centimeter long on every side, and each box is in the shape of a square," she answered.

I nodded. "I'll add *centimeter-squared paper* to our area and perimeter word list," I said, "and I'll tape a sheet to the list as a reminder." I knew

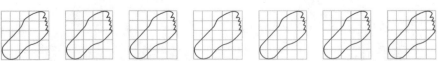

the students would be doing a good deal of writing during the unit, and I thought the reference would be useful to them.

Then I continued with the lesson. "This is an activity called *Foot Stuff.* You'll each figure the area of one of your feet, using a sheet of centimeter-squared paper. First, take off one shoe and place that foot on the centimeter-squared paper." I demonstrated as I gave directions. "Trace carefully around your foot. Hold your pencil vertically so you get as accurate an outline of your foot as possible. You may want to ask a partner to trace your foot and then you trace his or her foot." I held up the tracing of my foot for the class to see.

"What if your foot won't fit on the page?" Luke asked. Several children snickered.

"That may happen," I agreed, ignoring the laughter. "You might try rotating your foot just a bit so it fits on the paper, or tape two sheets together."

Since there were no other questions, I wrote the first direction on the board:

1. Trace around your foot (with your shoe off) on a sheet of centimeter-squared paper.

Then I continued. "Next, you'll figure the area of your foot by finding out how many square centimeters your foot covers. Notice that my foot partially fills some squares. Yours will too, so you'll have to think about how to count those bits and pieces. Your answer won't be completely accurate, since your foot is an irregular shape and your calculations are unlikely to be exact. Nonetheless, come as close as you can."

"If we have a partner, do we each do our foot, or can only one of us do it?" Malkia asked.

"Each of you should do your foot. That way we'll have more data to examine when we're done," I replied.

"Shouldn't everybody do the same foot?" Nathan wondered.

"Not necessarily. Either foot will do," I said.

There were no further questions.

"Once you've found the area of your foot, record it inside the outline of your foot. You can label it in one of two ways, *sq cm* or *cm*^{2}. Just make sure the label is large and clear enough to read from the back of the room if it's posted in front." I added *square centimeters* and the two abbreviations to the area and perimeter word list.

I wrote the second direction on the board:

2. Figure the area of your foot in square centimeters and record.

"This sounds fun. Can we start?" asked Brandon.

"Not yet. I have a few more directions for you," I responded, walking to the shelf where the string was kept. "After you've figured out the area of your foot, cut a length of string that's equal to the perimeter of your foot."

"You mean the outside of your foot?" Kathleen wondered.

"The length of the outline you drew," I clarified. I drew my finger around the perimeter of my foot tracing.

"Oh, I get it," Kathleen replied.

"Take the string that's the same length as the perimeter of your foot, shape it into a square, and tape it onto the same paper you traced your foot on. It's okay to overlap the string square and the outline of your foot.

NOTE When should we give students specific directions and when should they figure out what to do on their own? It's important to describe procedures clearly and, if possible, to model what they are to do. However, if an aspect of a task isn't merely procedural or organizational but requires students to think mathematically to solve a problem, then less information is better. We should give students as many opportunities as we can to think and reason mathematically for themselves.

Find the area of the square in square centimeters and record it inside the string square."

Up to this point, I had been giving the students specific directions and modeling how they were to proceed. However, I chose not to demonstrate how to make the string into a square, but to let them solve this problem on their own.

I recorded the two final directions:

3. Cut a piece of string equal to the perimeter of your foot. Tape your foot string, in the shape of a square, on the centimeter-squared paper.

4. Figure the area of the square and record the result.

Observing the Children

The students began to work. I walked around the room, helping them get started. Some children remembered my oral directions; others referred to the directions I had written on the board. Most children quickly got their paper and began tracing their foot.

However, I noticed that Sharnet was taking a long time getting started. She slowly untied her shoe and then dawdled at the pencil sharpener. Finally her friend Malkia urged, "C'mon, Sharnet, let's go!"

"But I don't know what to do," Sharnet replied plaintively.

"I'll help you, just hurry up and take off your shoe!" Malkia said. When Sharnet had her shoe off, Malkia handed her a sheet of centimeter-squared paper. "Now, put your foot on the paper and I'll help you trace around it." Sharnet smiled happily and placed her foot on the paper.

As I approached his table, Anfernee complained, "I can't count all these squares. I'll never keep track." Anfernee tended to give up easily, and I wasn't surprised by his comment.

"Does someone have a suggestion for Anfernee?" I asked his table-mates. Nathan, Nicole, and Rifka looked up from their work.

"Sure," Nathan replied. "Just put a dot in each of the whole squares you count."

"Oh, that's a good idea, Nathan," Rifka said.

"Yeah. Thanks," said Anfernee.

I noticed that most students approached the problem of figuring the area of their foot by counting each whole square inside the outline. Some children put a dot or some other mark in each square to help them keep track. JT, however, partitioned his foot into rectangles, finding the area of each smaller rectangle and then adding the partial squares that were left over.

After about 20 minutes, most children had found the area of their foot and were working on finding the area of their string square. I noticed that Doug's string square was markedly smaller than his tablemates'.

"Doug," I said, "your foot tracing appears to be about the same size as the others at your table, yet I notice that your string square is much smaller than theirs." Doug stopped working, as did Marcel, Kirsten, and Neshey.

"Hey, you're right," Doug exclaimed. "I wonder why?"

"Your string looks too short for your foot," Kirsten observed. "How did you measure it?"

"Measure it?" Doug replied.

JT partitioned rectangles within his foot perimeter and carefully accounted for each partial square.

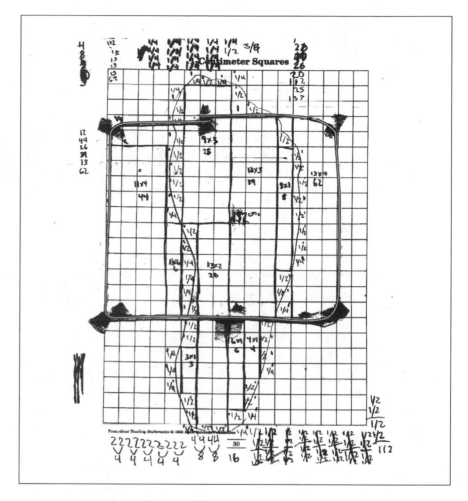

"Yeah, you know, put it along the perimeter of your foot," Kirsten said.

"We were supposed to put it along the foot perimeter? Oh. Now I know why it's too short. I just cut any old length," Doug said sheepishly. His tablemates giggled.

Malkia often tried to visit with her friends during math, but today she was focused and productive. She not only completed her work, but she also offered unsolicited help to Sharnet and anyone else nearby, thus satisfying her need to interact with others. "Do you have a way to keep track of the whole squares? Here, let me help you," she said to Sharnet.

Talon, too, was often unfocused, but today he was attentive to the task. "That's a rectangle," he said to Zak, who was sitting nearby and whose struggle to get his string into the shape of a square had produced instead a narrow rectangle.

"I can't get a square," Zak complained.

"Me, neither," called Brandon.

"I keep getting a rectangle!" Rachel said with frustration.

I decided to interrupt the class but had difficulty getting their attention. When the children were finally quiet, I said, "Several students seem to need advice on how to make the foot perimeter string into the shape of a square."

"Try doing one side at a time," Rifka suggested.

NOTE Circulating through the room as children work allows you to clarify directions, answer questions, and redirect those who have gotten off the track. It also can help you understand what students are thinking.

Erin added, "Or take the string and fold it in half. With a marker, mark that spot where you folded it, because it's one of the corners."

"Take a ruler and measure the length of the string. Then divide it by four and that's one of the sides," offered Luke.

"Are there any other suggestions?" I asked. There were none, so I said, "Anyone who is still uncertain about how to shape the string into a square can meet with me at the corner table."

Zak and Brandon joined me, bringing their paper and string. "Did you hear an idea that you might like to try?" I asked.

"Let's try folding the string," Brandon replied. Zak first helped Brandon even the ends of Brandon's string and tape it onto Brandon's paper. Then he made his own string into a square with ease.

"That's a good idea to fold the string," Zak said as the boys got up to return to their own seats.

There was a burst of conversation from Nathan's table, and I hurried over to investigate.

"You must have done it wrong!" Nathan exclaimed to Nicole.

"No, you must have!" Nicole retorted.

It was unusual for Nathan and Nicole to argue. "What's going on?" I asked.

"I only got 146 square centimeters for my foot. Nicole got a little more than 170. How is that possible? She's a girl!" Nathan cried.

"Girls can have bigger feet than boys," Nicole replied. "Besides, maybe you didn't trace right. It could be a measurement error."

"Wait! Stop!" Rifka commanded. "I don't think so, because I watched Nathan and he was really careful. But that's not the point. Look at your feet. Nathan, put your foot next to Nicole's. It's smaller." Nathan and Nicole compared feet and realized that Rifka was right.

"Oh. But what I don't get then is this. Is it possible to have a 182-square-centimeter square and a 146-square-centimeter foot?" Nathan asked.

Erin had been listening to the conversation with interest. "Wouldn't the square and the foot be the same size?" she asked me.

"What do you think?" I replied.

"Yes, they should be because all you did was take the squares off one place in your foot and put them somewhere else on the square," Erin said.

"I don't think so," Nicole countered. "You could have two shapes with the same area and different perimeters, like in that activity we did the other day."

"You mean *The Area Stays the Same?*" I asked.

"Yeah, that's it. I figure that if the areas can be the same and the perimeters can change, then the opposite must be true."

The other children were silent, thinking about Nicole's conjecture.

"I need to think about that some more," Nathan said slowly. "Let me see your papers," he said.

I interrupted the class again after hearing Nathan's comment. "When you've finished this activity, please post your papers on the bulletin board so we can take a look at your measurements," I said.

A Class Discussion

A few minutes later, all but three of the children had put up their papers. I told the three who weren't quite finished to post their work as soon as they were done but to listen and feel free to contribute to the class discussion we were about to have.

NOTE It's important for students to verbalize their thinking, because it helps them clarify and cement their understanding. Also, hearing other points of view can help stimulate their own thinking even though it can be difficult to follow others' reasoning.

After getting the children's attention, I said, "While I watched you work, I noticed that you used different methods for figuring out the area of the outline of your foot. Take a minute to share with others at your table how you did it."

Most of the children got involved in the table discussions. Many students pointed to their work or sketched ideas on paper. Some children, however, were quiet, listening or perhaps thinking about other things. I moved around the room, encouraging students to try to follow their classmates' reasoning, knowing that doing so is sometimes difficult.

After a bit I said, "Who would like to share?" About half the class raised their hand, and I called on Marcus.

"I wrote the numbers in the squares to keep track," he said. "Like, I put a 1 in the first square and a 2 in the second square and so on." I didn't notice it at the time, but later when I recounted Marcus's squares, I realized that he counted every square as a whole, even the partial squares. When I'm thinking mainly about my teaching I sometimes miss things about children's work that are incorrect or incomplete. When I do notice a mistake and feel the child won't be embarrassed by it, I'll sometimes bring it to the attention of the entire class. The next day I talked with Marcus privately about his work. He made a new tracing with my help and more accurately figured the area.

"Raise your hand if you numbered the squares like Marcus did," I said. Nobody raised their hand. "How else did you do it, then?" I asked.

A number of students now raised their hand, JT among them. I was pleased that he was volunteering to share his ideas. Usually he would talk at his table but remain silent during whole class discussions. Shyly JT said, "Well, I looked at my foot, and I didn't feel like counting all those squares one by one. So I counted off rectangles inside my foot and used multiplication to find out how many squares there were. Then I added the answers together and added the little pieces to that."

"Huh?" Eric said. "I don't get it."

"Show the class your paper," I urged JT, who quickly held it up.

"Oh! I get it now. You made smaller rectangles inside your foot. That's a good idea!" Eric said. JT beamed with pride.

JT continued, "Then I looked at all the little pieces left over when I was done with the whole squares. I thought that they were all halves or fourths, so I wrote the right fraction for each one in the little piece. It got hard because some of the pieces were pretty small," he said.

"What did you do next?" I asked.

"I wrote the number ½ down each time I saw one, and I ended up with four little ½s written one under the other. So that made 2. Then I counted up all my 2s to get 4s, and added all the 4s to get 8s, and added the 8s to get 16. Then I added all that to the whole numbers."

"Huh?"

"What'd he do?"

The class was clearly confused by JT's explanation.

"Why don't you unpin your paper and walk around and show everyone?" I suggested. JT walked around the room so everyone could see what he had done. I was impressed with JT's precision in counting, and the rest of the class was too. I was concerned, however, that some of his bits and pieces did not appear to be one-half or one-fourth of a square. I made a mental note to check later and get back to JT if necessary the next day.

"That's really good," said Nathan. "I counted fractions too, but I didn't write them down like JT. I used tallies. You can really tell how accurate he is because everything is written down."

Rachel agreed. "I thought it would look messy if I hung up my paper with all my dots on it for the partial squares, so I erased them before I put my paper up. But now I'm sorry I did."

JT was the only student who had partitioned his foot tracing into rectangles. The other students had counted the whole squares, one by one, marking them in some way as they counted.

Catheryne, for example, explained, "I saw Rifka putting a little circle in each square and I thought that was a good idea, so I did it too." Several children nodded agreement. "For the little bits I just looked and tried to see which ones I could put together to make a whole one," she finished.

Catheryne used circles to indicate whole squares. She drew lines to join partial squares that equaled a whole.

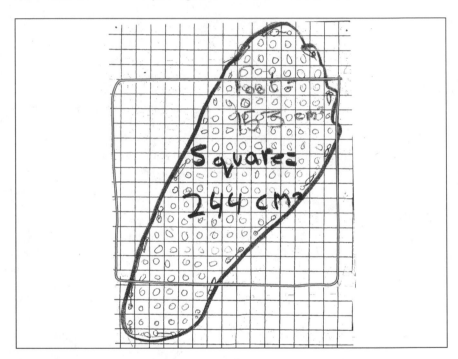

"Who counted like Catheryne and Rifka?" I asked. About half the class had.

"I used a tally," Nick said.

"Me, too."

"So did I!"

I had two or three more students explain their methods.

Then, changing the focus of the conversation, I said, "I'm interested in how you got your perimeter string into the shape of a square. What was your method? Share with your group and then be ready to share with the whole class." The room became noisy again as students compared methods. After a bit I asked for their attention.

"I folded my string in half and in half again, like this," Erin said, taking a piece of string and demonstrating.

"Why does that work?" I asked.

"Because the sides are the same length on a square, and this gives me four equal sides," Erin replied.

NOTE It's important for the class to hear different approaches so students have as many opportunities as possible to encounter an explanation that makes sense to them.

"Who made a square a different way?" I continued.

Kirsten offered, "Just take a ruler and lay your string along it. When you know how long it is just divide that number by 4. Then count centimeters on your paper and you've got your square."

"I like my method the best," Brandon announced.

"Which was?" I asked.

Brandon laughed and said, "Just move it around until it looks like a square." The rest of the class laughed.

"Would it be accurate?" I asked him.

"I don't know. Sure," Brandon replied.

"How would you check?" I prodded.

Brandon was silent, but Nathan chimed in, "Just count each side. You could adjust if you needed to."

"Oh, yeah," said Brandon.

"Were there other methods?" I asked the class. Nobody else volunteered.

"Okay, so now we've heard how some of you counted the squares in the outline of your foot and made your string into the shape of a square. How did the areas of your foot tracing and string square compare?" A number of students began talking at the same time.

"Wait, wait!" I said, "I can't hear if you all talk at once." The class quieted and about three-fourths of the children raised their hand. I called on Ann Maria.

"The area of my square was more than the area of my foot," she announced. The class immediately began talking loudly again.

With difficulty, I quieted the class and said, "Raise your hand if the same thing happened for you." Every student indicated that it had.

"Let's look at some of the areas," I said as I walked to the bulletin board. "Anfernee's foot area was 127 square centimeters and the area of his square was 196 square centimeters. Malkia's foot area was 172 square centimeters and the area of her square was 225 square centimeters. Rachel's foot area was 126 square centimeters and the area of her square was 185 square centimeters. What was your reaction when you found that the area of the square wasn't the same as the area of your foot?"

"I thought I'd done something wrong," Nathan said.

"Me, too!" Anfernee echoed.

Eric said, "I went back and counted both areas again to check."

"So did I," said Kathleen. "But then I looked at everyone else's paper at my table and theirs were all different too, so I felt better."

"But why wouldn't they be the same?" Nathan said.

"Talk about Nathan's question with your group," I suggested. "See if you can come up with some ideas about why the areas wouldn't be the same." If Nathan hadn't asked his question, I would have brought up this issue for discussion at this time.

The children talked for several minutes among themselves. As I circulated, I noticed that the question was engaging and challenging for some students, while other children had difficulty staying focused. This didn't surprise me, because I didn't expect every child to engage to the same degree with this mathematical question, but I wanted students to listen to one another's ideas.

After a few minutes I reconvened the entire class and said, "What does your group think is going on?"

Kirsten answered quickly, "I was talking to Rifka about how to get the least area with the same perimeter and the most area with the same perimeter. If you have a circle, everything goes away from the center, and that gives you the most area, and a line segment will give you the least area."

From her tone of voice it was clear that Kirsten felt she had some understanding of why the areas had differed. But I could tell from the expressions on many faces that Kirsten's explanation didn't make sense to the majority of her classmates. I asked the class, "Who can explain what Kirsten means?"

Rifka replied, "I think that what Kirsten means is that the foot doesn't have as big an area as the square because your foot area is kind of cramped together and the square is really open," she said.

On hearing Rifka's explanation Brandon exclaimed, "Oh, that makes sense. I just got it now. It's like, your foot is long and skinny, and the square is short and fat." Several students giggled at Brandon's characterization, but he continued. "So the square's got more room. That's why you didn't want us to put the string in a rectangle—it would be too much like our foot."

"That's true," I told Brandon.

Rachel raised her hand. "Our group wasn't really sure why the areas changed. But is it that when the perimeter stays the same, the area changes?" she asked.

Rifka turned to Rachel and said, "That's what seems to be happening."

"But I don't get it," Erin said. "Why does the area change when the perimeter stays the same?"

"Can another group help us make sense out of this?" I asked, wanting to hear from other students.

The class was unusually quiet.

Kirsten raised her hand again, and I called on her. "To get the most area you have to have the most space inside the shape. There's more space in a square than in a skinny rectangle like our foot," she said.

Erin replied, "But if you took a square you could add a centimeter on one side and take it away from the other without changing the area—that's why I don't get it."

Nathan blurted, "But you are taking it away … no, now I'm thinking like Erin. I don't get it."

"Sometimes when you think you understand something and you're presented with conflicting information, you get confused," I told the class. "It's a normal part of learning something new. When you're confused, often you want to find out what's really going on. I'm comfortable with your confusion because I know that you'll have many more experiences during this unit to help you make sense of what's happening. For now, I'd like you to write about why you think the areas of your foot and the square were different."

The children's papers revealed their confusion. I wasn't surprised when about two-thirds of the class indicated that they didn't know why. However, their attempts to reason it out were very interesting.

Hilda wrote: *Well I think because maybe its because the squares are in your foot cause you counted. Because your foot is biger achely [actually] the square is biger cause I got 180 and my feet is 170.*

Neshey was direct: *I think when I measured my foot I thought my foot was going to be the same size as the sqare and I'm still confused about it.*

NOTE Piaget said that the disequilibrium that results when something you think you know about the world is proved to be false is a natural part of the learning process. The greatest potential for learning exists when students are in a state of disequilibrium.

Erin's own logic confused her. She wrote: *My foot is 158 c.m.². My square is 225 c.m.². The square is odviosly bigger. I don't know why. I thought that both the square and the foot would be the same because every time you take off a square it comes on a different place.*

Erin's paper showed her confusion.

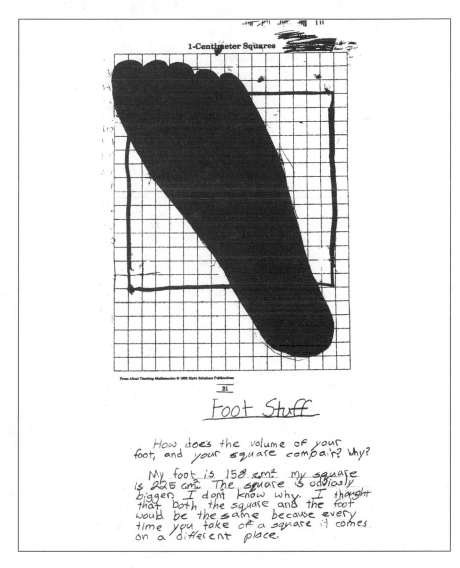

Ann Maria and Alex each made a connection to the activity *The Area Stays the Same,* but couldn't explain the connection. Ann Maria wrote: *Answers: I think that its just like the other project we did but I really don't know. Why, because I'm kind of in between and I don't know what to think.* Alex's paper revealed his preconception—a common one—that different shapes with the same perimeter should have the same area. He wrote: *The area of my square compares to the area of my foot because they are bolth made of the same string but I stil don't understand why the square is bigger because The Area Stays The Same unit the shape had the longer string.*

About a third of the class seemed to make some sense of why the areas differed. Kirsten's written explanation was similar to the one she had given in class. She didn't explain how she came to the conclusion about circles and squares, though. She wrote: *The area of my foot is a lot smaller then the area of the square, because if you want to get the most area you have to have everything going away from each other. To do this, you have to have a circle, it has the most area, a square has the second most area.*

The closer the perimeter is to itself, the smaller the area (like the foot.)

Kirsten had a sense of why the areas differed, but she didn't explain her conclusion about circles and squares.

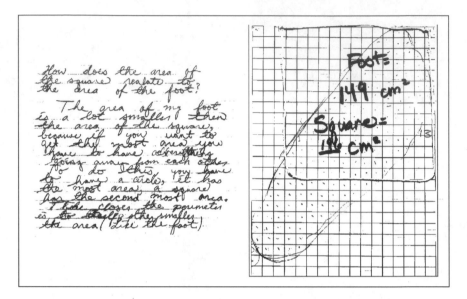

Brandon wrote: *1. The area of the square is 40 cm.'s bigger than the area of my foot. That is every little square and half square put together. 2. I think the area of the square changes because you are puting it in the shape of a square with both sides the same and feet are long and skinny, so I think if you put it in the shape of a rectangle it might be closer to the area of the foot.*

Rachel's explanation was brief: *They compare by the foot is 126 cm² and my square is 185 cm² so the foot is longer and skinner but the square is shorter, because changing the string into a square changes the area.*

Nicole loved to write, and she usually took a good deal longer than the rest of her classmates to finish. Today was no exception. Although some of her vocabulary was incorrect, she used an example to explain herself: *In* <u>Foot Stuff</u>, *my sqare is 225cm² and my foot is 170 cm². When I changed the foot into a square it changed the area, but not the perimeter. What I think happened is the perimeter was the same, but the shape was differerent so the area changed. Example:*

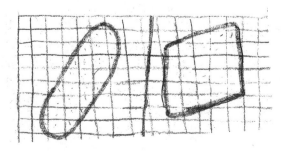

This oval is only 8½ cm². The dimond is 23²/₃ cm². They both have the same perimeter. As you may have already noticed, the oval is almost the same shape as the foot. The dimond is almost the same shape as the square. Since the dimond and the oval are totaly different shapes, then the oval has a whole bunch of different bits of squares along the dg like halfs, forths, etc. while the dimond may only have eights along the edg. I am making a guess that this is why my square is bigger than my foot.

Marcus began numbering every whole square.

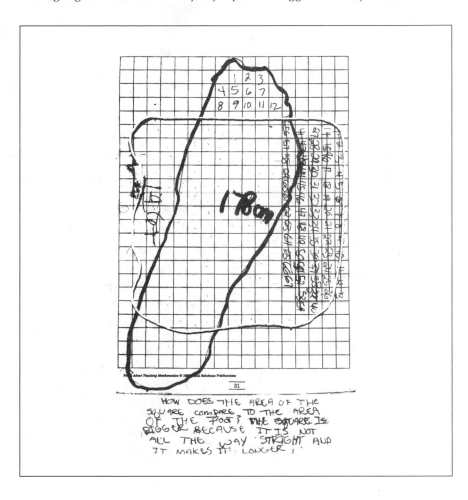

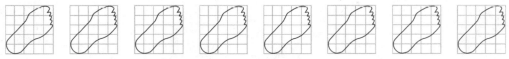

WHOLE CLASS LESSON   Spaghetti and Meatballs for All

Overview

Thinking about how to arrange tables and chairs to accommodate a large number of diners is a real-life context in which students can link the concepts of area and perimeter to the world around them. The story in *Spaghetti and Meatballs for All!*, a picture book written by Marilyn Burns and illustrated by Debbie Tilley, provides another opportunity for students to learn that different-shape rectangles with the same area can have different-length perimeters and that rectangles with different-length perimeters can have different areas.

After hearing the story and re-creating some of the table arrangements mentioned in it, students explore how many ways there are to arrange various numbers of smaller square tables into a large rectangular table that will seat exactly 32 people.

Before the lesson

Gather these materials:
■ A copy of *Spaghetti and Meatballs for All!* (Scholastic, 1997)
■ An ample supply of inch-squared paper (see blackline master, page 196)
■ Inch-square Color Tiles, approximately 70 for every group of four children
■ Overhead projector (optional)

Teaching directions

■ Read aloud the picture book *Spaghetti and Meatballs for All!* In the story, Mr. and Mrs. Comfort invite 32 family members and friends over for a reunion and set eight square tables that can seat four people at each, one on each side. As more and more people arrive, they try rearranging the square tables so that different-size groups can sit together. The story provides a real-world context for area and perimeter as the children investigate how different arrangements of eight square tables can provide seating for different numbers of people.

■ After you have finished reading the story, ask the children to describe the problems the Comforts faced as they rearranged tables in order to accommodate more and more guests.

■ Ask the students to take four inch-square Color Tiles and put them together in as many table arrangements as they can. Explain the rule that whenever a tile is joined with another tile, the two tiles must touch along the length of an entire side. Point out that touching only at the corners is not acceptable. Illustrate several correct and incorrect arrangements on an overhead projector or on the board.

■ After the children have made various arrangements, have them report on what they built. Re-create their arrangements on the board or on the overhead projector. For each arrangement, demonstrate how to count the exposed sides to figure out how many people could be seated. Introduce the concept and definition of congruent figures when children suggest figures that are shaped the same but whose position orientation is different (i.e., upside down or "flipped"). Add *congruent* to the area and perimeter word list.

■ Now ask the children to eliminate the table arrangements that are not rectangles. You may choose to have them define what a rectangle is. Be sure to tell them that a square is a specific kind of rectangle, one with four equal sides. Add *square* and *rectangle* to the area and perimeter word list.

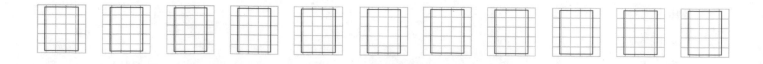

■ Introduce the concept that we can label a rectangle by identifying its length and width: 1 by 4, 2 by 2, etc. Again, reemphasize the concept of congruence, that is, that a 1-by-4 rectangle is the same as a 4-by-1 rectangle but in a different orientation.

■ Use eight tiles to build a 1-by-8 rectangle and ask how many people can sit at a table of that size and shape. Rearrange the eight tiles into a 2-by-4 rectangle and again ask how many people could sit there.

■ Tell the children to imagine that Mr. and Mrs. Comfort want to sit all 32 of their guests at one solid rectangular table created by joining a number of small square tables. Present the problem: how many different tables can they create that will sit exactly 32 people? Ask students to draw their solutions and record the dimensions of each table.

■ After students have had adequate time to work on the problem, use the following suggestions to hold a class discussion:

Help the students see a pattern in the dimensions of the rectangles: 15-by-1, 14-by-2, 13-by-3, 12-by-4, 11-by-5, 10-by-6, 9-by-7, 8-by-8. (Beyond this point the pattern reverses itself, but the rectangles are congruent with ones already formed.)

Ask: Which rectangular table would be the least expensive for the Comforts to create if they have to rent the individual square tables? Which would be the most expensive?

■ After the discussion, give the children a writing assignment to answer the following questions:

1. What did you notice as you worked? What patterns were helpful?

2. What arrangements are the most and least economical if you're renting by the small square table?

3. What do you notice about the areas and perimeters of the arrangements you made?

FROM THE CLASSROOM

"I'm going to read a story to you that can help you think more about area and perimeter," I told the class. "In this story, Mr. and Mrs. Comfort invite people over for a family reunion but run into problems because everyone wants to sit together. Listen while I read the story aloud, and think about the problems the Comforts faced."

I read the story to the class. Then I asked, "What was Mrs. Comfort worried about?"

I waited until about two-thirds of the students had raised their hand. Then I called on Nicole.

"There's not going to be enough room, because when you push tables together you lose chairs," she said.

"What do you mean?" I asked.

"It's like, if you put two together, you lose the seats that would be there where the tables touch. It's hard to explain." Nicole drew two tables in the air, pointing to the sides where they met.

"I understand," I replied.

David said, "She had a plan, but Mr. Comfort kept ruining it. He just should have listened to her."

"Yeah, he was pushy," added Ann Maria.

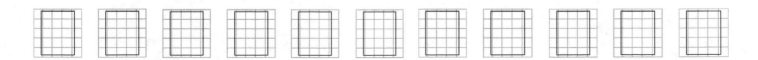

"What else did you notice?" I asked.

Nathan volunteered, "At the end, everything got done like Mrs. Comfort planned."

"There were four people at first, and they pushed two tables together to fit them and the Comforts. They kept pushing more and more tables together so they only had two seats at each table," Eric said.

"How did they end up with two seats at each table when they pushed them together?" I asked Eric.

"Well, it's like what Nicole said earlier. Where the tables touch, you lose one seat from each table where they touch on the left, and one seat where they touch on the right," Eric replied.

I sketched three adjoining squares on the board. "You mean Mrs. Comfort lost seats here?" I asked, drawing arrows that pointed to where the sides touched.

"Yes," Eric said.

Rifka added, "And then they kept dividing the tables for more people."

"Yeah, it was like they kept dividing the tables in fractions," said Sharnet.

"What do you mean by fractions?" I asked Sharnet.

"You know, dividing them in half and stuff," she replied. "Like if there was eight tables, divide them in half and get four."

Building Rectangular Arrangements

I turned on the overhead projector, on which I had placed four Color Tiles. "Imagine that these tiles are small square tables like the ones that Mr. and Mrs. Comfort rented. When they are used individually, four people can sit at each one, one on a side. Let's explore the different ways to arrange four tables to seat people. Let's follow the rule that if tiles attach, they do so along the length of an entire side. Attaching parts of sides or only corners is not okay." I pushed together four tiles to demonstrate my instruction.

"This arrangement follows the rules because where tiles touch, they touch along the entire length of a side," I told the class. "Here's one that doesn't work." I put four more tiles on the overhead in a stairlike arrangement.

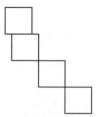

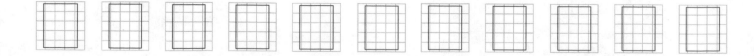

"Why doesn't this work?" I asked.

"Because some of those touch on the corners and you said they couldn't," Brandon called out. "And besides, you said they have to touch on the two whole sides and two of those only touch parts of the sides."

"That's true," I agreed.

"How about this arrangement?" I asked, as I rearranged four of the tiles.

There were conflicting opinions.

"It's not okay. One of them isn't touching."

"That's all right. There are two tables."

"I don't think that follows the rule."

"Yes, it does. No corners are touching."

I interrupted to clarify. "This arrangement is fine. The rule is that sides that touch must touch completely. But you can make separate tables."

Then I completed my instructions. "Use the tiles I've placed on your table. Share them with everyone in your group and build the different ways to arrange four tiles. Be sure to follow my rule."

The students immediately began working.

I circulated around the classroom, watching what the children were doing and making myself available to answer questions.

"Did you make a shape like this one I made?" Talon asked Zak, pointing to an L-shape arrangement.

"Not yet," Zak replied, and proceeded to build the shape.

At another table, Nicole had methodically arranged several groupings of four tiles each: a 1-by-4 rectangle; a 1-by-3 rectangle with a 1-by-1 square; and two 1-by-2 rectangles.

"I'm trying to be logical," Nicole told me cheerfully. "First I made a 1-by-4, then a 1-by-3 with a 1-by-1, then two 1-by-2s."

As I looked at Nicole's work, I heard a commotion at Nathan's table and went over to investigate.

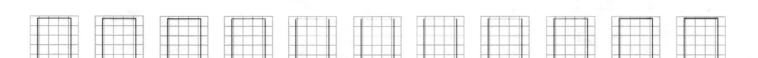

"She's hogging all the tiles and won't let us use them," Nathan complained, pointing accusingly at Malkia, who had all of the tiles in front of her, her arms circling them protectively.

"It's not fair," added Catheryne, another of Nathan's tablemates.

"But I need them," Malkia said. She was the oldest of several children in her family, and I was well aware that she often resented having to share things with her siblings.

I told Malkia, "Sometimes we worry we won't have enough of something, and we take more supplies than we actually need. I put enough tiles at your table so everyone will have plenty to use. Can you think of a way to share the tiles?"

"No," Malkia grumbled.

"Does someone else have an idea then?" I asked.

"Let's just put them all in the middle of the table and take what we need," Nathan suggested.

"Or we could count them out one by one so we each get the same," said Catheryne.

"But that would take too long," Malkia replied, eyeing the large pile. "Oh okay," she relented, "just take them." She pushed the tiles to the middle of the table.

After a few more minutes I asked for the entire class's attention.

"What arrangements did you make?" I asked. "One person describe an arrangement so I can build it with tiles on the overhead." I switched on the machine.

"You can make a straight line," Brandon suggested.

"How many tiles wide?" I asked him.

"One across and four in a row," he replied. "It's a little boring, but it works." I arranged a 1-by-4 rectangle on the overhead.

"Make a square with all four of them," Rachel said. I built a square using four tiles.

"You can make four separate tables," Nathan said.

"I did a three and a one," Nicole said.

"What do you mean?" I asked.

"One little table like one of Nathan's," Nicole explained, "and then a 1-by-3."

NOTE Even though we talk as a class throughout the year about how to share materials and space, the children still occasionally need help putting their ideas into practice. If Malkia had not decided to share the tiles, I would have had the students at Malkia's table dole out the tiles equally.

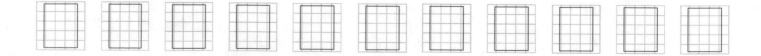

"You could make the letter T," Zak said. "Put three in a line and put the last one underneath the middle one." I duplicated Zak's arrangement.

"I made that too, but mine's upside down," said Eric. I built his arrangement under Zak's.

"Is Eric's arrangement the same as Zak's?" I asked the children. "Talk it over with your neighbor." The students talked among themselves. After a minute or two, I said, "What do you think?"

"They're the same, because all you have to do is flip Eric's and you get Zak's," Erin volunteered.

"I don't know if this is different, but it seems like they're the same because it's the same arrangement, just upside down," Kathleen said.

When the class fell silent, I told the children, "When you can flip, rotate, or slide a shape so that it fits exactly on another shape, the shapes are congruent. We'll consider congruent shapes to be the same." As I added the term *congruent* to the area and perimeter word list, some students nodded in agreement.

"I remember that."

"Oh, yeah."

"So, since I can rotate or flip Eric's arrangement so that it exactly matches Zak's, we can say that Eric's and Zak's arrangements are congruent and aren't different." I flipped Eric's tiles, placed them on Zak's, and then removed them from the overhead. "Who has another arrangement?"

Students volunteered different arrangements until the overhead was filled.

Even though not every child had contributed an idea, I stopped at this point because I knew there was enough variety here to satisfy my next instruction, which was to eliminate those table arrangements that weren't rectangles.

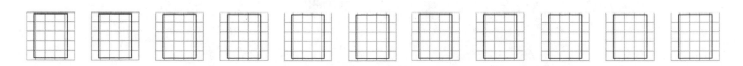

"What if I said that the only arrangements we could use were single rectangular tables made from all four tiles? What shapes would we have to remove?" I asked.

Rifka said, "Take off the one that looks like the letter T."

"Isn't it a rectangle?" Nick asked.

"No," Rifka replied.

"Why not?" Nick asked her.

"I think because it's made with two rectangles but it's not in the shape of one," she said.

"What is a rectangle?" I asked. "Talk about it at your table and be ready to share in a minute or so."

While the students talked with one another, I added the word *rectangle* to the area and perimeter word list. Then I called on Luke.

"It has four square, or 90-degree, angles," he offered. I wrote the word *rectangle* on the board, writing *has four 90-degree angles* underneath it.

"Four sides, it has four sides," Sharnet offered. I listed *has four sides* underneath Luke's idea.

Kirsten said, "Write that opposite sides are parallel."

"What do you mean by that?" I asked.

"The opposite sides have to be parallel, like the same distance apart," Kirsten replied. "Like railroad tracks." I listed *opposite sides are parallel* underneath Sharnet's idea.

"Anything else?" I asked the class. They were silent. "So then based on what you know about a rectangle, what about Eric's and Zak's arrangement? Is it a rectangle?" I asked.

"No," Rifka replied. "Even though it's made from two rectangles, it's not one because of the square sticking out below the three other ones."

"But it has four 90-degree corners," Nick protested.

"How many sides does it have?" I asked.

Nick squinted and pointed at the shape on the overhead, counting aloud. "One, two, three … 10. Oh, I guess it's not a rectangle."

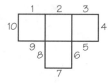

"How did you get 10?" I asked.

Nick said, "Easy. Just count each one of the little sides on the shape."

"But that'd give you the perimeter, not the number of sides," Rifka corrected Nick.

"Oh, yeah, you're right. I'll count again. So it's one, two, three … eight sides. Not a rectangle," Nick finished.

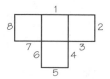

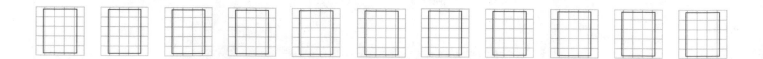

I removed the T arrangement from the overhead.

"What else can we eliminate?" I asked.

"Take off mine," Nicole said. "It's not a single rectangle." I removed the 1-by-3 rectangle with the separate 1-by-1 square.

Erin raised her hand and said, "The one that looks like the letter Z. It's like Zak's and Erik's because it looks like it's made from two rectangles but it isn't one."

"I agree."

"Take it off."

I removed the shape from the overhead.

"Take off the square, too," suggested Malkia, "because a square's not a rectangle."

Conversation erupted, with support expressed for both sides of the issue.

"Yes, it is!"

"No, it isn't!"

"There seems to be a difference of opinion here," I said. "Let's have someone explain what they think and why."

Brandon said, "A square isn't a rectangle, because it's a different shape."

"I disagree," Erin countered. "A square fits the definition of a rectangle."

"Yeah, but on a square the sides have to be the same and on a rectangle the sides aren't the same," Kathleen said.

"That's not true," Erin replied.

"Yes, it is!" Kathleen said.

I intervened. "A square is a rectangle," I explained. "It's a special kind of rectangle because it has four equal sides. Its sides are all the same length."

"So a rectangle doesn't have to have sides the same length but a square does?" Brandon asked. I nodded. "I didn't know that. Well, okay," he replied.

"So let's look at a square," I said, isolating a single tile. "Does it have four 90-degree angles, like a rectangle?"

The class chorused yes.

"It has four sides, which is a characteristic of all rectangles," I continued, indicating the four sides on the square. Running my finger along two opposite sides I asked, "Are the opposite sides parallel to each other?"

Again, students nodded and said yes.

"So that means the square stays!" Nathan said happily.

"But the L shape has to go for the same reason as the Z and the T," added Neshey.

"Why is that?" I asked.

"It's made of rectangles, but it isn't one," Neshey answered. I removed the L arrangement.

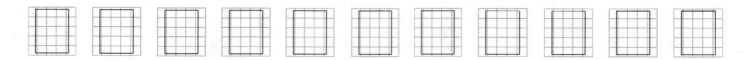

Returning to the overhead, I suggested, "We need to have a way to describe the two rectangles left on the overhead." I pointed to the 1-by-4 rectangle and said, "I could call this a 1-by-4 rectangle. Who can explain why that makes sense?"

After a minute I called on David.

"It's 1 square wide and 4 squares long," he said.

"What if I make another 1-by-4 rectangle but I rotate it 90 degrees so it's vertical? Can I still call it a 1-by-4 rectangle?" I made a second 1-by-4 rectangle on the overhead, orienting it vertically instead of horizontally.

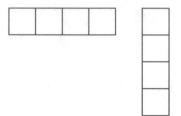

"Sure," Rifka replied. "It's the same rectangle no matter how it is on the overhead because it's the same shape."

"I can write 1 by 4 two ways," I said, and wrote on the overhead:

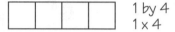

"Could I also call it a 4-by-1?" I asked.

After a moment I heard several "yeah's" and "it's okay's."

"It's just the same as the 1-by-4, except you're saying how long it is first and then how wide," Nathan commented.

"So it doesn't matter if I call it a 1-by-4 or a 4-by-1 because I can place one on top of the other and the sides and angles will match exactly. They're the same rectangle, and they're congruent with each other," I said.

I pointed to the square. "How should I label this?" I asked.

"Two-by-2," several children called out. I recorded this two ways:

Counting the Perimeter

I pointed to the 2-by-2 square table. "If one person sits on a side of a small square table, and no one sits at the corners or on the cracks between tables, how many people can sit at this table?" I asked.

"Easy. Eight," replied Nicole. "Just count two people on each side times 4."

"Did anyone count a different way?" I asked. Several students had.

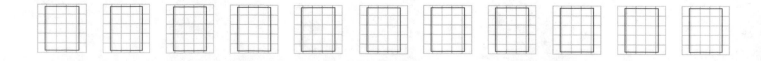

"I counted one by one, all the way around the square," Catheryne announced.

"I went two, four, six, eight," David said.

"I just looked at it and saw right away it was eight," Luke said.

"When you count the number of people who can sit at the table, you're actually finding its perimeter," I explained. "That's because each person sits at one side of the smaller squares and takes up one unit of length. So the perimeter of the 2-by-2 rectangle is 8 units."

"The perimeter of the 1-by-4 table is 10," Eric said.

"Yeah, 10 people can sit at that one," Anfernee added. Others nodded.

I then arranged the eight tiles into a 1-by-8 rectangle and said, "Let me ask a different question. Suppose Mrs. Comfort pushed the eight small square tables she rented into a straight line, one table wide, making a rectangle with no gaps or holes in it. What could she call this rectangle?"

"She could call it a *1-by-8* rectangle," Rifka suggested.

"Or an 8-by-1," said Nicole.

"Right," I replied, "you can take an 8-by-1 rectangle and put it on top of a 1-by-8 rectangle and they'll match exactly. They're congruent."

I labeled the rectangle *1 by 8* and asked, "How many people could the Comforts seat at this table?"

There was a buzz of conversation. Some students built the rectangle with tiles to figure the answer, and others looked at the rectangle on the screen, pointing and counting.

"I think there are 16," Nick ventured. "If you have one long row of tables, people at chairs where the tables meet have to go away."

Nicole announced, "No, it's 18! There are eight tables right? Eight on a side times 2 sides is 16, plus a person at each end makes 18."

David said, "I think there's 18 too. I built the rectangle and counted."

"Oh! I get it. I mean 18," said Nick.

"So the perimeter of the 1-by-8 table is 18 units. The Comforts could seat 18 people at this table," I recapped.

I put six more Color Tiles on the overhead. "Suppose Mrs. Comfort had rented 14 small square tables and arranged them into a rectangular table like this." I made a 2-by-7 rectangle with the tiles.

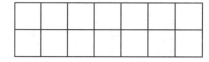

"How many people could the Comforts seat at that table?" I asked.

Again, conversation broke out. I called the children to attention.

"Eighteen," Ann Maria said confidently.

"How do you know?" I pushed.

"Seven plus 7 is 14, and then 2 and 2 is 4. Add the 4 and 14 and you get 18 people," she replied.

"Or you could count 7 plus 2 plus 7 plus 2," added Mike.

"That's weird," Zak said. "You added more tables but you didn't fit any more people."

"Yeah," Malkia added. "There were 18 at the 1-by-8 table and 18 at this one, too."

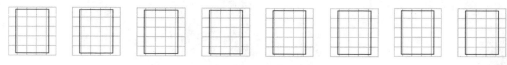

"Yes, it's possible to seat the same number of people at different-size and -shape rectangular tables. The area changes, but the perimeter stays the same," I told the class.

Next, I explained the problem I wanted the class to tackle. "Imagine that Mrs. Comfort wants to have all 32 guests sit at one large, solid rectangular table made from small square tables. How many different-size and -shape tables can seat all 32 people?"

"Does each table have to fit exactly 32?" JT wanted to know.

"Yes," I replied.

"Can we use more tiles?" Catheryne asked.

I said yes.

"How many tiles do we use?" Malkia asked.

"It will depend on the tables you build," I responded.

"Can we work with a partner?" Nicole asked.

"Sure," I replied. "I'll write the problem on the board." I wrote:

> Find all the different-size and -shape rectangular tables made from small square tables that will seat exactly 32 people.

"Use the tiles, but draw your solutions on a piece of paper," I added. "Be sure to record the dimensions of each table and the number of people it will seat."

Observing the Children

Kathleen began by making a 16-by-2 rectangle. I watched and listened as she thought out loud. "Hmm, 32 people, let's see. This should work, because 16 times 2 is 32." She frowned with concentration as she counted the exposed sides of the squares one by one. Then she looked up at me in surprise.

"I don't get it," she said. "I counted 36 seats. But that doesn't make sense, because 16 times 2 is 32. Maybe I miscounted." She counted the sides again, one by one.

"Still 36. Huh." She shrugged, mixed the 16 tiles back into the pile in the middle of her table, and began building another rectangle.

"What are you doing?" I asked her.

"Well, I must have messed up 'cause the first one I made didn't work, so I'm going to try something else," Kathleen replied.

"What are you going to try?" I asked.

"I don't know. I'm just going to mess around and see what happens," she said.

I watched as Kathleen began placing square tiles in a long row one square wide. She kept counting the sides one by one each time she added a new tile. Finally she smiled.

"It works! This one seats 32 people. It's a …1-by-15. Now to record it." Kathleen wrote the word *table* and listed *1) 1 x 15* below it. She then began sketching the rectangle on her paper.

Alex was sitting across from Kathleen.

"I found that one too," he said. "Now I'm trying a 2-by-something."

"Oh," Kathleen responded. She began trying to assemble a rectangle that would be four squares wide. Again, she used trial and error, adding tiles and counting the perimeter as she did so.

"That looks interesting," Alex said as he continued to build a 2-by-something rectangle. "Did it work?"

NOTE When faced with a problem whose solution is not evident, students need to be able to try different approaches. I've learned to resist telling students how to solve a problem or showing them what I think is a simpler or more efficient approach. Time to "mess around" is valuable for students' learning and should not be discouraged.

"Hold on," Kathleen said. Then she quickly added, "Yup, 32 people. A 12-by-4."

"You seemed to count the perimeter of this table more quickly than the last one," I said.

"Yeah. See, I realized that you can just count a long side, just one of the sides, and double it. Then you can add the seats at the end," Kathleen explained. She recorded the table dimensions and sketched the rectangle.

Nathan came up to me.

"I'm not drawing rectangles on my paper like everyone else," he said. "I decided to use Xs instead. But Luke told me it was wrong. Can't I draw Xs if I want to?" Nathan held his work out to me.

Nathan used Xs to represent the rectangular arrays of tables he built with tiles.

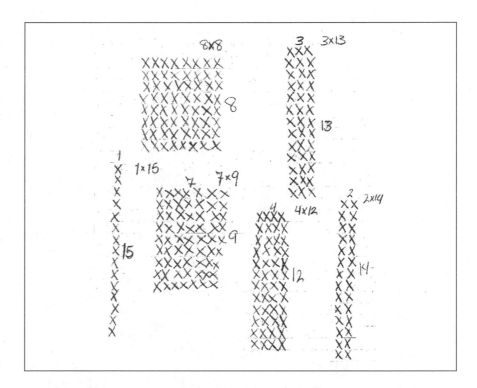

"Tell me about your paper," I suggested.

"First I used the tiles to make an 8-by-8 square, because 8 on each side equals 32. So instead of drawing little squares, I just put Xs for each tile instead. It comes out the same, in the end," Nathan explained.

"What you've done makes sense to me, too," I replied.

Nathan ran back to Luke. "See? I told you she'd say it was okay."

Talon and JT were working together and recording their work on two separate sheets of paper. Both boys liked having a partner and rarely chose to work independently.

"I found a 3-by-13," Talon said with pride. "I don't think anyone else found it."

"Yeah, and I helped him!" JT added. Talon had used a ruler to draw a 3-by-13 rectangle, which filled most of his paper. In the remaining space he drew the other rectangles he and JT had found.

"Then we found a 2-by-14," JT continued.

"And then a 1-by-15, and a 4-by-10, and a 6-by-12," Talon said.

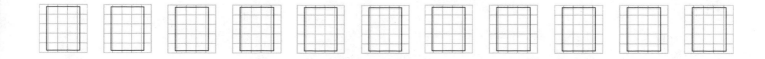

JT and Talon began recording by drawing a rectangle that measured 3 inches by 13 inches, the size of the rectangle they built with tiles. They switched to drawing small-scale rectangles so they could all fit on their paper.

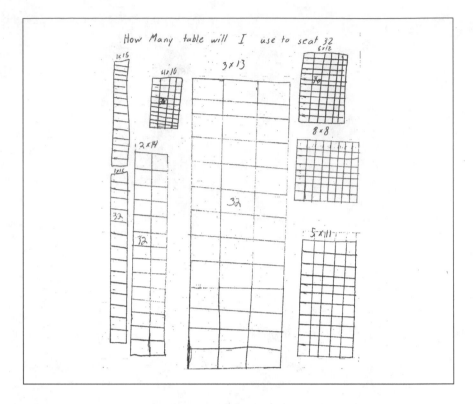

They appeared to have been following a sequential pattern of rectangles—a 1-by, then a 2-by, and so on—but then had deviated from it.

"How did you come up with each rectangle?" I asked.

"We just tried different things," Talon answered.

"How did you make sure each rectangle seats 32 people?" I asked, noticing that some of their rectangles would seat more than that.

"Huh?" JT asked. He seemed to have forgotten about the directions for the task. "Oh, yeah! We'd count each side one by one to see how many people could sit there."

I hesitated. Talon and JT both struggled occasionally with understanding directions. I debated whether or not to push them to find tables that seat exactly 32 people. It seemed as though the task of creating rectangles and determining the number of people who could be seated at each table was appropriate for both boys. However, I decided to hold off asking them to focus on tables for 32 until they had explored the problem further.

Nicole noticed a pattern in the dimensions of her table arrangements.

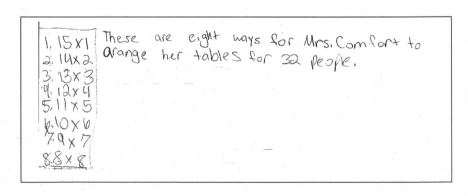

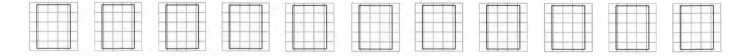

"Hey! I found a pattern!" Nicole cried loudly. Several students around her stopped working and looked at her. "It goes 15 times 1, and that gets 32 seats. Then it goes 14 times 2, for 32 seats, and 13 times 3, and it keeps going! Every time one number goes down in order the other goes up." Nicole excitedly held up her paper for her classmates to see.

"Cool!"

"Oh, I didn't know that."

"Good idea."

Nicole's discovery spread quickly around the classroom. Soon many students were trying this idea and discovering that it worked. Nick wrote: *What I found out was that the bigger the number the bigger the rectangle gets. And the bigger [the rectangle] gets the retangle turns into a square. Then I figured that there was a pattern. The pattern was that each time 1 number got higher ex 1 then comes 2. And in the other one it goes lower. Example 15 then 14. And the 2 & 14 are rectangles.*

A few minutes later Nicole interrupted everyone again. "Hey, look, once you get to 8-by-8, the pattern reverses itself. Instead of 7-by-9 you get 9-by-7. But you shouldn't count it twice," Nicole advised, "because it's the same rectangle." Again, her announcement caused a flurry of conversation.

Nicole realized that although the pattern sequence continued beyond 8 times 8, the resulting table arrangements were congruent with the ones already formed.

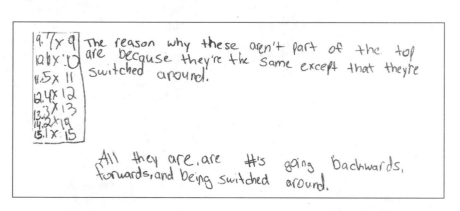

Neshey said, "You have to stop at 8 because you would start making congruent rectangles."

The concept made sense to Malkia, too: "Oh, so that's when it starts repeating."

A few minutes later, math class was over for the day. While the children put the tiles away, I collected their papers. Later, when I read the children's work, I saw that about half the class had found all eight possible ways for seating 32 people.

The Next Day

At the beginning of class the next day, I told the students, "Think about these questions: If Mr. and Mrs. Comfort have to rent each small square table, what's the least expensive way to seat 32 people at one large rectangular table? What's the most expensive way? And how do you know? Yesterday about half of you found all the ways for 32 guests to sit at a rectangular table, but some of you will need to find more table arrangements in order to answer this new question."

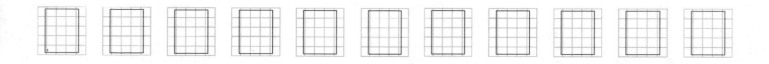

Then I checked back with JT and Talon.

"I get it now about the 32 people," JT told me when I asked him about the work he and Talon had done yesterday after I had left them. "You're trying to see how many tables can hold just 32 people. We did that and found eight different ones. Some of the ones we did yesterday were wrong."

"How did you know there are eight?" I asked.

"Well, hearing about Nicole's pattern really helped. We started looking at 1-by-15, then 2-by-14, and so on. When we got to 8-by-8 and then they started repeating, we thought we got them all," JT replied.

"We looked at Kirsten's paper too, to help," Talon added.

"What about the ones you said were wrong?" I wondered.

JT replied, "Well, we just left them on the paper, because it would be messy to erase them."

"C'mon, let's go," Talon urged. He began building a 1-by-15 rectangle. "Let's see how much this one would cost."

Kirsten came up and said, "You know, the cheapest table would be the 15-by-1. It would save more room too. If you got an 8-by-8 it would be really expensive. I think the Comforts would be foolish to get that, because it would cost so much. But since Mr. Comfort didn't seem to get it, I wonder if he would have ordered that? Better leave the ordering decision to the women." She smiled and winked.

After a few more minutes I called the students together for a discussion, asking them to bring their papers with them.

A Class Discussion

"From what I noticed as you worked on finding how many different-size and -shape tables you could arrange to seat exactly 32 people, there seem to be several ways," I told the class when they had brought their chairs and papers to the front of the room. "If we were the Comforts, what options would we have?"

Most of the students raised a hand, and I called on Rachel.

"They'd have a bunch, eight to be exact," Rachel said.

"Did everyone get eight different tables that would seat 32 people?" I asked. Most of the class nodded or said yes.

"Can someone describe each table's dimensions?" I asked. "I'll record them on the board."

Eric said, "One-times-15, 2-times-14, 3-times-13, 4-times-12, 5-times-11, 6-times-10, 7-times-9 and 8-times-8." As Eric called out the size of each table, I recorded the dimensions on the board and sketched the corresponding rectangle (see opposite page).

"Oh, I see a pattern!" Anfernee said. "Can I show it?" I nodded, and Anfernee came to the board and said slowly, "From the top to the bottom it goes 1, then 2, then 3, then 4, then 5, and so on, up to 8."

"And the other side goes down," Ann Maria contributed.

"Oh, yeah, I didn't see that," said Anfernee. "Yeah, 15, 14, 13, and on and on." He sat back down.

I wanted to see what the students would say about reversing the factors, so I asked, "Shouldn't the list keep going, then? Shouldn't a 9-by-7 rectangle come next?" I wrote 9 x 7 on the board.

"You've got that one already," Malkia said.

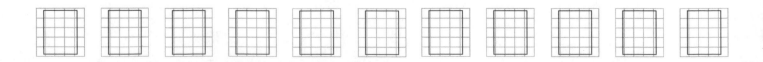

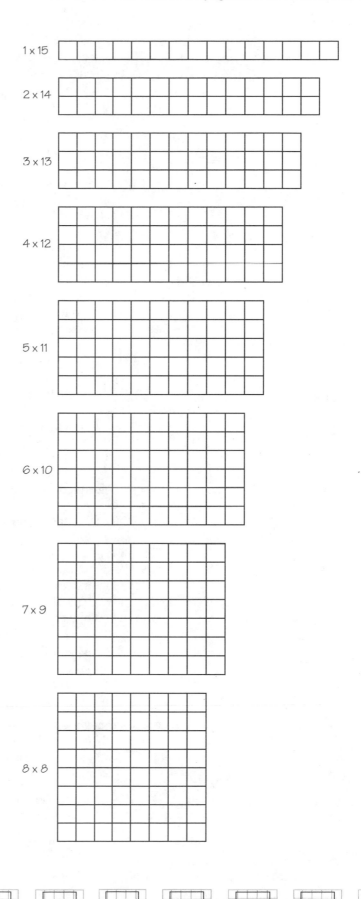

1 x 15

2 x 14

3 x 13

4 x 12

5 x 11

6 x 10

7 x 9

8 x 8

"Yeah, 9-by-7 and 7-by-9 are the same," Nicole added.

I crossed out the 9 x 7 I had written and wrote 10 x 6 beneath it. "What about a rectangle with these dimensions?" I asked.

"No, it's already there," Nathan said.

"You can't switch them around," Kirsten said.

"Why not?" I asked.

"The ones that come after 8 times 8 are repeats," Kirsten replied. The rectangles are congruent, so you can't count them. See, it doesn't matter if I call a rectangle a 2-by-14 or a 14-by-2. It's the same rectangle. So if I write it down twice, it's like it's a different rectangle and it's not."

"Erase 9 x 7 and 10 x 6," Brandon called.

"Yeah, erase them," chorused several other students, and I did, leaving the original eight.

"How did you find all eight possibilities?" I asked. "Take a minute to explain your method to a neighbor." As I listened, I heard several students say they had found a pattern and used it to figure out the possibilities. I called for the students' attention and said, "Tell us how you found them all."

"I decided to be logical. I went long and skinny to short and fat," Luke replied, triggering giggles from his classmates, which I chose to ignore. "My first one was the 1-by-15. I saw that it gave you 32 seats. So I thought, let's try 2-by-14. I kept going like that."

"I did too," said Nicole. "Then I saw a pattern to help me find them all."

"Did anyone have a different method?" I asked.

JT said, "When Talon and me started, we kind of messed up, 'cause we were just finding any old rectangle. They didn't all fit 32 people. Then Nicole said that thing about that pattern, and when I got confused, Kirsten let us look at her paper. Then we got it."

"Did anyone try some rectangles at first that didn't work?" I asked.

Kathleen laughed and said, "Sure. I thought you should do 16 times 2 because 16 times 2 is 32. But it didn't work."

"Yeah, me too," said Rachel.

"What was your reaction?" I asked the girls.

"I was surprised," said Kathleen. "It didn't make sense. It should have worked. But then when I tried other rectangles, I saw the pattern and found the tables."

"Let's think about how many tables Mr. and Mrs. Comfort would have to rent to make each of the rectangles you mentioned," I said. "If they wanted to arrange a 15-by-1 table, how many small square tables would they have to rent?"

"Fifteen. Easy," several students called.

I wrote = 15 next to the 1 x 15 on the board.

$$1 \times 15 = 15$$

"What about 2-by-14? How many tables would the Comforts have to rent if they wanted that arrangement?" I continued.

"Twenty-eight," many children called. I recorded this as well.

$$2 \times 14 = 28$$

"What about the 3-by-13 arrangement?"

The class was quickly catching on to what I was doing.

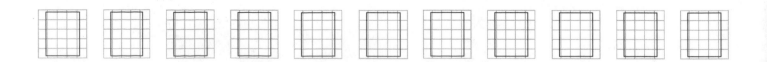

"You're just multiplying," Rifka said. "Just do that for all of them—28, 39, 48, 55, 60, 63, and 64." I recorded the products as she read them off. When I was done, the list looked like this:

$$1 \times 15 = 15$$
$$2 \times 14 = 28$$
$$3 \times 13 = 39$$
$$4 \times 12 = 48$$
$$5 \times 11 = 55$$
$$6 \times 10 = 60$$
$$7 \times 9 = 63$$
$$8 \times 8 = 64$$

"Do any of the solutions call for 32 tables?" I asked.

"No," the children answered.

"Huh. They all seat 32," Nicole said. "So the number of people who can sit there is the same but the number of small tables is different each time."

"What do you notice about the shape of the large tables?" I asked.

Malkia said, "The 8-by-8 is a square, and all the rest are rectangles."

"But the 8-by-8 is a rectangle too, remember?" Erin reminded Malkia.

"Huh? No, it's not," Malkia began, then covered her mouth. "Oops! Yes, it is. But it's a special kind. Let's not start that whole conversation again, okay?"

"Okay," Erin grinned.

A Writing Assignment

"Which arrangement is the best value if the Comforts have to pay for each small square table?" I asked.

"Fifteen by 1."

"One times 15."

"Look," Brandon said. "If they arrange a long, skinny rectangle for 32, then they can do it with only 15 tables. It'd be cheapest that way."

"And they'd save space, too, since the 1-times-15 takes up the least amount of space," added Sharnet.

"You'd need a long room, though," Nicole added, "like for a king's banquet."

"If you were trying to save money, which arrangement would you absolutely not want to use?" I asked.

Doug said, "The 8-times-8 uses the most tables, 64. So it'd be expensive, and you'd have all those tables in the middle that no one could sit at!"

"You probably wouldn't want to use the 7-by-9 or 6-by-10 either," added Ann Maria.

"So that I can better understand your thinking about these problems, I'd like you to do some writing," I then explained. "On the paper where you recorded the tables that can seat exactly 32 people, write about what you noticed as you worked and describe the patterns that were helpful to you. Also record what arrangements are the most and least economical if you're renting by the small square table. Finally, write about what you notice about the areas and perimeters of the arrangements you made." As the students got ready to begin writing, I recorded the questions on the board:

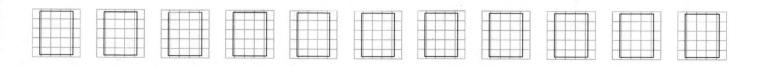

1. What did you notice as you worked? What patterns were helpful?

2. What arrangements are the most and least economical if you're renting by the small square table?

3. What do you notice about the areas and perimeters of the arrangements you made?

The Children's Writing

Brandon addressed all of the questions: *I saw a pattern which started with 15 by 1. Then subtrat 1 from 15 to get 14 and add that one to 1 and get 2 and it would be 14 by 2 and that worked. So I kept on repeating the pattern and trying it out by counting the sides and it kept working. I stopped at 8 by 8 because if I subtracted one from 8 I would get 7 and if I added one to 8 it would be 7 by 9 and I would just be repeating my tables. The only difference would be it would be congruent but backwards.*

I feel 15 by 1 is more economical because it will save space and money for renting the tables. I feel 15 by 1 is the least tables you can buy to fit 32 people. I feel that 8 by 8 is a perfect square. 15 by 1, the most economical is a long and skinny rectangle. This makes me think that maybe a square wastes space compared to a long skinny rectangle because the most economical one was a long skinny rectangle and the least was a square rectangle. Maybe this is a lesson saying when you want to arrange things in groups the most economical shape would be to arrange them in a long skinny rectangle shape rather than a square rectangle shape.

On some #'s the perimeter is smaller than the area and the perimeter always is the same. A square number like 64 for 8 by 8 has a larger area than perimeter except for the square #'s 1 and 4. That is a fact.

Rachel commented on the pattern she saw: *I predict the numbers on the left hand side will keep increasing, as the numbers on the right hand side will keep decreasing.*

My prediction is correct.

Also, the perimeter will stay the same, 32, but the area inside changes.

If we had to pay for each table, I'd probably go with 1 x 15 because it's cheapest.

Doug focused on table cost: *The most expensive rectangular table is the 8 x 8 because there are are 64 squre tables. I figured that out by multiplying 8 x 8 = 64.*

The least expensive rectangular table is the 1 x 15. Because there are only 15 square tables. I figured that out by multiplying 1 x 15 = 15.

Mike was terse: *I would pick 15 x 1 because you would only have to buy 15 tables!*

The 8 x 8 cost the most because you would have to buy 64 tables 8 x 8 = 64!

I saw a pattern by like 1, 2, 3, 4, 5 and 15, 14, 13, 12, 11 and like 15 x 1, 14 x 2, etc.

The area of each table is different. it is the multiple of each set like 15 x 1, 15 by 1 it's the multiple!

The perimeter of each table is 32 because their has to be 32 people at each set of tables!

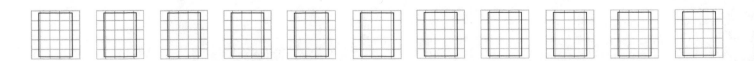

Erin explained why the pattern repeated itself after reaching 8-by-8: *I ended up with 8 tables, first I tried a table straite across and ended up with 15 x 1. I was thinking for a little bit and I decided to start going down from 15. After I was done with the whole thing I figured out that the number's were in a pattern.*

Like 15 x 1, 14 x 2, 13 x 3, 12 x 4, 11 x 5, 10 x 6, 9 x 7, and 8 x 8. When I got to 8 x 8 I knew it was done because when you end up with two numbers that are the same your really finished. Some shapes are big and some are small. If Mrs. Comfort had to pick one I would tell her to pick 15 x 1 because it saves up much more room and also saves up money. If she picked 8 x 8 she would've took up much more room and also spent much more money. So it would be much more better if she just did the 15 x 1.

Erin drew all eight table arrangements that would seat exactly 32 people but didn't discover the pattern until she had finished.

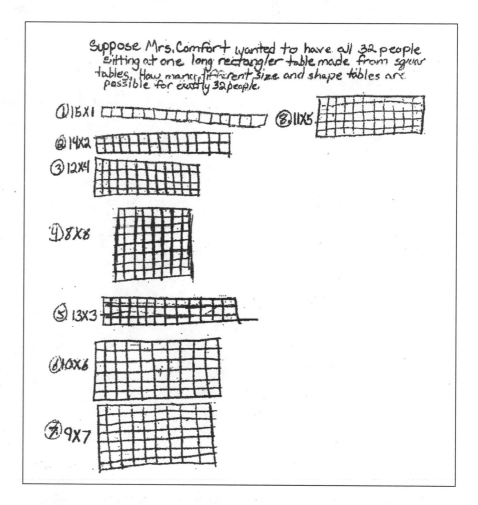

Malkia focused exclusively on the differences between the areas and perimiters of the rectangles: *I noticed that the perimiter is the same as any perimiter, they all add up to 32, but the area is very different, no area can be the same. I also noticed that they all have different shapes, and no shape is alike.*

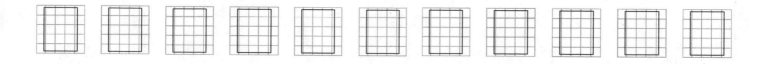

Ann Maria drew some conclusions about the areas of the various table arrangements.

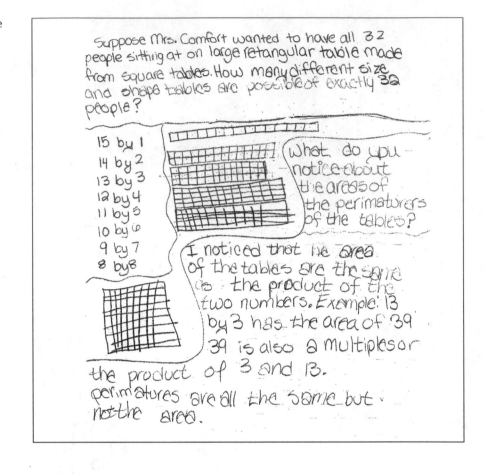

Suppose Mrs. Comfort wanted to have all 32 people sitting at on large retangular table made from square tables. How many different size and shape tables are possible of exactly 32 people?

15 by 1
14 by 2
13 by 3
12 by 4
11 by 5
10 by 6
9 by 7
8 by 8

What do you notice about the areas of the perimaters of the tables?

I noticed that he area of the tables are the same as the product of the two numbers. Example: 13 by 3 has the area of 39. 39 is also a multiplesor the product of 3 and 13. perimatures are all the same but not the area.

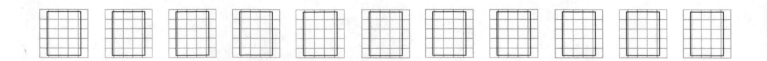

CONTENTS

MENU ACTIVITIES

The activities on the menu were selected to offer children a variety of ways to think about area and perimeter. The menu was constructed bearing in mind that not all students engage with or experience concepts in the same way; it includes activities that appeal to different interests and aptitudes.

The menu activities offer opportunities for children to extend the experiences they have in the whole class lessons. *The Perimeter Stays the Same, Part 1; The Perimeter Stays the Same, Part 2;* and *Perimeter with Cuisenaire Rods* extend ideas in the whole class lesson *Foot Stuff. The Banquet Table Problem* extends the whole class lessons *Spaghetti and Meatballs for All* and *The Area Stay the Same.* In *Round Things,* students explore the relationship between the circumference of a circle and its diameter. *Double the Circumference* gives children ways to think about how increasing the circumference of a circle affects its area.

The menu approach has several benefits in the classroom. It solves the problem of what students can do when they finish activities more quickly than others. It responds to students' individual needs by allowing them to work at their own pace. Using the menu also helps children learn to make choices and manage their own time. In addition, when students are working independently, the teacher can work with individuals, pairs, or small groups and initiate discussions that give valuable insights into students' thinking, reasoning, and understanding.

A variety of materials is used for some of the menu activities. In *The Perimeter Stays the Same, Part 1* and *The Perimeter Stays the Same, Part 2,* students draw polygons on centimeter-squared paper. Inch-square tiles are used for making tables in *The Banquet Table Problem.* An assortment of round objects are used in *Round Things* and *Double the Circumference.* The students use Cuisenaire rods in *Perimeter with Cuisenaire Rods.*

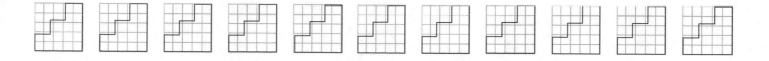

The Importance of Class Discussions

While the menu activities provide experiences with area and perimeter, class discussions are essential for cementing and furthering student learning. Class discussions help students express their ideas, learn about others' ideas, and develop and strengthen their understanding. These discussions also provide the teacher with opportunities to receive feedback about activities and assess what students have learned.

As a general guideline, it's beneficial to encourage students to explain their thinking whenever they offer an idea or give an answer in a class discussion. Probe with prompts such as:

Why do you think that?

Tell some more about that idea.

Explain how you figured that out.

It's important to have children explain their reasoning even when they give correct responses. Having students explain their thinking not only provides useful information for assessing their understanding, it also gives the message that their thinking and reasoning are important and valued in all situations. Also, hearing other students' ideas provides children with different points of view and can stimulate their thinking.

A class discussion is most beneficial after students have had time to work on a menu activity and think about the area and perimeter ideas. The "From the Classroom" section for each menu activity contains valuable suggestions for leading class discussions. The situations described in these sections will not, of course, be the same in your classroom, but they are representative of what may occur, and the teacher's responses in the vignette are useful models for working with students during menu time.

Classroom Suggestions

"Notes About Classroom Organization," on pages 6–10, includes information about organizing the classroom for menus. Here are some additional suggestions.

Because the menu activities relate to previous instruction in whole class lessons, students are somewhat prepared for them. However, menu activities need to be introduced carefully so that children understand what they are to do. When students are clear about what is expected of them, they're more able to function as independent learners. Specific teaching directions are provided in the "Getting Started" section of each menu activity.

Also, it's best to introduce just one or two activities at one time. "A Suggested Daily Schedule," on pages 11–13 offers one possible schedule for introducing menu activities and structuring menu time for the unit.

Giving clear directions by itself will not help children learn to work independently. You'll need to devote your time and attention to it. From time to time you may need to remind children that information about a menu activity is available on the written menu tasks. For example, menu activities that require students to work in a group are marked with a G in the upper right-hand corner; those that require a partner are marked with a P, and those that can be done individually are marked with an I. You may need to review directions several times, on different days, to be sure that the students understand and remember what to do.

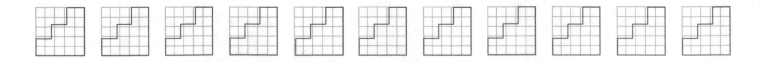

Providing Ongoing Support

From time to time, before the children begin work on menu activities, you might want to have a discussion about working with partners. Have the children talk about how they can help one another. Ask them to bring up problems they've encountered and either describe how they resolved them or ask the class for suggestions. You may want to report what you've observed about students working independently and cooperatively. These discussions are invaluable for helping the children become productive learners.

Although students are encouraged to make choices and pursue activities of interest to them during menu time, every student should be required to do every menu activity. However, students respond differently to different activities and children do not all get the same value out of the same experiences; individual students will engage fully with some activities and superficially with others. This is to be expected and respected.

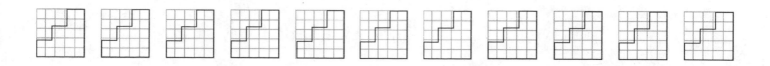

MENU ACTIVITY

The Perimeter Stays the Same, Part I

Overview

In *The Perimeter Stays the Same, Part 1*, children compare the areas of shapes that all have the same-length perimeter. The activity helps children see that shapes with the same-length perimeter can have different-size areas. In the lesson *The Area Stays the Same*, children made several shapes with the same area and compared the perimeters to find that shapes with the same area can have different perimeters. While the area remains constant in *The Area Stays the Same*, the perimeter remains constant in *The Perimeter Stays the Same*.

This activity has an additional problem-solving challenge. Children are required to draw three different shapes on centimeter-squared paper, each shape having a perimeter of exactly 30 centimeters. Children typically use trial and error to draw the shapes, adjusting to make the perimeter the correct length. Through this process, they have the opportunity to see that adding squares to a shape increases its area but doesn't necessarily increase its perimeter, and that removing squares from a shape decreases its area but doesn't necessarily decrease its perimeter.

189

The Perimeter Stays the Same, Part 1

You need: Centimeter-squared paper

1. Draw at least three different shapes on centimeter-squared paper, following three rules:

   (a) When you draw the shape, stay on the lines.

   (b) You must be able to cut out the shape and have it remain in one piece. (Only corners touching is not allowed.)

   (c) Each shape must have a perimeter of 30 centimeters.

2. Record the area of each shape you draw.

From *Math By All Means: Area and Perimeter, Grades 5–6* ©1997 Math Solutions Publications

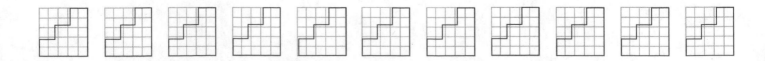

Before the lesson

Gather these materials:
■ An ample supply of centimeter-squared paper (see blackline master, page 195)
■ Blackline master of menu activity, page 189
■ Transparency of centimeter-squared paper (optional)

Getting started

■ Read aloud the menu directions.
■ Then model for the students what they are to do. First draw a 13-by-2 rectangle on centimeter-squared paper. (This rectangle has a perimeter of 30 centimeters.) Ask students to check that it meets each of the three rules in the directions. It's helpful to have students suggest different ways to figure out the length of the perimeter so that they have several options. Show students how to record the shape's area and perimeter.

■ Then draw another shape, as shown.

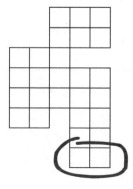

After students verify that it follows the first two rules but that the perimeter is 32 centimeters, talk with the class about how you could alter the shape to change the perimeter to 30 centimeters. One way to do this is to remove the two bottom squares:

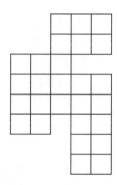

■ Instead of holding a class discussion about this activity, after the students have made their shapes, introduce *The Perimeter Stays the Same, Part 2.*

FROM THE CLASSROOM

I posted on the board an enlarged copy of the directions for the menu activity *The Perimeter Stays the Same, Part 1*. Holding up a sheet of centimeter-squared paper, I said, "Your job is to draw three shapes on a sheet of centimeter-squared paper, following three rules. First, stay on the lines when you draw. Second, you must be able to cut your shape out and have it all in one piece. Finally, each shape must have a perimeter of exactly 30 centimeters. After you've drawn each shape, figure the area in square centimeters and record it on the shape."

I then placed a transparency of a sheet of centimeter-squared paper on the overhead and turned it on. "To draw a shape here with a perimeter of 30 units, I might start by drawing a rectangle on the paper, being careful to stay on the lines." I drew a 13-by-2 rectangle. (I had thought about this ahead of time, so I knew that a 13-by-2 rectangle has a perimeter of 30 units.)

"That's cool," Rifka remarked.

"Let's see if it fits the rules," I said. "Can someone come up to the overhead and check the perimeter?" There were many volunteers, and I called on Kathleen. She came up to the overhead projector and carefully counted the perimeter.

"Yup. Thirty centimeters!" she said, and returned to her seat. I wrote in the rectangle:

$$P = 30 \text{ cm}$$

"What about the other rules?" I asked.

Nathan replied, "It fits, because you stayed on the lines and didn't cut through any boxes."

"And it could be cut out and it wouldn't fall apart," Malkia added.

"What's the area of this shape?" I asked. Again, many students raised their hand, and I called on JT. He came to the overhead and softly counted each square one by one as he touched each unit within the boundaries of the shape.

"Wait, let me count again," he said. After he had done so, he told the class, "It's 26. Do you want me to write it on the shape?" I nodded and told JT to write *A = 26 sq cm* in the middle of the shape. After he did, he returned to his seat.

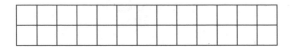

"The shape you draw doesn't have to be a rectangle though," I explained. I drew a 13-sided polygon, the perimeter of which I knew was 32 units, and therefore too long (see top of next page).

"Let's check the menu directions to see if this shape fits the rules," I said.

"Okay on the first one," Eric said. "You drew on the lines."

"And you can cut it out and it will be in one piece," Nicole added.

"Who would like to count the perimeter?" I asked. Ann Maria eagerly came to the overhead and began counting. After counting all around the

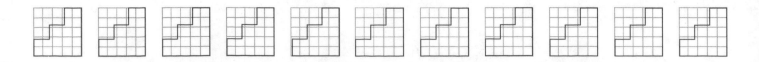

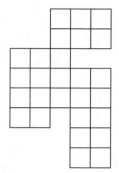

figure, she lost her place. "Does someone have an idea for keeping track of each unit of length you've counted?"

"Put a little number next to each one," Erin suggested.

"Or just put your finger on the one that you start on," Luke added.

"I'll try that," Ann Maria said, placing her finger on one of the centimeter units to mark her place. As she counted using her other hand, however, she found that she had trouble seeing around her finger. "This isn't working," she said.

Erin said, "I told you, just put a little number next to each one."

"Nah. That takes too much time," Ann Maria said.

"How about another idea for keeping track, then?" I asked the class.

"Put a dot next to each side!" Brandon suggested enthusiastically.

"You could also tick off each unit of length," I suggested, illustrating what I meant.

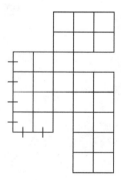

"I like Brandon's idea," Ann Maria said decisively.

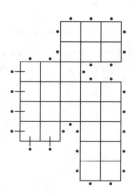

"It's too long," Ann Maria announced. "It's 32." She returned to her seat.

"So it looks as if I need to adjust the figure a bit to make the perimeter exactly 30 centimeters," I theorized. "Maybe I'll take off these bottom two squares and see what happens." I drew a circle to illustrate.

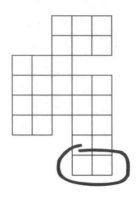

"Wait!" Luke said. "Won't that give you a perimeter of 28? Because you're taking off four."

I hadn't anticipated this. "Take a few moments to talk about Luke's idea with the people at your table," I instructed. Anfernee looked confused.

"What do you think about Luke's idea?" I asked him.

"I don't get it. What does he mean that you're taking off four?"

"Come on up to the overhead for a minute," I said, and Anfernee followed me. "If I erase all of these, Luke thinks that I'm erasing four units of length from the perimeter of 32," I explained, tracing my finger over the units I planned to erase.

"But you're not," Anfernee said. "You still have these two across the bottom. You only took off one on each side."

"That's what I think, too," I replied.

"So you mean Luke is wrong?" Anfernee's eyes widened. He looked at my shape again to confirm his thinking and called, "Hey, Luke!" Then he headed over to Luke's table to share his discovery.

After a few more moments I called the class to attention.

"I was wrong," Luke announced. "Anfernee showed me that if you take off the bottom like Mrs. Rectanus was going to do, you only take one off each side and you still have two across the bottom."

"It's weird that you can take off two squares with four sides and it's only two less," Malkia said.

"What do you mean by 'it's only two less'?" I probed, wanting to push Malkia to clarify her thought.

"The perimeter," she said. "Why isn't it four less?"

"Does someone want to respond to Malkia's question?" I asked. Four hands went up. I waited a moment, but no one else raised a hand. I called on Nathan.

"I thought it should be four less, too," he said, "but look. You take off the bottom lines, but there still are bottom lines. All that's really missing are the side lines."

"I don't get it," Malkia said.

"Can I show her?" Nathan looked at me. I nodded yes.

"See," he said, pointing to the bottom squares on my shape. "When you take off these, you're taking off four sides, but then there are two new sides where they were touching. So you only really take off two."

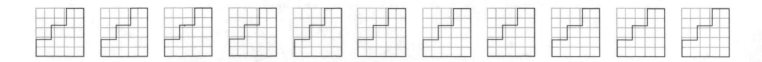

Conversations broke out in the room. Often students need to say something aloud to themselves in order to be able to understand it, and that's what seemed to be happening now. After a moment I asked for their attention.

I erased the two squares and said, "Let's check. Erin, would you like to count the perimeter?" She nodded and came up to the overhead, ticking off each unit of length as she counted it.

"It's 30," Erin announced. I recorded on the shape:

$$P = 30 \text{ cm}$$

"What's the area of this shape?" I asked.

Erin quickly counted the area. "Twenty-five. Should I write it?" I nodded, and Erin recorded A = 25 sq cm in the middle of the shape.

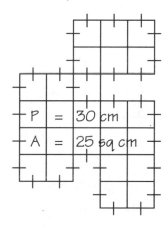

"Can we have a partner for this activity?" Doug asked. "I think I'm going to need one."

I pointed to the I in the corner of the menu directions and explained, "Each student has to do the activity individually. That means you each need to draw shapes on your own sheet of centimeter-squared paper. But you're free to ask one another for help."

"Can we start? This looks like fun," Ann Maria said.

I said yes, and the students began to work.

Observing the Children

This was a popular activity. All the students worked alone, although some of them checked with a classmate from time to time. I noticed children doing a variety of guess-and-check drawings. Anfernee and Luke sat together and helped each other count the perimeter of each shape they drew, adjusting their shapes as necessary so that the perimeters came out to exactly 30 centimeters. Anfernee didn't see himself as being strong in mathematics, but he worked competently and confidently, although more slowly than Luke did.

"Can you help me?" Catheryne asked when I walked by her table. She often wanted adult assistance even before she'd tried an activity on her own.

"What do you need?"

"I'm trying to draw a rectangle with a perimeter of 30 but I can't make one," she replied.

"What have you tried so far?" I asked.

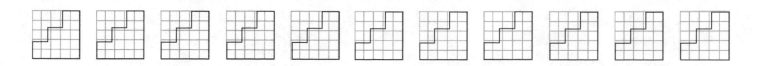

"First I did a 1-by-15, because 15 plus 15 is 30. But that didn't work. Then I did a 1-by-16, and that didn't work either," she said, her frustration obvious.

"Let's take a look at the perimeters of the rectangles you tried and see whether we can use that information to help solve this problem," I suggested. "When you counted the perimeter of the 1-by-15 rectangle, what did you get?"

"Thirty-two," Catheryne said.

"And the 1-by-16?"

"Thirty-four."

I thought looking for a pattern might be helpful, so I drew a chart on a piece of paper. "Let's list the dimensions of each rectangle you made on the left side of this chart, and the perimeter of each rectangle on the right."

Dimensions of rectangle	Perimeter
1 x 15	32
1 x 16	34

"Now what if you made a 1-by-17 rectangle? What do you think the perimeter would be?" I asked.

"I don't know," Catheryne replied.

"Try it," I said, and she drew the rectangle on her centimeter-squared paper and counted the perimeter carefully, using dots to keep track.

"Thirty-six," she announced, and I recorded the dimensions and perimeter in the appropriate columns.

Dimensions of rectangle	Perimeter
1 x 15	32
1 x 16	34
1 x 17	36

"As you increase the length of the rectangle each time, how much does the perimeter increase?" I probed.

"Oh! Two!" Catheryne said.

"What do you think the perimeter of a 1-by-18 rectangle would be?" I pushed.

Catheryne looked at the chart and confidently replied, "Thirty-eight, because they all go up by 2."

"But you're not trying to get a perimeter of 38. You're trying to find a rectangle with a perimeter of 30," I reminded her. "Could this chart help you do that?"

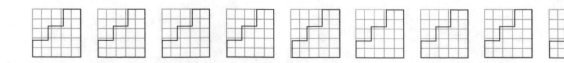

"I get it. It must be 1 by 14, because it goes in a pattern. I'm going to try it and see. Thanks!" Catheryne dismissed me with a wave of her hand, and I moved on to another table where Nicole, Eric, and Rachel were sitting.

"This is harder than it looks," Eric announced.

Nicole agreed. "Yeah, I had trouble with a shape I made. It was too big, and I kept taking squares out to try to make a perimeter of 30, but for a while I kept getting the same too-big perimeter. It was weird."

"Why do you think that happened?" I asked.

"Rachel showed me that even though it looked like I was taking off squares, I really wasn't changing the perimeter at all," Nicole said.

"So what did you do then?" I asked.

"I just completely changed where I took stuff off, and that helped. It was hard for a while, but I finally got it."

It was tricky for some students to adjust shapes so their perimeters were exactly 30 centimeters. Students ran into pitfalls and some became frustrated. But with trial and error and help from classmates, everyone was able to complete the activity.

MENU ACTIVITY

Round Things

Overview

In *Round Things* students look at how the perimeter of a circle, the *circumference*, relates to that circle's *diameter*. This experience sets the stage for children to compare the area and the circumference of a circle.

With a partner or in a group, students choose a variety of circular objects and use appropriate tools and units to measure the circumference and the diameter of at least 10 of them. After recording these measurements on a chart, students investigate the relationship between the circumference and the diameter of each circular object. This activity gives students the opportunity to see that the circumference of a circle is a little more than three times as long as its diameter. It therefore sets the stage for them to learn about pi.

Before the lesson

Gather these materials:
■ Ample supplies of rulers, tape measures, and string
■ A variety of circular objects
■ Blackline master of menu activity, page 190

190

Round Things

You need: Something to measure with

1. With a partner or a group, find at least 10 circular objects. For each one, measure its diameter and its circumference.

2. Record your results on a chart.

Object	Diameter	Circumference
1.		
2.		
3.		
4.		
5.		
6.		
7.		
8.		
9.		
10.		

3. Look for a relationship between your diameter and circumference measurements that you could use to predict the circumference of a circle if you know its diameter. Write about what you notice.

Getting started

■ Talk with the class about circles to introduce (or reinforce) the following ideas and terminology:

The perimeter of a circle is called the *circumference.*

The *radius* is a line segment that joins the center of a circle to its circumference.

The *diameter* is a line segment that passes across a circle through its center.

Add the new terminology to the area and perimeter word list.

■ Present the menu directions. First, tell the children they are to find 10 circular objects and measure the diameter and the circumference of each.

■ Explain to the children that they should record their measurements on a chart. Draw a sample chart on the board:

Object	Diameter	Circumference
1.		
2.		
3.		
4.		
5.		
6.		
7.		
8.		
9.		
10.		

■ Ask the students to suggest ways they might be able to measure circular objects. (The ways may include rulers, flexible measuring tapes, or string.) Also ask them to think about appropriate units of measurement they might use.

■ Reinforce the idea that they must use the same unit of measurement for both the diameter and the circumference of any one circular object. (If they measure the circumference in inches, for example, they must measure the diameter in inches; if the circumference is measured in centimeters, the diameter must be measured in centimeters; etc.)

■ Tell the children that after they record their measurements, they should look for a relationship between the diameter and circumference so that they can predict the circumference of any circle from its diameter.

■ After all the children have finished measuring their circular objects (perhaps several class periods later), hold a class discussion centering on measuring tools, measurement units, and the concept of pi. You may want to use questions like the following as prompts:

What measuring tools did you use?

What units of measurement did you use? (You can take this opportunity to introduce units of measure with which the children may not yet be familiar.)

What did you notice when you compared the circumference and diameter of the objects you measured? (If students have not discovered that the circumference of each circle is a little more than three times the diameter, and that the diameter is a little more than one-third the circumference, ask them to divide each circumference by its diameter.)

■ Explain that the relationship between the diameter and circumference of any circle is always the same no matter the size of the circle. When the circumference of a circle is divided by its diameter, the result will always be approximately 3.14, and this number is known as pi.

■ Ask the children to write about what they understand about the relationship between the circumference and diameter of a circle.

FROM THE CLASSROOM

It was a beautiful spring morning when I called the class to attention to introduce this menu activity. Reluctantly the class settled down. "This menu activity is called *Round Things.* In it, you'll measure the perimeter of circular objects. Does anyone know what mathematicians call the perimeter of a circle?" With my finger, I traced the circumference of a circle I had drawn on the board. About a third of the students raised their hand. I called on Talon.

"Circumference," he said confidently.

"Oh, yeah," several other children murmured.

I recorded the word *circumference* on our area and perimeter word list. "What should I write to help you remember what it means?"

Kirsten suggested, "Why don't you draw a circle with an arrow pointing to the perimeter—I mean, to the circumference?"

"Or you could just write, 'perimeter of a circle,'" Luke said.

There were no other ideas.

"I'll do both," I said.

"You need to measure circles in this activity," I continued. Is there anything circular on these scissors?" I held up a pair of adult-size scissors. I chose the scissors purposely, because they had no circular parts. Students can learn as much about a concept from thinking about what it isn't as they can from seeing examples of what it is.

"Maybe that part where your fingers go," Anfernee said. But then he corrected himself. "Never mind. They're not circles."

"They're sort of oval," Nathan observed.

"A circle is like a wheel," Catheryne offered. "That shape wouldn't roll."

"The scissors handles aren't round," Neshey added. "They're squished."

"What makes a shape a circle?" I asked.

After a few moments, Brandon spoke up. "A circle has to have everything the same distance from the middle," he said.

"Tell us more about that idea, Brandon. Do you need to draw something to help us understand what you mean?" I prodded.

Brandon nodded and came up to the board. He placed a dot at the center of the circle I had drawn on the board. "See, here's a circle and here's the middle. I know it's a circle because if I draw a line from the middle to anyplace on the outside, kind of like a spoke ..." He stopped and looked at me. "Is that a radius?" he asked.

I nodded.

NOTE When children explain their thinking or listen to another student doing so, they gain a better understanding about the mathematics. Also, the teacher learns more about what students understand.

"Okay, if I draw a radius from the middle to the outside, no matter where I draw it to, it's always going to be the same length." Brandon drew several radii to illustrate. "That's why a circle is a circle, I think," he concluded, returning to his seat.

I added the word *radius* to the area and perimeter word list and defined it as, *Line segment joining the center of a circle with any point on its circumference.* I drew a circle and a radius next to the definition to illustrate it.

"What circular objects might you measure?" I asked. The class had many suggestions: soda cans, masking tape loops, water bottles, garbage cans, plant containers, paper cups.

Neshey, sensing an opportunity to go outside and enjoy the sunny weather, asked slyly, "Can we go outside to the yard? There's a tire swing I'd like to measure." The class tittered.

I smiled, shook my head no, and went on with my instructions. "In the *Round Things* activity, you also need to measure the diameter of the circular objects you've chosen," I explained, writing the word *diameter* on the area and perimeter word list.

Anticipating my question, several children raised their hand. Erin called out, "It's the distance across a circle."

To be sure the students all understood, I asked Erin to come up to the board and draw a picture to explain. She drew another circle and carefully labeled the center. Then she drew several diameters.

"It's like a radius all the way across," Luke noted.

Erin said, "It doesn't matter where the diameter is. It can be horizontal or vertical or on a slant. What matters is that you go through the middle." Nobody asked for clarification and Erin returned to her seat.

I wrote Erin's definition on the word list and drew a circle with a diameter line segment as illustration.

Next, I posted an enlarged copy of the menu activity and read the first two directions aloud, stopping where it said to record the results on a chart. I drew a chart on the board:

	Object	Diameter	Circumference
1.			
2.			
3.			
4.			
5.			
6.			
7.			
8.			
9.			
10.			

I was curious about how the children thought they might measure circular objects and wanted to be sure they all had a way to do so. I asked, "How can you measure around something?"

After a few moments of silence Kirsten raised her hand. "You could take string and lay it around the circle, like we did for our feet. Then cut it so it's exactly the same length, and lay that string against a ruler."

"Any other suggestions?" I asked.

Malkia said, "Well, I think you could do it like Kirsten, but you don't have to cut the string. That's a waste of string. Just cut a long piece and mark with your finger instead of cutting it. Then you can use it again."

"How about another idea?" I asked. The children were silent, so I moved on to the third direction. "After you've measured 10 circles, look at your measurements of the diameters and circumferences and see how the two numbers relate. Then try to figure out how you can use this relationship to predict the circumference if you know the diameter."

"Can we start?" Sharnet was eager to get to it.

"In a minute," I replied. "First, what unit of measurement might you use? Miles?"

The class giggled, and several children called out inches or feet.

"You should pick units that make sense for what you're measuring," I continued. "What units might you use if you measured the inside loop on the roll of masking tape?"

"Inches."

"Centimeters."

"Both make sense to me," I said. "But whatever unit you use to measure the circumference, you need to use the same unit to measure the diameter. That way, you'll be able to compare two like measurements."

"Do you have to use centimeters for everything if you use it for the first thing you measure?" Luke wanted to know.

"No," I answered, repeating, "as long as you use the same unit of measure for the diameter and circumference of each circular object. Don't switch units for the same object."

Observing the Children

Over the next few days, the students measured and recorded with enthusiasm. Everyone used string to measure the circumferences and the diameters. When their string was longer than the straightedge, some children added another ruler or two, while others marked the string and then moved the straightedge.

Zak and Anfernee started slowly. After measuring around a marker cap, Zak said to Anfernee, "Got your sheet out? The first object should be 'marker end.' It's spelled m-a-r-k-e-r e-n-d. Write '1½ cm' for the diameter." He paused while Anfernee laboriously recorded the information. Then Zak continued, "Now put '5½ cm' under circumference."

Zak wrapped the string around each object they measured while Anfernee held it in place. Once Zak had marked the circumference or diameter, both boys carefully laid the string against a centimeter ruler and Zak read the measurement.

When they measured the Frisbee they found the string wasn't long enough.

"It's too short!" Anfernee exclaimed with surprise. After cutting a longer piece of string and again measuring the Frisbee, the boys laid the string along their ruler.

"Now the ruler's too short! I can't believe the string is way longer than the ruler," said Anfernee. "Let's get more rulers." He jumped from his seat

Zak and Anfernee used centimeters for all of their measurements.

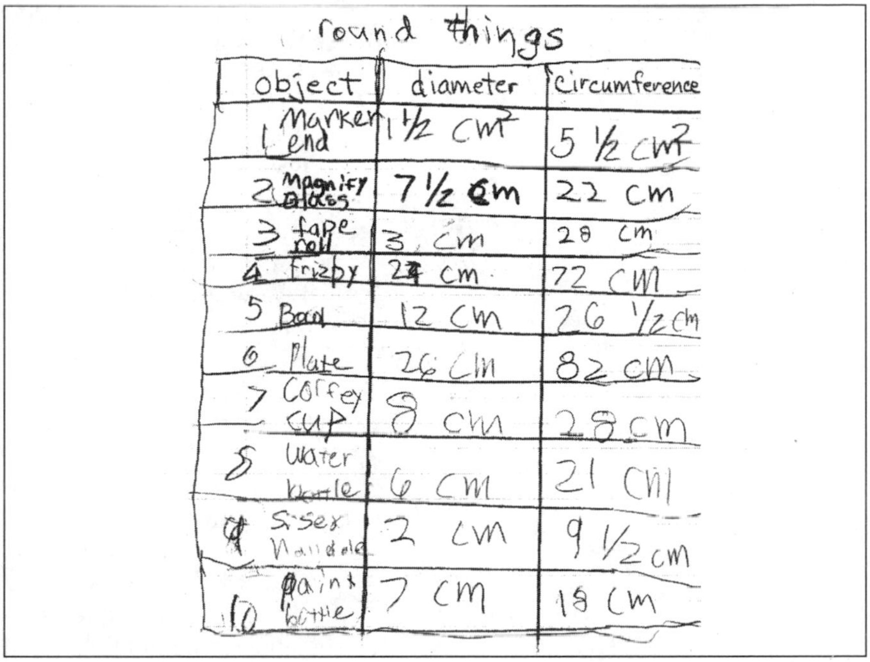

object	diameter	circumference
1. Marker end	1 ½ cm	5 ½ cm?
2. Magnify glass	7 ½ cm	22 cm
3. tape roll	3 cm	28 cm
4. frisby	23 cm	72 cm
5. Ball	12 cm	26 ½ cm
6. Plate	26 cm	82 cm
7. Coffey cup	8 cm	28 cm
8. water bottle	6 cm	21 cm
9. S-sex handele	2 cm	9 ½ cm
10. paint bottle	7 cm	18 cm

round things

and went to the ruler box. He returned with two more, which he carefully laid end-to-end along the string.

"Hey, Zak. Each ruler is 30 centimeters, right?"

Zak nodded.

"So 30 plus 30 equals 60, plus 12 more is 72, right?"

"Yup, let's record it," said Zak.

I then observed Nicole and Kathleen studying their chart. They had recorded the diameter and circumference of 10 objects.

NOTE Measurement tasks can provide a natural context for computation.

From the chart, Nicole later noticed that the circumference of each object she and Kathleen measured was about three times longer than its diameter.

Round Things

Objects	Diameter	circumference
Water bottle	2⅞ in.	9 ⅜ in.
Marker	10/14 "	1 5/14 "
Round fractions	2 ½ "	11 ⅛ "
Plastic party plate	9 4/14 "	29 3/14 "
"cool whipcool"	5 13/14 "	17 ¾ "
Pencil	6/14 "	1 "
Dixua cup	2 ½ "	7 ½ "
Chair leg	1 ⅞ "	3 ⅞ "
Jar top	13 ¾ "	11 ⅞ "
tape roll	¾ "	10 ½ "

"Okay, so how do the circumferences and diameters compare?" Nicole mused. After a moment she continued. "I think I kind of get it. The diameter is always less than half but more than a fourth of the circumference."

"Maybe if we subtract all the diameters from the circumferences we'll be able to find something," Kathleen suggested.

Nicole replied, "I don't know why, but I think we need to divide to find out, not subtract."

"Okay," said Kathleen, yielding. The girls took out their calculators and began entering data.

I was curious. "Nicole, Kathleen, this looks interesting. Explain what you're doing."

Nicole stopped pushing buttons on her calculator and looked up at me.

"Oh, Kathleen and I are trying to find out what the connection is between the diameters and circumferences of stuff. So we're dividing the circumference by the diameter," she said.

"What buttons are you pushing on the calculator?" I asked.

"Well, say the circumference is 42 and the diameter is 13. You push '42 ÷ 13 =' and you get your answer."

"What will your answer tell you?" I persisted.

"Probably nothing for just one thing. But if it's the same number for all the things, then it might be the connection between circumference and diameter," said Nicole.

The girls divided 42 by 13 on their calculators. After a moment, Kathleen said, "It's 3.2307692. Oh, my goodness." She looked at Nicole and the girls began laughing.

"What's so funny?" I asked.

"I thought … I didn't think we'd get a weird number like this! I was hoping for something even!" Kathleen said.

I suspected she meant "whole" instead of "even," so, in order to find out more about Kathleen's number sense, I said, "Even? As in divisible by 2?"

Kathleen looked confused. "No, not exactly. It's hard to explain," she said.

"I wonder if you didn't mean 'whole' instead of 'even.' Something without a decimal," I explained.

"Yeah, that's it!"

"So what does the decimal number tell you?" I pushed.

"Uh, that it's more than 3 but less than 4," Kathleen replied.

Just then Rifka interrupted us. "We're having a really important conversation, and I think you need to hear it," she said to me. I followed her to find Kirsten, Erin, and Rachel talking passionately.

"But *I am* trying to understand, and you guys go too fast and aren't explaining what you're doing!" Rachel said, with obvious frustration.

Kirsten responded, "Well, I'm trying to explain it, but every time I do you say you don't know what I mean and walk away!"

Erin, who had no problem being blunt, said, "Rachel, if you just tried to understand and contributed something to the group, maybe you would get it."

Rachel retorted, "I'm trying to get it, and just when I do, you take off on some other idea."

I intervened. "What's happening here occurs sometimes in groups. You think you're with the group and following the ideas when all of a sudden someone takes off in a direction you didn't anticipate and you can't immediately follow her thinking. That can be frustrating."

NOTE Menu tasks provide many opportunities for teaching and learning. Such opportunities often emerge from what particular students are doing and allow for teaching directly to children's specific needs.

"Boy, tell me about it," said Rachel.

"I want to remind you that sometimes it's hard to follow somebody else's reasoning," I added. "Sometimes in class when you're explaining your ideas they make perfect sense to me, and other times I don't have a clue what you're saying."

The girls giggled with recognition.

"So," I continued, "everyone has some responsibility when that happens. Rachel did the right thing by speaking up. When it isn't clear to you what someone means, you have to say, *Hey, wait a minute, slow down.* Or, *I'm having trouble following your reasoning—can you explain it a different way?* Let the others know you're confused.

"And as a part of the group, your job is to slow down and respond to the person's request. It can be hard if you're hot on an idea, but on the other hand, you have a responsibility to your team members and know how much better your thoughts are when they're collective and part of the group."

I have conversations like this one with groups throughout the year. Children need help learning how to work in groups, and I don't mind repeating the guidelines. It's necessary.

"Okay, so tell us about what part isn't clear to you, Rachel," Rifka said calmly and evenly.

"Why are you dividing the circumference by the diameter?" Rachel asked.

Kirsten answered, "Because we're trying to find the connection between the circumference and the diameter, and that's how you do it."

"Can you explain why you divided?" I asked.

"The circumference is always bigger," Kirsten said, "so I was trying to figure out what to do to it to get the diameter. Dividing makes it smaller."

"We tried subtracting first," Erin said, "but we got numbers all over the place."

"Excuse me a minute," Kirsten said. She went over to talk to Luke and Doug, who were waving her over to where they were sitting.

"But what about the .32 stuff?" Rachel persisted.

Rifka took over. "See, the garbage can circumference is 61 inches. We know the diameter is 20 and a third inches. We're trying to figure out what to divide the circumference by to get the diameter. Twenty times 3 is 60, right?"

"Uh-huh," Rachel said, calmer now.

"We're trying to get a little more than 60—we need to get 61. Does that make sense?" Rifka asked.

Rachel nodded. "It makes sense. I just don't get where the .32 comes from."

Rifka replied, "Erin thought we needed to multiply 20 by more than 3. So we tried 4. Twenty times 4 is 80—"

"Way too big," Rachel interrupted.

"Right. So now we're trying numbers in between 3 and 4. Erin thought 3.32 would be close."

"Oh," Rachel said with a shy smile.

"Tell me why it makes sense now," I said to Rachel.

"I was really confused by the decimal. I couldn't figure out where it came from," Rachel explained.

"Where does it come from?" I probed.

"Well, I think it's a number between 3 and 4. Like 3.5 would be 3 and a half," she replied.

"About how much is 3.32?" I asked.

"I don't know. Maybe less than 3 and a half?" Rachel said tentatively.

"Tell me why you think that," I pressed. I wanted to see where her understanding broke down.

Slowly Rachel answered, "If .5 is half or 50 percent, than something less than .5 should be less than half. But I'm not very good in decimals. When I left my old school we hadn't done them yet, and when I came here, this class had already studied them."

It was almost time for recess. Still concerned about Rachel, I asked her to write about what had happened. She wrote, *I got confused when they started coming up with things like the decimal for figuring out how to divide the circumference to get the diameter. It made me mad because they said stuff like I'm not trying to understand when I am. I feel stupid because when they said stuff I got really confused, and Erin kept on saying that if I would contribute to the group maybe I would get it. Erin, Rifka and Kirsten have always made me feel stupid during math because they always understand stuff I don't get at all, then when I come up with an idea they already thought of it and so then I feel even more stupid. Right now I'm feeling like people are expecting too much out of me and are expecting me to understand what I can't understand yet.* I made a note to check with Rachel the next day to see how she was doing.

A Class Discussion

At the beginning of class about a week later, I initiated a class discussion by having the children share at their tables what they enjoyed about the activity. The children talked for several minutes. Then I asked for everyone's attention and asked, "What did you like about this activity?"

"I had fun," Sharnet said. "I liked finding things and measuring them."

"Me, too," said Zak.

Anfernee raised his hand and said shyly, "Me and Zak worked real good together. We were a good team."

"How did you work well together?" I asked.

"We'd both hold the string and help each other with the spelling and stuff," Anfernee replied.

"I liked choosing objects," Neshey said.

"We were trying to measure 3-D objects like the globe and it was hard, so we erased it and got new objects," Hilda added.

Nathan asked Hilda, "How would you figure the diameter of the globe?"

"You'd have to split it open in half. That's why we got new objects," Neshey answered for Hilda.

I then asked, "What measuring tools did you use?"

Students immediately began shouting out what they had used.

"Wait. Hold on, one person at a time," I said. I called on David.

"A ruler," he said.

"A meterstick," Doug reported.

Nobody else had used any other tools, so I asked, "What units of measurement did you use?"

Several children shouted, "Inches."

Catheryne said, "I used centimeters."

Talon and JT primarily made their measurements in inches, but they also used centimeters.

"Feet," Rifka said.

"Did anyone use a meter or a yard?" I wondered.

"I could have, but I didn't," Luke said. "The garbage can in the hall was 62 inches, which is more than a yard, but since I only had a twelve-inch ruler, I just kept using it over and over again to measure the string."

"Did anyone use millimeters?" I prodded.

"What's a millimeter?" Rachel whispered surreptitiously to Nathan.

"A millimeter is one-tenth of a centimeter. That means it takes 10 millimeters to equal a centimeter," I replied.

"Wow, that's really small," JT commented.

Not surprisingly, nobody had used them.

I changed my line of questioning. "What did you notice when you compared the circumferences and diameters of the objects you measured? Talk with your group," I instructed. The children noisily began sharing their results. After a few minutes I called the room to order.

"It's kind of cool, but at my table, for most of the things the circumference was around three times more than the diameter," Nathan said.

"We found something different," Brandon said. "Eric and I found that the diameter is about one-third of the circumference."

"Same with us," David called out.

Kirsten said, "Hey, everybody, we're saying the same thing. One-third of the circumference is the same thing as three times the diameter."

To make sure that all students had a chance to understand what Kirsten had said, I asked her to give me an example using something she had measured.

"Let me think," she said, pausing for a moment. "Well, we measured a masking tape loop, and the circumference was about 6 inches and the diameter was almost 2 inches."

On the board I wrote:

Masking Tape Loop   Circumference ≈ 6"

Diameter ≈ 2"

"Nathan said that the circumference was around three times more than the diameter," I said. "Watch as I abbreviate a little here." I wrote:

$$C \approx 3 \text{ times } D$$

"The C stands for circumference and the D stands for diameter. The wiggly lines mean that the circumference is about equal to 3 times the

diameter. I can abbreviate a bit more, though. What's the symbol for multiplication?"

"X," several children shouted.

I wrote:

$$C \approx 3 \times D$$

"I can read this sentence as, *Circumference equals about three times the diameter*," I said. I recorded this on the board:

$$C \approx 3 \times D$$

Circumference is about equal to three times the diameter.

"So, what about this masking tape loop. What's its circumference?"

"About 6 inches," the class said.

"And the diameter of the tape loop?"

"About 2 inches."

"So the circumference, about 6 inches, is about three times the diameter, which is almost 2 inches," I concluded.

"Yup. That's cool!" JT cried.

"Brandon noted that the diameter was one-third the circumference," I reminded the class. I wrote:

Diameter is about one-third of the circumference.

"I can write, $D \approx \frac{1}{3} C$. If we look at the tape loop again, is 2 a third of 6?"

Several hands shot up, but I waited until about half the class had their hand raised before calling on Erin.

"Yes it is, because 2 plus 2 plus 2 equals 6, and each 2 is a third of 6," she said.

I changed the focus a bit. "Raise your hand if your connections between circumference and diameter are always close to three or one-third." Almost everybody raised their hand.

"Do you think that would always happen if we measured different circles?" I asked. "Let's say you went home and asked your parents to measure the circumference and diameter of many circles. Would they also find that the diameter is about a third of the circumference and the circumference is about three times the diameter?"

"I guess so. It makes sense," Rifka said.

"I've never thought of that," Nathan chimed in. "But it should. I mean, if 28 people in a room come up with the same thing … We're pretty smart as a class, even if one or two people mess up."

"So why do you think that would happen?" The class was quiet.

"Mathematicians would say that if you did the same activity, *Round Things*, that we just did, you'd always come up with the same relationship between the diameter and the circumference, no matter what circle you measured. The circumference would always be a bit more than three times the diameter. That number that is a little more than 3 is a special number with its own name. It's called pi," I explained.

Luke had been quiet so far, but now he spoke up. "I asked my mom about this activity the other night and she said something about it having to do with pi, too. Doug and I were talking about this in the hall yesterday," he said.

"Pie? I love pie!" chirped Nicole.

"Not that kind of pi, Nicole," Luke admonished. "P-i."

"I heard about it from my older sister. She told me some neat things about it," Rifka added.

I wrote pi on the board, along with the symbol used for it—π—and explained, "When you divide the length of the circumference of any circle by the length of that circle's diameter, the result is always pi. It will always be about 3.14." On the board I wrote:

$$Pi \approx 3.14$$

Pi is the result of dividing the circumference by the diameter of any circle. The circumference will always be about 3.14 times as large as the diameter.

Several students looked confused, so I said, "One way you might think about pi is this. Imagine you have a coke can in your hand." I took a can from our recycling bag and grabbed a piece of yarn. "If I take this yarn and wrap it around the circumference of the can, pi means that the circumference length of yarn should go across the top of the can, the diameter, a little more than three times." I wrapped the yarn around the can and showed how it fit across the diameter three times, with a bit hanging off the end.

"Oh," Nathan said, "that little bit hanging off is the .14!"

"Right, approximately .14," I replied.

"If I don't quite get this stuff yet, does it mean that I'm dumb?" Nathan wanted to know.

Kirsten answered for me, "Rifka's sister didn't learn this stuff until high school. So don't worry."

Nathan and several of his classmates looked relieved.

Kathleen wondered aloud, "So what does pi have to do with perimeter and area?"

I replied, "The perimeter of a circle is called circumference, so pi is the relationship between the diameter and perimeter of a circle. It also helps you figure out the area of a circle."

Ann Maria raised her hand. "Is perimeter circumference?"

"Yes."

"So is area pi?"

"No, but it has to do with it. Don't worry about that for now. You'll get to that later. Are there more questions?" The class was quiet, so I said, "Now I'd like you to write about what you learned from doing this activity and our discussion."

The Children's Writing

The children's writing revealed their differing understanding.

Kirsten wrote: *We notice that when we divid the circumference by 3, we get the diameter and a little bit more.*

If you multiply the diameter by 3.14 it's the circumference. PI is the connection between circumference and diameter.

David and Mike were brief: *We think that diameter is usually close to a third of the circumference. The recording sheet shows that information.*

Eric and Brandon wrote: *We noticed on first few objects that the diameter is always about one third of the circumference. We then noticed this on all of the objects. So no matter what, the diameter is all ways ⅓ and a little more of the circumference. So now we can always find about the circumference, by just looking at the diameter.*

Eric and Brandon's paper listing their measurements and describing what they noticed.

ROUND THINGS

OBJECT	diameter	CIRCUMFERENCE
1 DREAMCATCHER	14 INCHES	42 INCHES
2 CLAY POT	3 INCHES	9 INCHES
3 COFFE POT	6 INCHES	18 INCHES
4 JAR	3¾ INCHES	12 INCHES
5 TAPE ROLL	4⅛ INCHES	4 INCHES
6 WATER BOTTLE	3 INCHES	9 INCHES
7 WHITE OUT	1⅛ INCHES	4 INCHES
8 GARBAGE CAN	21 INCHES	63 INCHES
9 DOOR NOB	2⅓ INCHES	7 INCHES
plastic 10 GARBAGE CAN	22 INCHES	66 INCHES

We noticed on first few objects that the diameter is always one third of the circumference. We then noticed this on all of the objects so no matter what, the diameter is all ways ⅓ and a little more of the circumference. So now we can always find about the circumference, by just looking at the diameter.

Talon and JT commented on how they had learned from a classmate: *We learn that the diameter is close to a ⅓ of the circumference. And we got help from are friend Eric.*

Doug and Luke's writing didn't reflect the rich explanation they'd given during the class discussion: *We talked about pi in the hall. We figured area and volume of the trash can. We figured out that π is the relationship between circumference and diameter and it's 3.14. We also concluded that without multiplying or dividing pi is just another number.*

Then we looked in a dictionary and found a way to find the area of a circle using pi. The formula for that is $A = \pi r^2$ with r meaning radius and A meaning area.

Nicole's writing usually tended to be conversational, and this piece was no exception: *When I did "round things" I had no idea what kind of pattern I would find. (Actuaily, I didn't think ther was a pattern to find.) Well anyway, I thought it was just a big bunch of bolony!*

But, when I finished working on finding round things to measure, I realized that I should find our how much bigger the circumference compared to the diameter to see if that was what the relationship was. What I found was that if you take the diameter of any round object and times it by three (sometimes its a little higher than that) then you get the circumference! Example: Chair leg: 1.14 x 3.45 = 3.93.

Nicole was skeptical about the activity at first, but noticed the consistent relationship between the diameters and the circumferences.

When I did "round things" I had no idea what kind of pattern I would find. (Actually, I didn't think ther was a pattern to find.) Well, anyway, I thought it was just a big bunch of bolonys

But, when I finished working on finding round things to measure, I realized that I should find out how much bigger the circumference compared to the diameter to see if that was what the relationship was. What I found out was that if you take the diameter of any round object and times it by three, (sometimes its a little higher than that) then you get the circumference! Example:

Chair leg: 1.14 × 3.45 = {3.93}

Rachel, Erin, and Rifka wrote: *We noticed that when you divide the circumference by the 3.14 you get the diameter. This is called pi (π). Pi is the relationship between circumference and diameter (3.14) The reason 3.14 is the pi is that the diameter goes into the circumference 3.14 times.*

We also found that to get the area of an object, you multiply the pi by the radius squared. We are not sure why you multiply those by each other yet. When we find out we will add it on to this.

Also, 6.28 divided by 2 is 3.14, pi!

Without multiplying or dividing, 3.14 is just a number.

MENU ACTIVITY

The Banquet Table Problem

Overview

This activity gives students another opportunity to explore the areas and perimeters of rectangles and think about the idea that different-shape rectangles with the same area have perimeters of different lengths. Using one-inch square tiles that fit together to make rectangular "banquet tables," children find the number of people who can be seated at tables with areas of 12 square units and 24 square units. They compare results during a class discussion.

Before the lesson

Gather these materials:
■ An ample supply of Color Tiles
■ Ample supplies of centimeter-squared or inch-squared paper (see blackline masters, pages 195 and 196)
■ Blackline master of menu activity, page 191
■ Overhead projector and overhead Color Tiles (optional)

191

The Banquet Table Problem

You need: Color Tiles
Squared paper (1" or 1 cm)

A banquet table can be made by fitting together small square tables to make one larger rectangular table.

1. Arrange 12 square tiles into as many different-shape rectangular "tables" as you can. Draw your arrangements on squared paper and indicate the number of people each arrangement can seat.

2. Do the same for 24 tiles.

Extension:

The 100-Table Problem. If 100 small square tables are arranged into different-shape rectangular tables, what is the greatest number of people that can be seated? What is the fewest number?

From *Math By All Means: Area and Perimeter, Grades 5 – 6*   ©1997 Math Solutions Publications

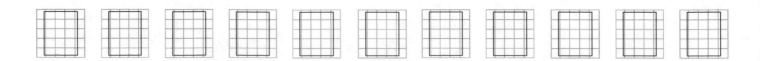

Getting started

■ Discuss with the class the word *banquet*, so that they all know that a banquet is a meal for a large group of people.

■ Introduce the activity by reviewing what the class experienced in the whole class lesson *Spaghetti and Meatballs for All*. Place eight Color Tiles on the overhead projector and ask the class to suggest a way to arrange all of them to make one rectangular table. Then ask how many persons can be seated at the table. Repeat. (There are two possible rectangular tables that can be made from eight tiles—a 1-by-8 that seats 18 people and a 2-by-4 that seats 12 people.)

■ Present the menu directions. Be sure to include the extension.

■ After students have completed the activity, hold a class discussion. Questions like the following can help you guide the discussion:

How did you find all of the rectangles for each number of tables?

What do you notice about the shapes of rectangular tables and the number of people they can seat?

What do you think are the greatest number of seats and the fewest number of seats there can be for a rectangular table made from 100 tiles?

■ After the class discussion, ask the students to write about what they learned from doing this menu activity.

FROM THE CLASSROOM

To prepare for the lesson, I posted an enlarged copy of the menu task and put eight overhead Color Tiles on the overhead projector. I also placed a sheet of centimeter-squared paper nearby to have available for showing the class how to record the work they would be doing in this activity.

"This activity has to do with banquet tables, and it relates to what you did in our lesson about the Comforts' spaghetti-and-meatball party," I told the class. "Raise your hand if you've heard of the word *banquet*." About two-thirds of the class had. "Who would like to explain what a banquet is or give an example?" I waited a few moments to give the children a chance to think, and then called on Eric.

"We had a banquet at the end of baseball season. It was this awards ceremony thing," he said.

"We had one in soccer too," added Nicole.

"Was there food at your banquets?" I asked Eric and Nicole, who nodded enthusiastically.

Several children began talking at once.

"I went to a banquet once for basketball."

"My brother had one for baseball."

After the children quieted down, I said, "A banquet is a ceremony of some sort for a group of people, with a meal served. Usually banquets are held in banquet halls—a large room in a hotel or restaurant."

Ann Maria asked, "Do people have weddings at banquet halls? I'm not sure but I think my sister had hers at one."

"Yes, sometimes they do," I answered, and I turned on the overhead projector, showing the eight Color Tiles I had placed there. I arranged the tiles so they formed a 1-by-8 rectangle.

NOTE Asking students to talk as a small group gives more children a chance to voice their ideas. Also, some children are more willing to share their thinking or ask a question in a small group rather than address the whole class.

NOTE Asking children who had a different way to solve a problem reinforces the idea that there are many ways to solve problems. Students increase their chance of hearing something that makes sense to them when many approaches are shared. It also gives teachers insights into what children are thinking.

NOTE It is important that children have the opportunity to decide whether a problem has another solution. Determining for themselves when all possibilities have been found, rather than having you tell them, helps children develop logical reasoning skills.

Then I said, "When we did the *Spaghetti and Meatballs for All* lesson, we talked about how many people could sit at a rectangular table like this made from the eight small square tables Mrs. Comfort rented."

"Yeah," Erin commented. Others nodded.

"This could be a banquet table," I continued. "How many people can be seated at this banquet table? Think about this for a moment and then share your idea with your neighbor." After a minute I called on Brandon.

"Eighteen," he said. "You can seat eight on each side and two at the ends."

"Did anyone else get 18 people?" I asked the class. Most of the children indicated they had. "Raise your hand if you thought about the problem the same way Brandon did, adding 8 and 8 and then 2 more for the ends." All but about 10 children raised their hand.

"Who solved this a different way?" I asked the class.

"You can just count all around the sides," offered Catheryne, "Like, 1, 2, 3, and so on until you get to 18. That's what I did."

"Who counted, like Catheryne?" I asked, counting the tile edges in the perimeter one by one. About a third of the students raised their hand.

"Did someone find 18 a different way?" I prodded, wanting to allow anyone with a different approach to share. The class was silent.

I sketched the 1-by-8 rectangle on a sheet of centimeter-squared paper, wrote the number 18 inside it, and held the page up for the class to see.

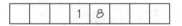

"So, we know you can arrange eight tiles into a 1-by-8 rectangle. What about a differently shaped table? How else could we arrange eight small tables to make one rectangular table?" I asked the class.

"Make a 2-by-4 table," Kirsten suggested.

As I rearranged the tiles on the overhead, Kirsten continued, "You can seat 12 people at a 2-by-4 table, four on the sides and two at the ends. So 4 and 4 is 8, and 2 and 2 is 4, and 8 and 4 is 12 people." Many students nodded or called out their agreement.

"Count one by one to be sure," Catheryne suggested, and I did.

"I'll record this rectangle on the centimeter-squared paper as well," I said. I drew Kirsten's rectangle and wrote inside it the number of people who could be seated.

"How else could we rearrange the tiles to make a rectangular table?" I pushed, even though I knew there were no other ways.

After a few moments, Rifka raised her hand and said, "I don't think there are any other ways, because there aren't any other rectangles that can be made from eight tiles."

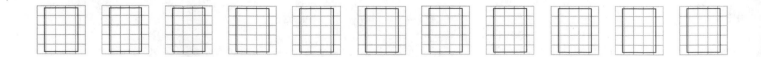

"I agree," said Luke.

"What about arranging the tiles like this?" I asked, and pushed the tiles on the overhead into an L shape.

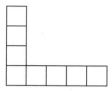

"No," many children chorused.

"Why not?" I asked.

"It's not a rectangle."

"The two people in the inside corner would bump up together."

"It's an L so it doesn't fit the rules."

"Then how about this?" I asked, and formed the tiles into a square with a space in the center.

"You can't do that, because the people sitting in the middle would have to crawl under the table to get to their seat," Kathleen said, giggling. The rest of the class laughed.

"So the rectangle has to be solid," I reminded the children.

Then I pointed to the menu directions I had enlarged and posted. "For this menu activity, arrange 12 tiles into as many different rectangular banquet tables as you can and figure out the number of people that can be seated at each." I held up a sheet of centimeter-squared paper. "Record each rectangle you make on squared paper and write inside it how many people can be seated. Then do the same using 24 tiles." I pointed to the I, P, and G written in the upper right-hand corner of the menu task sheet. "Remember that I stands for individual. You can work individually if you want. P stands for partner, and G stands for group. You can also choose to work with one or more of your classmates." I ended by asking whether there were any questions.

Eric ventured, "No offense, but this seems too easy. What part of this activity takes thinking?"

I was a little surprised by his question, but fifth and sixth graders do tend to blurt out exactly what's on their mind. I considered asking Eric to tell me more about what he meant, so I could understand why he felt the task didn't involve thinking. Or I might have provided a grown-up's mathematical rationale: Exploring this problem helps develop ideas about relationships between area and perimeter, connects factors and multiples to a geometric activity, and provides the opportunity to generalize information to new situations.

NOTE Most children prefer making decisions about which activity to do and with whom to work. Providing these opportunities gives students choice and control over their learning and encourages them to invest in their work.

Before I could say anything, however, Luke said emphatically, "But this is real life! People who run banquet halls have to figure this stuff out."

Rachel, who had been quiet all morning, said, "So it's like *Spaghetti and Meatballs for All,* but we don't know how many people will fit. That's what we figure out."

Kirsten said. "I think it's like *Area Stays the Same.* The area stays constant but the perimeter changes."

"Oh, I get it," said Eric, relieving me of having to respond. Nevertheless, I was glad to be able to introduce the extension to the menu task at this point.

"There is an optional extension that you may want to investigate for an extra challenge," I began. "If 100 small square tables are arranged into as many versions of a large rectangular table as possible, what are the greatest and fewest number of people who can be seated?"

"Cool," said Nathan.

There were no more questions, and the students got to work.

Observing the Children

The students enjoyed this activity. Not only did they like working with the Color Tiles, but their previous experience with the lesson *Spaghetti and Meatballs for All* made them feel comfortable.

Sharnet and Kathleen worked together. Sharnet took 12 tiles and began placing them in clusters of two, spaced equidistant from each other.

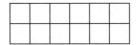

"No, no! That doesn't follow the rule," cried Kathleen. "You need to push them all together." She pushed several together until Sharnet got the idea and took over for Kathleen, making a 2-by-6 rectangle.

"How about this?" Sharnet asked.

"Yup, it works. I'll write it down," Kathleen replied. She took a sheet of centimeter-squared paper and drew the rectangle. "How many people can sit at it?" she asked.

Sharnet counted the edges of the tiles on the perimeter one by one and replied, "Sixteen." Kathleen recorded the number inside the rectangle she'd drawn.

"Okay, let's make another one," said Sharnet. She took the tiles, shuffled them, and made another 2-by-6 rectangle.

"No, we already did that," Kathleen told her. Leaning over, she took five tiles from Sharnet's pile of 12 and arranged a 1-by-5 rectangle. After

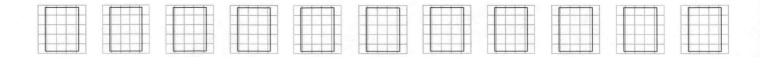

thinking a moment, Kathleen made an identical rectangle, placing it parallel to, but not touching the first.

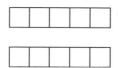

Then she took the remaining two tiles and used them to connect the two rectangles.

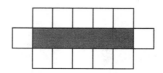

"Does this fit the rules?" Kathleen asked Sharnet.

"No, it's got a hole in the middle. Let's try something else," Sharnet said.

Kathleen took the tiles and made another rectangle while Sharnet began watching something going on in another group. Soon Kathleen had made a 3-by-4 rectangle, and she started to count the sides one by one. Sharnet was becoming even more distracted by the group nearby, edging her chair toward them. Kathleen didn't seem to be bothered by this, but I was. I was often unsure how to deal with Sharnet's lack of interest in math. She responded well to one-on-one instruction, and I checked with her frequently during menu time.

"Sharnet, Kathleen, I'm confused," I said. "You began working together, but now it looks like you've chosen to work alone, Kathleen. What's going on?"

"I was just ... I got distracted!" answered Sharnet good-naturedly as she returned to her table. "C'mon, Kathleen, let's get to work."

"Okay," Kathleen replied with a smile, and she began silently manipulating the tiles again while Sharnet watched. A minute or so later, Sharnet again began watching the other group.

"Look," I interrupted the girls. "Working together means sharing the materials and the thinking. Kathleen, when you use the tiles without telling Sharnet what you're thinking, it's easy for her to become distracted. And, Sharnet, part of sharing the materials here means that you need to try to make some of the rectangles too."

"Okay," replied Kathleen, and she pushed the tiles over to Sharnet, who made a 1-by-4 rectangle, then attempted to enlarge it.

"Oh, this is hard!" Sharnet cried. "Let's make it fatter." She began to add tiles randomly, here and there.

"No, no—see, it has to be one rectangle," explained Kathleen, reaching for the tiles and then stopping herself and glancing at me. Sharnet was clearly having trouble making sense of the activity, and Kathleen wanted to do it for her.

"Sharnet, tell me what you need to do for this activity," I said, to see if I could find out about her confusion.

"Well, first you take the tiles and lay them all out and find the rectangles," she said.

"Can you be more specific?" I asked her.

NOTE Students sometimes need help learning that working together doesn't mean that one person does the thinking and work while the other person simply puts her name on the completed paper.

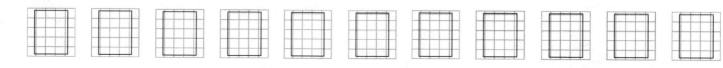

"Uh ... I think you need 12 tiles. Yeah, 12 tiles. You put them in order and find how many there are," she responded.

"What do you mean when you say 'find how many there are'?" I probed.

"How many tiles?" Sharnet asked.

Kathleen slapped her forehead in mock frustration and groaned, "There are 12 tiles. You said so yourself. You need to find how many people can sit there. You know, one person on a side of a tile."

"One person?" Sharnet repeated.

"Yeah, you have to pretend that the tiles are a table, like the one we're sitting at," Kathleen said as she pointed to the rectangular table she and Sharnet shared with two other students.

"How many people can sit on your side of the table?" I asked Sharnet. "Two."

"And the other side?" I pointed to where her tablemates sat. "Two."

So how many people can sit at your table?" I asked.

"Four," came Sharnet's confident reply.

Kathleen said, "Sharnet, just pretend that the tiles are like our table. But you can sit on all four sides of one tile. See?" She placed a tile in front of Sharnet and counted the sides.

"Oh, I get it!" said Sharnet excitedly. "So if you do that big table we did first—what size was it?"

"Two-by-6," Kathleen answered, quickly creating the shape.

"So one person sits on each side. So that's ... ," Sharnet was momentarily silent as she counted the edges of the tiles one by one, "... 16!"

"Right!" answered Kathleen.

"What do we do next?" Sharnet asked Kathleen.

I felt confident that Sharnet had a better understanding of the task, so I moved on to another table, where Anfernee had made a 1-by-3 rectangle with the tiles.

"How do you count this rectangle?" Anfernee asked. "Do you count 1, 2, 3, 4, 5, 6, 7, 8?" He indicated the tile edges in the perimeter. "Or 1, 2, 3?" He indicated the three tiles that made up the area.

"Well, first of all, what are you trying to find out?" I asked.

"Uh, how many people can sit there," Anfernee said.

"Okay. So you have two choices. You can count each unit around the rectangle, or count each tile. Imagine that the tiles are tables. Do you sit around the table or on the tables?"

"Oh, I see. Around the tiles. Because if you counted 1, 2, 3, you'd be sitting on the table, and you can't do that in a restaurant." Anfernee grinned.

"So tell me how many people can sit around the table you've made," I said.

"Eight. Three on each side and one on each end," Anfernee replied.

Anfernee was not using the correct number of tiles, and I addressed this next. "I notice you have three tiles. Let's read the menu task together to make sure you're using the correct number of tiles." After we had reviewed the directions, Anfernee added 9 more tiles to his pile to make 12, and began making a 1-by-12 rectangle.

Catheryne now brought me her paper, where she had carefully drawn two shapes.

NOTE Menu tasks engage children with reading and writing as well as with mathematics. It is helpful to reinforce for students that necessary information for the activity is written in the menu instructions. However, some students may need help reading them.

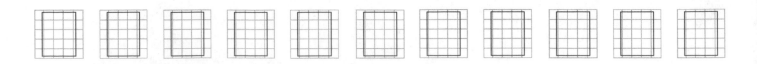

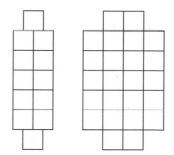

"I'm working alone," she said. "Are these shapes okay? Because I thought they were, but now I don't think so."

"Why don't you think so?" I asked, to find out what made her doubt her work.

"Kirsten said they weren't okay. She said they weren't rectangles because of the tiles sticking out at the ends," Catheryne responded.

"What did you think about that?" I asked.

"I think she's probably right, because she's pretty smart and all," Catheryne replied.

"How many sides does a rectangle have?" I asked.

"Four."

"And how many corners does a rectangle have?" I asked.

"Four," Catheryne said again.

"Watch as I count the sides and corners on the shapes you made," I said. Catheryne's eyes widened as I did so.

"Oh boy, I guess these aren't rectangles!" she exclaimed and wheeled around toward her seat. "Thanks!" she called over her shoulder.

I noticed that Talon was working alone. He had recorded a 2-by-6 rectangle on his centimeter-squared paper. Nicole, who was sitting nearby, was working on the same activity. I watched Talon as he completed a 3-by-4 rectangle. He said aloud, "Hmm, four on each side and three on each end. That's 8 times 6. Let's see ... 48 people."

Then he stopped and looked carefully at the rectangle he had arranged on his table. "That can't be right," he commented. Looking up at me he said, "I just realized that instead of multiplying you should add."

"How did you realize that?" I asked.

"When I multiplied, the number seemed too high," Talon responded. He pointed to the 2-by-6 rectangle he had drawn on his paper. "That one seats 16 people." Talon grabbed his centimeter-squared paper, drew a 3-by-4 rectangle, and counted the perimeter units. When he was done recording that 14 people could be seated at the table, Talon began rearranging the tiles.

"Oh! You can make a 12-by-1," he discovered. "That's a long one. I bet lots of people can sit there."

"Try 26," suggested Nicole, who had been listening to our conversation and now gathered up her materials and moved closer to Talon and me.

"You're right!" he said.

"Do you have all the rectangles I have?" Nicole compared her paper with Talon's. "Let's see, 1-by-12, 2-by-6, 3-by-4. Yup, all there," she said.

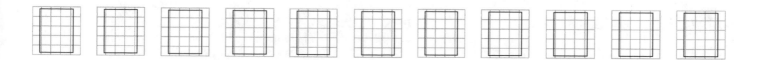

Ann Maria overheard and called, "Nicole, how do you know those are all the ways?"

Nicole replied, "Well, first I made a long skinny rectangle that's 1-by-12. Then I cut it in half and made a 2-by-6. Then I cut the six in half and made a 3-by-4. But then, I couldn't cut the three in half because it's odd, and when I cut the four in half, I could only make a 2-by-6 again." Nicole's response indicated that she reasoned well, both logically and mathematically.

Working on the 100-Table Extension

Over the next several days, almost half the class tried the 100-table problem, Sharnet and her partner, Kathleen, among them. Sharnet wanted to use 100 tiles, while Kathleen was comfortable approaching the task abstractly. Sharnet took a tub of tiles and dumped them out on the floor. She got down on her hands and knees and began making a 1-by-100 rectangle. Kathleen attempted the problem on centimeter-squared paper, quickly finding out that she needed to tape several sheets of paper together to make it long enough to draw 100 squares.

"Sharnet! That's more than 100," Kathleen called as she glanced up from her paper.

"How do you know? I've been keeping track. It's right," said Sharnet. She stopped momentarily and sat up.

"Because when we did 12 and 24 tiles the lines looked a lot shorter than I expected. That looks too long. Anyway, we really don't have to lay them out because we know 100 in a line is 100. So is 50 and 50 or 20 in five rows or ten rows of 10," Kathleen replied.

"Well, I wanted to lay these out just to be sure," Sharnet responded.

Kathleen continued, "So, the most people you could seat would be on the 1-by-100 table. And when we did the 1-by-12 and the 1-by-24 tables, the seats were way more than 12 and way more than 24, so I think it will be a lot more people than 100 that can be seated, like 150 or 200."

"Let's count 'em," suggested Sharnet. She began counting the tile edges in one side of the 1-by-100 rectangle. Kathleen joined her on the floor and counted the other side. I thought it was interesting that while Kathleen could think abstractly about the problem and make a prediction by connecting the problem to a similar problem, she chose to count to be certain of the number of people who could sit on one side.

"Two hundred people!" Sharnet gasped.

"No, 202!" countered Kathleen. "Don't forget the two ends. I knew it would seat a lot."

"This is fun!" cried Sharnet. "Let's write 202 down." Kathleen recorded the information on a sheet of notebook paper and then said, "Let's try a 10-by-10." Sharnet immediately began building the rectangle.

When I approached Erin's table, Erin announced to me, "I found out that for the 100 table, you can use multiplication to find the rectangles."

"Tell me more," I urged.

"Well, it's simple. I did a 10-by-10 square and remembered that 10 times 10 is 100. So I thought, 25 times 4 is also 100. I bet that works, too. And I tried it and it did!" Spotting Nicole, Erin skipped off. "Hey, Nicole—guess what I found out?" I laughed at Erin's obvious excitement and appreciated her discovery of a connection between multiplication and geometry.

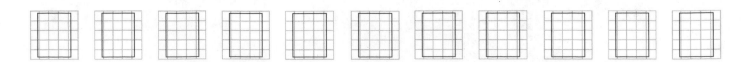

A Class Discussion

I began our discussion of this activity by asking, "How did you find all of the rectangles for each number of tables? Share your ideas with your group."

After a few minutes I asked for volunteers to share their methods. JT waved his hand insistently and I called on him.

"First we messed around with the tiles. Then Eric and I were doing 24 tiles. We made a 2-by-12 rectangle. I knew that 12 plus 12 is 24 and so we added both sides and came up with 24. Then, when we added the ends, we got 30," he said.

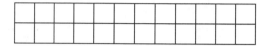

"So the area was 24 and the perimeter 30?" I asked.

"Yeah," replied JT.

Eric added, "Then we did the same for 12 tiles. We knew that 6 plus 6 was half of our 12-by-2 rectangle, so that made it easy. But the rectangles got a little fatter when they weren't 1-by rectangles."

"I saw that too," called Nicole, "except that I found an easier way to do it. I broke the tiles in half each time to find the rectangle."

The rest of the class looked confused.

"Why don't you use some tiles on the overhead to show what you mean," I suggested. Nicole came to the overhead projector and placed 12 tiles in a 1-by-12 rectangle.

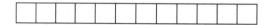

"I'm going to use 12 tiles because 24 probably won't fit. See, this is a 1-by-12 rectangle, and you can seat ... um ... 26 people because there's 12 people on each side and one on each end. Then you can just break the 12 in half to get six tiles, and put them next to each other." Nicole made a 2-by-6 rectangle with the tiles.

"That's six on each long side and two on each end, so it's 16 people you can get there. And like Eric said, the rectangle is a little fatter," she noted. Next, Nicole took the 2-by-6 rectangle and rearranged it to make a 3-by-4 rectangle.

"This one was the fattest, and it seats only 14 people. So the banquet hall people won't fit a lot in if they use it. They should use the long skinny tables," she finished and sat down.

"How did someone else find the rectangles for each number of tables?" I asked. After a few moments I called on Kathleen.

"Me and Sharnet did the 100-table problem and the 12- and 24-table problems," she began. "There wasn't a big difference in them because if you knew how to do the 12 and 24 problems it was easy to do the 100-table problem."

Eric interrupted. "That's what I was trying to say when Mrs. Rectanus introduced the activity."

"Anyway, me and Sharnet found that you could use rows to solve the problem. We did a row of 12 first, two rows of 6 next, and three rows of 4 for the 12-tile problem. Then with 24 tables you could do the same, a row of 24, two rows of 12 and so on," Kathleen continued.

"What do you notice about the shapes of rectangles and the number of people they can seat? Talk with your neighbor," I told the class. The class discussed the question for a few minutes.

"What did you notice?" I asked after I had called the children to attention again.

"The long skinny ones seat more people," Doug said.

"And the fat ones don't seat very many people," Catheryne added.

"It's kind of like *Perimeter Stays the Same,*" noted Nicole. "The same thing happened in that activity, too."

"Let's look at 100 tables," I suggested. I was curious how those who had not explored the 100-table problem might now apply their understanding about 12 and 24 tiles to a new situation. "Talk with your group. Based on what you know about rectangles with 12 and 24 tiles, what's your conjecture or theory about the dimensions of the table with the greatest number of seats and the fewest number of seats for 100 tiles?"

The children's conversations were animated as they discussed the question. After a few minutes I called the students back to attention.

"I think the most people is 202," said Zak. "On each side is 100 people, plus the two ends. The lowest is 50 people, because you have 25 people sitting down on top."

I didn't understand Zak's second answer, so I asked how he had arrived at it.

"Uh, I guessed," he said with a grin.

Nathan said, "I disagree. I think the least number is 40 people sitting at a 10-by-10 table. I think this because the one with the most squares inside fits the least people." Several children applauded Nathan's idea.

"How did you get 40 people?" I asked Nathan.

"Easy. Ten on each side, so you go 10 plus 10 plus 10 plus 10 equals 40," he answered.

"The square one seats the least," Kirsten agreed. "It's a square number too."

"Explain what you're thinking, Kirsten," I said.

"Sure. When you take 100 tiles and arrange them 10 by 10, it makes a square. So it's a square number because it's 10 by 10."

Kathleen raised her hand. "If you do a 9-by-9, do you get a square number? Like what you multiply together by itself, the answer is a square number?" she asked Kirsten.

"Yes," Kirsten replied.

"I didn't know that," Kathleen replied.

"Me, neither," said JT.

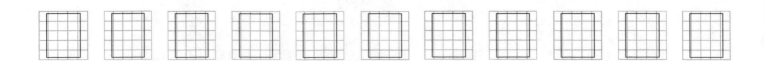

NOTE Hearing one another's thoughts helps students clarify their thinking and gives them ideas for what to write about.

I chose to stop the conversation because it was nearing the end of math time and I wanted students to write about what they had learned. To prepare the children I said, "I'm curious about what you've learned from this activity. Talk to your neighbor and then be ready to share with the class."

After a bit I called the children together: "What did you learn?"

Nicole said, "The banquet table problem teaches you more than the best way to seat people. It shows you about square numbers, because you can take a certain number like 6, and if you can't make a square out of those tiles, it's not a square number."

"I saw that when it's long like a snake, you can fit a lot of people on it," said Anfernee slowly. "And if it's fat like a cookie, you can't."

"It's like long and skinny tables have more perimeter than short fat ones," Rachel added.

"The longer the perimeter, the more people can sit there," Ann Maria said.

Doug had been silent during the class discussion, but now he raised his hand and said, "I've been thinking. If you know how many people are sitting at a banquet table, you can subtract 2 and divide by 2 to get the long skinny table. Like, take 50 people. Subtract 2 and you get 48. Divide it by 2 you get 24. Take 24 tiles and put them in a straight line. You have 24 people on a side with 2 people on the ends."

Rifka immediately added, "The way to seat the most people no matter how many tables you have is to take one times the amount of tables you have because two people can sit at each table plus the two ends. A quick way to find out how many can sit is, you double the number of tables and add the two ends. You go, tables times 2 plus 2. My mom helped me."

After everyone who wanted to had offered ideas, I asked the students to write about what they had learned.

The Children's Writing

Almost half the class commented on how multiplication helped them understand the banquet table problem.

Talon wrote that he learned more about multiplication and group work: *I think that Banquet table problem was cool because it taut me how to use multiplication. And I learned how to work in a group (Nicole) and I learned how to arange tables by using multiplcation.*

Nathan noticed that there were different approaches to solving the problem. He wrote: *I learned that many people have ways to find the combination for this activity. Some are harder then others some are easier. The easiest and most logical for me is to just write down all the factors for 12 and 24.*

Erin, Nicole, Eric, and JT all referred to Kirsten's insight about square numbers. Erin explained how to find square numbers and included examples. She wrote: *I learned that if you can take a number of tiles and make them into a square that number is square. Like if you take nine tiles you can make them into a square, so 9 is a square number. One way to tell if a number is square is use your muliplication facts. First do 1 x 1 = 1 so 1 is a square number. then do 2 x 2 = 4, that makes four a square number.*

Nicole wrote: *I learned that the B.T.P. (Banquet Table Problem) teaches you more then the best way to pick out square goodie-holders for a lace and flower ceremony (in other words, a wedding). What it is, is the eaistest way to find out if a diget is a square number.*

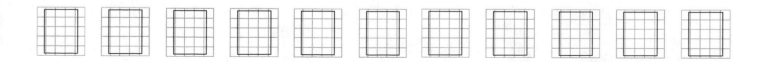

Nicole used an example and a sketch to communicate her thinking.

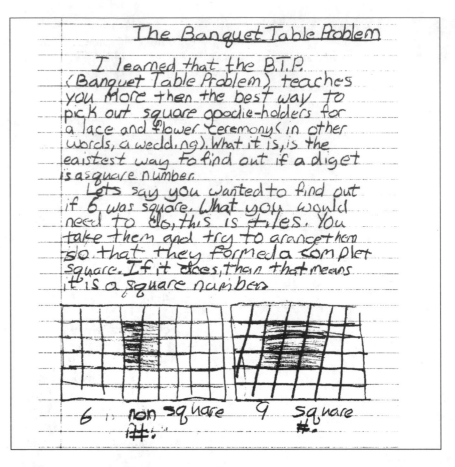

The Banquet Table Problem

I learned that the B.T.P. (Banquet Table Problem) teaches you More then the best way to pick out square goodie-holders for a lace and flower ceremony (in other words, a wedding). What it is, is the eaistest way to find out if a diget is a square number.

Lets say you wanted to find out if 6 was square. What you would need to do, this is tiles. You take them and try to arange them so that they formed a complet square. If it does, than that means it is a square number.

6 non square #.   9 square #.

Lets say you wanted to find out if 6 was square. What you would need to do, this is tiles. You take them and try to arange them so that they formed a complet square. If it does, than that means it is a square number.

Eric commented on the connection between multiplication and area and perimeter, and used his knowledge of factors to check his answers: *I learned after friday about the multables. It realy helped even if I had all the anwsers, it helped me check them over. It also could have got me the anwsers quicker. I noticed that banquet table problem can help you with your square numbers.*

Eric's knowledge of fractions helped him verify his solutions.

The Banquet Table Problem

I learned after friday about the multables. It realy helped even if I had all the anwsers, it helped me check them over. It also could have got me the anwsers quicker. I noticed that banquet table problem can help you with your square numbers.

Rachel, Luke, and Mike focused on the shape of the tables and the number of people each would seat. Rachel wrote: *I noticed that the long and skinny banquet tables have more perimeter than the short and fat ones. And it helped me understand square numbers better.* Luke provided an explanation for why the square tables seated fewer people: *I noticed that the long skinny tables seated the most people because since each table had some perimeter more than 1 person could be seated at each table. The squarish "fat" tables seated the least because the tables in the middle couldn't be sat at.* Mike was terse, but clear: *I noticed that the tables that were skinny could seat more people because more parts of the squares are exposed.*

Rifka generalized for any number of tables.

> ## The Banquet Table Problem
>
> I learned that the way to seat the most people, no matter what number, would be a table with the dimensions of 1 × the amnt. of Tables because 2 people could sit on each side of a table, plus 2 on the end tables. Example
>
> A quick way to find how many people can sit at the table would be to multiply the # of Tables by 2 (2 sides) and add 2 (the 2 ends). In algebra that would be, (T×2)+2 = # of people who can sit there.

Rifka's paper showed that she was able to generalize from the experience. She wrote: *I learned that the way to seat the most people, no matter what number, would be a table with the dimensions of 1 x the amnt. of tables because 2 people could sit on each side of a table, plus 2 on the end tables.*

A quick way to find how many people can sit at the table would be to multiply the # of tables by 2 (2 sides) and add 2 (the 2 ends). In algebra that would be (T x 2) + 2 = # of people who can sit there.

Malkia wrote: *I learned that the bigger the table (long) the more people can fit. I also learned how to do peremiter better and Area.*

Sharnet's writing showed that the problem was not as difficult for her after getting clarification from her partner: *I learn that the Banquet table problem is not as hard as you think it is. And I learnd onece your start it you get use to it and it starts to get fun. I also learn the the Banquet table problem is useing a little bit of fraction but not very many. But when I playd Banquet problem it was eazy fineding tables when I playd the game with Kathleen and onece I got use to it it did not sem so hard anymore.*

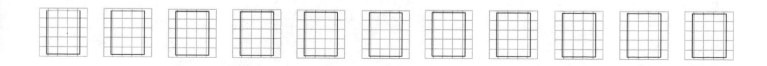

MENU ACTIVITY

Double the Circumference

Overview

This activity gives children the opportunity to look at the relationship between the circumference and the area of a circle. The activity builds on students' experiences with *Round Things* (see page 86).

With a partner or group, students trace a circular object on centimeter-squared paper, find its area, and measure its circumference. Children then draw two new circles, one with a circumference double that of the original circle and another with a circumference half that of the original circle. After first predicting the areas of the two new circles, the students calculate them and record all their measurements on a class chart.

Before the lesson

Gather these materials:
- ■ Ample supplies of rulers, tape measures, string, and tape
- ■ An ample supply of centimeter-squared paper (see blackline master, page 195)
- ■ Blackline master of menu activity, page 192

192

Double the Circumference P or G

You need: A small circular object
Centimeter-squared paper
String
Tape
A partner or group

1. Trace the circular object onto centimeter-squared paper. Figure the area and record it inside the circle (___sq cm or ___ cm²).

2. Use string to measure the circumference of the circle you traced. Cut a piece of string that is twice the length of the circumference and use it to form a new circle on the paper. Tape the string in place. Predict the area of the new circle and then figure it. Record the area in the circle.

3. Discuss how you could describe the relationship between the circumference and area of each circle.

4. What do you think the area will be for a circle with a circumference that is half the length of the original circle? Predict first and then find out.

5. Record all of your data on the class chart.

From *Math By All Means: Area and Perimeter, Grades 5–6* ©1997 Math Solutions Publications

Getting started

■ Post a class recording chart on a wall or draw one on the board:

	Groups / Teams										
	1	2	3	4	5	6	7	8	9	10	11
Area of circle with half the circumference (cm²)											
Area of original circle (cm²)											
Area of circle with double the circumference (cm²)											

■ Present the menu directions. First, tell the students that they are to find a small circular object (for example, a roll of tape, a jar lid, or a bottle), trace around it on a sheet of centimeter-squared paper, figure out the area (in square centimeters) of the resulting circle, and record the area inside the circle.

■ Talk about the mathematical shorthand used to indicate square centimeters: sq cm or cm2.

■ Tell the children that they then are to cut a length of string that is twice as long as the circumference of their original circle and use it to form a new circle by taping the string to the centimeter-squared paper. They should predict the area of this circle, figure it out (in square centimeters), and then think about and describe the relationship between the circumference and the area of the two circles.

■ Tell them that next they are to predict what the area will be of a circle with a circumference equal to half that of the original circle; then they are to use string to make the circle and figure out its area.

■ Give the reminder that they are to record their results on the class chart.

■ After all the children have recorded their data on the class chart, hold a class discussion about this activity. Questions like the following can help you guide the conversation:

> What did you think the areas of the larger and smaller circles would be before you actually measured them?

> How did you figure out the area of the circles?

> How did you account for the partial squares in the circles?

> What do you notice from the data on the chart? (They should notice that the area of each middle circle is approximately four times the area of the smaller circle and one-fourth the area of the larger circle. You may need to prompt students by suggesting that one way to investigate the relationship between the circles is to divide each area by the area above it on the chart.)

> Why do you think the area of a circle quadruples when its circumference doubles? (It may help to work through a similar example using a square.)

■ Give the students an assignment to describe in writing how they found the area of each circle and to explain why they think the area of a circle quadruples when its circumference doubles.

FROM THE CLASSROOM

NOTE Children need guidelines for the care and storage of materials. Keeping materials in a central location such as on a shelf or a table makes it easier for students to locate them. Labeling both containers and the place where they belong helps keep your classroom orderly.

"This menu activity is called *Double the Circumference*," I told the class. I had posted an enlarged copy of the menu activity on the board. I pointed to the letters P and G in the upper right-hand corner of the menu task and reminded the children: "These letters mean you can choose to work with a partner or with a group."

"You need several materials for this activity, including a small circular object to trace, like this," I continued, holding up a roll of masking tape and pointing to the circumference. "You also need some string, which is on the supply shelf. Instead of taking the whole spool of string to your place, cut a length about 2 feet long to take to where you're working. Then people won't have to figure out who has the string."

Walking to the cubbies that held our paper supply, I said. "You also need a sheet of centimeter-squared paper and some tape."

I continued reading the menu instructions. "Trace around the circular object onto the centimeter-squared paper. Figure the area in square centimeters and record it inside the circle."

"This sounds sort of like *Foot Stuff*," interrupted Rachel. "In *Foot Stuff* your toes were round on the ends like a circle and that made it hard to count."

"Interesting point, Rachel," I told her. "Like in *Foot Stuff*, you'll notice that your circle partially fills some squares, leaving you with the problem of finding a way to count the partial squares as well as the whole ones."

Catheryne asked, "Why would you measure it in square centimeters if it's a circle?"

Neshey raised her hand, and I told her she could reply. "Each box on the paper is a square, and it's also a centimeter on each side. That's why it's called square-centimeter paper, and that's why we're measuring the area in square centimeters," she explained patiently. "We don't have circle paper." Neshey was often impatient with Catheryne's questions, and I was pleased by her kindly tone.

I continued with the directions. "Use the string to measure the circumference of this circle, but don't cut it. Then cut a piece of string double the length of the circumference of the circle and shape it into a new circle on the paper." I demonstrated. "Tape it in place. Predict the area of the new circle and then figure it out. Then discuss with your partner or group how you could describe the relationship between the circumference and area of the two circles." I knew I'd just given the class a lot of information, so I asked, "What questions do you have so far?"

"Why do we have to predict the area of the second circle before we figure it?" Nicole wanted to know.

Rifka replied, "If I know Mrs. Rectanus, it's probably because what we think is going to happen won't!" The class laughed. They had learned that some tasks appear to be deceptively simple but are quite complex.

"Predicting allows you to think about what should happen based on the experiences you've had with area and perimeter," I said. One of my goals is for students to make connections between activities, and I wanted to reinforce that idea.

Then I finished presenting the directions. "What do you think the area will be for a circle with a circumference equal to half the circumference of the original circle? Predict first and then find out. Finally, record your data on a class chart." I indicated a large chart I had posted on the wall.

	Groups / Teams										
	1	2	3	4	5	6	7	8	9	10	11
Area of circle with half the circumference (cm²)											
Area of original circle (cm²)											
Area of circle with double the circumference (cm²)											

"Write your group's or team's data here," I told the class. "Record the area of the original circle in the box in the middle." I again modeled two ways to indicate square centimeters: *sq cm* and *cm².* "Record the area of the circle with half the circumference in the top box and the area of the circle with double the circumference in the bottom box."

Zak asked, "Can I cut another string that's half the circumference of the half-circumference string?" He giggled.

I smiled and told Zak he could, as long as he continued to follow the rule of predicting first and writing about the relationship he noticed. There were no further questions and the class began working.

Observing the Children

JT and Talon chose to work together, which was unusual. Talon and his best friend, Marcel, were usually inseparable and often spent their time together having fun but not being very productive. However, Marcel was absent. It was wonderful to hear Talon's careful thinking when he worked with another partner.

JT spent a lot of time carefully positioning and then tracing a tape loop on the centimeter grid paper. He began counting the whole squares but lost track of how many he had counted, so Talon took over.

"I'll bet we have 200 squares!" JT guessed enthusiastically.

"I bet 180 something," replied Talon.

Talon finished counting the whole squares and began to write the total in the middle of the circle.

"Wait!" JT stopped him. "We forgot to count the half squares!" They giggled as they realized their error, and Talon erased the total he'd written. I found it interesting but not surprising that JT referred to all of the partly filled squares as halves. Fifth and sixth graders often struggle to understand fractions.

JT began counting the partly filled squares. "I'm matching up the ones that seem like half with the others that seem like half. So we'll have to use fractions to figure this out," he said aloud.

"What about that one?" asked Talon, pointing to a square that was about three-quarters filled.

"Easy. Just put it with that little one," JT said, pointing to a square that was about one-quarter filled. As he worked, JT tallied each equivalent whole square while Talon looked on in silence. Finally, Talon counted JT's tallies and added them together mentally to find the area of the circle.

"So it's 52 square centimeters," remarked Talon as he recorded the area in the middle of the circle. I noticed the large discrepancy between the boys' prediction of 200 square centimeters and the actual area, but they seemed unaware of how far off their guesses had been.

JT and Talon's work shows how they kept track of whole squares and partial squares.

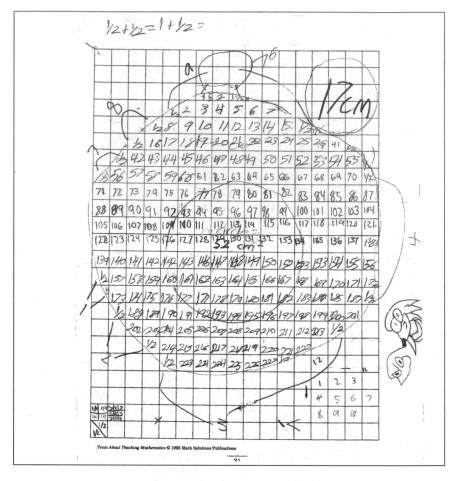

From *About Teaching Mathematics* © 1992 Math Solutions Publications

"Well, I think since we're going to double the string, then the area should double. That would make it 104 centimeters," JT said.

Talon agreed: "Yeah."

"Let's get paper and record our prediction," said JT, as he opened his binder. I was impressed with JT's competence. He didn't often perceive himself as being "smart" in math, and his leadership was positive. Both JT and Talon recorded and explained their predictions. JT wrote: *The area of the original circle is 52 cm We think the area of the circle with double the circumference will be 104 cm We think this because when you add 52 + 52 you get 104* Talon wrote: *The area of are original circle was 52 cm². We thought the area of are doubled circle would be 104. We thought this because when we measured the original circle was 52 and we thought 52 + 52 = 104.*

Several other students were working on *Double the Circumference* that day. After a new menu task has been introduced, many students are eager to try it out, even if they have previously been working on another activity.

Ann Maria chose to work alone, despite my instructions to work with a group. She approached me while I was observing Talon and JT. "Do you measure the whole entire circle?" she asked.

Overhearing Ann Maria's question, JT stopped working long enough to look up and say, "First you figure out the original area and record it. Then double the circumference string, predict the area of the new circle, and figure that."

Ann Maria thanked him and went back to her table.

When a student asks me a question that other students can answer, I usually suggest that he or she check with a classmate. Sometimes all that's needed is clarification. Hilda and Sharnet were just sitting at their table.

"We don't know what to do," Hilda said plaintively.

"Did you read the directions on the menu instruction sheet?" I asked.

"Yeah, we did that," Sharnet replied. "It says to double the circumference of the original circle."

"Did you do that?" I prodded.

"No, how do you do that?" Hilda asked.

Sharnet quickly answered, "Take the string that we used to measure the circumference of the circle. Make it twice as long and put it on the paper and make a new circle."

"So what you need to do is …?" I prompted.

Hilda smiled. "Double the string and make a new circle!" She and Sharnet went back to work.

As I circulated through the room, I noticed Ann Maria working intently. She had counted the whole squares and was staring at the partial squares. "I know! I'll count the halves and put two together to make a whole," she said to no one in particular. "Then, with the tiny ones left over I can trace them to see how much more I need to make a whole." She worked with precision and patience.

A while later I noticed JT and Talon concentrating on their paper.

"What should we predict for the circle with half the circumference?" Talon asked JT.

"Well, we're not going to predict that the area will be half 'cause we were wrong on the last one. Look, the area of the original circle was 52 and the doubled circle area was 233. Get your calculator," JT responded.

Talon took out his calculator. "Two hundred and thirty-three divided by 2 equals 122," he told JT, who seemed confused by this information.

"Here, let me see that," JT said, reaching across the table to take the calculator. "Look, all you have to do is divide 233 by 52 to find out how many times greater the area of the double string circle is than the original circle." He entered the numbers. "Hmm, 4.48."

"That's $4.48, which is close to $4.50. Fifty cents is half of a dollar so the area of the double circumference circle is four and a half times greater than the original circle," Talon finished.

JT said excitedly, "Since we multiply by 4 ½ for the double circumference circle, that means we divide 52 by 4 ½ to get the area of the circle with half the circumference. But let's just divide by 4. The .48 is less than half, so it rounds down to 4." He entered 52 divided by 4 on the calculator and said, "Thirteen."

"So the area of the half circle should be about 13!" Talon concluded. The two boys immediately made the new circle and began counting.

"Ten whole squares," said JT.

"Let's do part squares now," Talon said. "Should I break these into thirds because they're not halves?" JT seemed unsure.

"Let's split the little ones into halves, fourths, and ninths. Maybe that will help," JT said to Talon as he drew a tiny 3-by-3 grid inside one of the square centimeters to indicate ninths.

After a great deal of checking and rechecking, both boys seemed satisfied. "Yup, it's 17 square centimeters," said Talon, "I'll record it on the class chart." He did this while JT finished recording their predictions and results on a sheet of notebook paper.

A Class Discussion

"I'm curious about what you predicted would happen in *Double the Circumference*," I told the class several mornings later. I had waited until everyone had entered their measurements on the class chart.

Eric immediately blurted out, "I thought the area would double for the doubled string!" Several children nodded in agreement.

"Why?" I asked.

"Well, it is called *Double the Circumference*," he explained.

"How many of you thought the area would double, like Eric said?" I asked. About a fourth of the class indicated they had.

"Did someone have a different prediction?" I asked.

Catheryne raised her hand. "I thought it would get a little bigger but it got a lot bigger!"

"I thought it'd double," offered Nathan, "but I knew it wouldn't be that easy."

Erin chimed in, "I thought it would triple."

"Why?" I asked.

"When you made the new circle it looked like you could fit three of the original circles inside it," she responded.

"I wasn't really sure if it would double or not," Nicole said. "I got really confused, because if you change the perimeter, then the area was supposed to stay the same. I learned that in the activity we did where the area stayed the same. But in this situation it didn't happen."

"So what did happen?" I prompted.

Nick said, "When the circumference doubled, I think the area doubled."

Rifka clarified, "The circumference doubled, but the area quadrupled!"

Eric and Brandon began keeping track of the square centimeters by writing numerals in each square. They later abandoned that technique and instead put dots in each square.

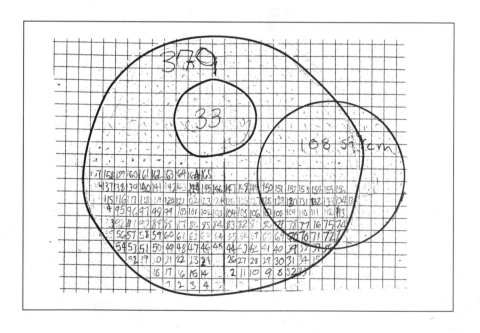

JT agreed. "It was four times as big or four times as small as the original circle."

"Before we look at our class chart, I'm curious about the way you counted the squares to figure the area. How did you accomplish that?" I said.

Eric raised his hand. "Brandon and I took turns counting the squares and the fractions of the squares," he said. "We counted the fractional squares by halves, fourths, and thirds."

"Yeah," Brandon agreed. "And I would put a dot in each of the squares so I would know which ones I did."

"When I saw a half of a square or a fourth, I added them together to make a whole," Nathan contributed.

Sharnet elaborated on this idea. "After I counted all the whole squares, I looked at the ones that weren't whole. I would look at one and find another that was the same size and put them together to count as one square."

I then redirected the students' attention to the class chart, which looked like this:

Groups / Teams

	1	2	3	4	5	6	7	8	9	10	11
Area of circle with half the circumference (cm²)	4	13	5	24	11	28	10	16	22	31.5	99
Area of original circle (cm²)	17	52	20	99	44	108	32	39.5	73.5	14	26
Area of circle with double the circumference (cm²)	65	233	79	404	182	425	116	175	280	57	384

"Let's look at the data you gathered to see what we notice," I said. I saw that one group had recorded their data in the wrong boxes: "I see some data that doesn't seem to be written in the correct boxes. What do you think? Look carefully."

After a few seconds Brandon said, "Hey, I notice that the 99–26–384 doesn't look right. It seems like the 99 should be the area of the original circle and the 26 should be the area of the circle with half the circumference. What do you guys think?"

"Oh, yeah," Marcus agreed, "you're right."

I knew that each circle's area wouldn't increase (or decrease) by exactly four each time, because the children had approximated the areas by counting the squares. I was curious, though, whether the students would notice.

"Do you think the areas increased or decreased each time by exactly four times?" I asked.

"Ours did," replied Alex.

"Raise your hand if you think the area increased or decreased by exactly four times for every circle," I said, and about half the class did.

Nicole asked, "How could we find out?"

"You could divide the largest circle's area by the original circle's area to see whether they all increase by about the same amount. Then do the same with the original circle's area and the smallest circle's area," I suggested.

"Oh, I get it. Let's just round things and estimate," Brandon responded.

Nathan said, "Look at the first column—4, 17, 65. Seventeen is pretty close to 20, and 65 is close to 60. So the area increased by about three times. And 4 times 4 equals 16, which is one less than 17. So when you went from the area of the circle with half the circumference to the original circle, the area quadrupled, but when you doubled the circumference it was about three times greater. That's weird."

"Try the next one," I urged the class, wanting to encourage the children's mental computation skills.

"The difference between the first two in the second column, 13 and 52, is like 15 into 60. It's close to four times larger. And 233 is like 250, so 50 into that is 5," said Rachel.

Nicole wasn't pleased. "Wait a minute. We're not being exact enough. If we spent all this time counting the area as accurately as possible, it doesn't make sense to estimate. Let's use calculators."

"What will you enter into the calculator?" I asked.

Erin called out, "Easy. The larger area divided by the next larger area."

"Give us an example," I told Erin, to be sure the rest of the children understood her.

"Start with the number on the bottom row, like 233. Divide it by the number right above it in the middle row. See what you get. Then do the same for the middle-row number. Divide it by the one above it in the top row." I wrote 233 ÷ 52 = ? and 52 ÷ 13 = ? on the board to model Erin's instructions.

There was a quiet hum of noise as the children took out their calculators and performed the divisions. As students came up with answers I recorded them underneath the chart:

Groups / Teams

	1	2	3	4	5	6	7	8	9	10	11
Area of circle with half the circumference (cm²)	4	13	5	24	11	28	10	16	22	31.5	26
Area of original circle (cm²)	17	52	20	99	44	108	32	39.5	73.5	14	99
Area of circle with double the circumference (cm²)	65	233	79	404	182	425	116	175	280	57	384

4.25 4.0 4.0 4.13 4.0 3.86 3.2 2.47 3.34 4.0 3.80

3.82 4.48 3.95 4.08 4.14 3.94 3.63 4.43 3.8 4.07 3.88

"Do you notice any data that doesn't seem to fit?" I asked.

"I think the 2.47 is wrong," replied Catheryne. "It's so much lower than the others." The rest of the class agreed, and Luke suggested I cross the number out.

"In mathematics, that can be okay to do," I said. "Often when we look at statistics, there's a piece of data that is an outlier, like this. Ignoring it makes it easier to analyze the information that remains." I crossed out the number.

Nicole spoke up again. "Now that we've got these numbers, let's find out the average."

"How do we do that?" I asked.

"Add all the numbers and divide that number by how many numbers were added," said Nicole.

"Will you read them to us so we don't have to keep looking up at the chart?" Doug requested. I began reading the numbers.

When I finished, Nicole said, "Everybody divide the answer by 21 since there are 21 numbers."

The result was 3.94, and a lot of students called it out.

"Close to 4," observed Erin.

I wanted to refocus the discussion, since I suspected that several children had lost sight of why we were doing these computations. "What does the 4 tell us?" I asked.

Kathleen said, "It means that the area quadrupled each time from the smallest circle to the largest."

"Why?" I prodded. The class fell uncharacteristically silent. "Talk with a neighbor and see what you can come up with," I instructed.

After several minutes I called for everyone's attention. "Why does the area quadruple each time?" I asked.

David raised his hand. "I think you can fit four small circles into one large one when you double the circumference," he said.

"Why do you think that?" I probed.

"It just looked like it when we did it," David replied.

"Maybe if I can explain something similar it will help you make sense of why the area is quadrupling," I replied, placing an overhead Color Tile on the projector and turning it on.

NOTE The homework assignment *Double the Perimeter* is based on this same example and is effective when given after this activity.

"Here's one tile with an area of one square unit. What's the perimeter?" I asked the class.

"Four," several students called. I counted each side to verify their answer.

"Right. In this activity, the circumference doubled. Now remember that circumference is the perimeter of a circle. So if the perimeter of my square doubles, from 4 to 8, I need to add more tiles to make a square with a perimeter of 8 units. Let's see how I could do that." I arranged four tiles in the shape of a square.

"Have I doubled the perimeter?" I asked.

"Yes," the class chorused.

"What happened to the area?" I asked.

Several children gasped and Nathan shouted, "It's four! Four times as large! Just like what happened to our circles. Just pretend the squares are circles, and voilà!"

Several students called out, "Oh, I get it!"

"I think I get it. It's like you doubled the height and width," Nathan said.

I knew that my explanation was helpful for some children but not for others: teaching by telling doesn't guarantee understanding. I felt it was time to try to get an insight into what they were thinking. "You've heard several explanations for why the area quadrupled when the circumference doubled, and I'd like to know what you think at this point. On a piece of paper, write about two things: how you figured out the area of your circles and why you think the area quadrupled each time."

Rifka wrote: *To find the area of each circle, I used pi and the formula A = πR2. The area quadruples because if there were rays expanding from the center of the circle, there is room for them to quadruple when the circumference only doubles.*

JT explained his use of fractions: *If you know what fractions are then this activead well be easy because when you have a pice like this [Illustration] you will have to use it as a ½ or when you have a pice like this [Illustration] it will be a ⅓ or if you hav a pice like this [Illustration] it will be a hole.*

JT described how he used fractions to figure out the area of his circle.

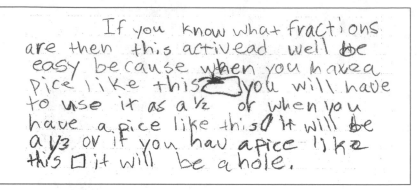

Marcus was matter-of-fact, if confused: *I just counted the hole squares and the parchail squares. I'm not sure why the area quadrupled but I think it's because you have to make the circle doubled and it is triple and the circle inside the big circle that you doubled.*

Nathan explained: *The way I found the area was I just counted the squares. When I saw a half of a square or a fourth etc. I added them together to make a whole. I realize there is a pi version to find it but I did not do that. I think the reason why the area quadrupled each time is because you double the highth and width.* He included an illustration:

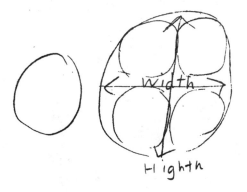

Erin disagreed with the idea that the area quadrupled: *The way I would find the area of each circle, is I would measure the diamiter. Then I would do the diameter times pi, that would give me the circumfrance. Then I would do circumfrance times diameter.*

I don't think the area quadrupaled. I think it went up by π each time. I don't know why I think this but it might be that the smaller area goes into the original area 3.14159 times.

Nick wrote: *My group counted each square and when we came to a partial square we would match it with another square like it. I think it quadrupled because each time you measure one/forth of circumference the area goes up a whole.*

Nick had a conjecture for why the area quadrupled, but he didn't explain the reasoning behind his idea.

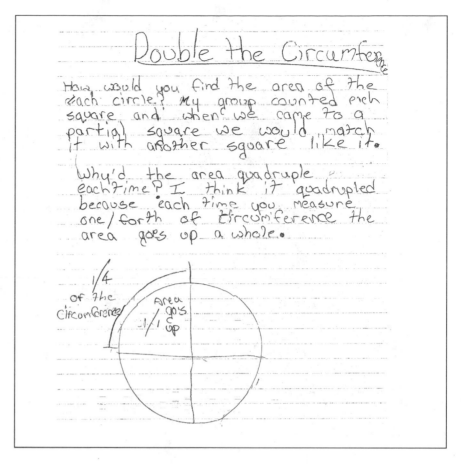

Malkia wrote: *Kristen told me how to do it. She told me to cut a piece of string and than double it and make a circle. How I know it was right is that I count the squares.*

I don't have a clue but I'm going to guess, because we counted it wrong.

Eric offered: *Brandon and I would take turns counting the squares and fractions of squares. We counted the fraction of squares by half, forth and third.*

Why I think the area quadrupled because a square just widens. But a circle widens and gets taller or else its a ovel.

ASSESSMENT The Garden Problem

This assessment requires children to apply what they have learned so far about relationships between area and perimeter to a new situation. Given three scenarios for enlarging the area of a garden, students write about which one makes the most sense, explaining their reasoning. Reading the students' papers helps reveal how they think and what they understand. The assessment should be used after children have worked on most of the activities in the unit; it allows you to see how students apply what they've learned to a new problem.

Holding a class discussion after students have written down their ideas expands the assessment into an instructional opportunity. Some children may change their opinion after hearing others' ideas.

To prepare for the assessment, write the following problem on the board, make an overhead transparency of it, or distribute individual copies for students to read at their seat (see blackline master, page 188):

The Garden Problem

Bill, Kathy, and John are working together to make the following garden plot larger.

Bill says, "We have to buy more fencing, because if we increase the area of the garden, our current fence won't go all the way around."

Kathy doesn't think so. "That's not true," she says. "We don't need any more fencing. We can move the fence we have into a different position and still make the area of the garden larger."

John disagrees with both Bill and Kathy. "I know a way that we can make the garden larger," he says, "and use less fencing than we currently have."

Who do you think is right—Bill, Kathy, John, all of them, or some of them? Explain your reasoning. Include sketches to explain your answer.

FROM THE CLASSROOM

To prepare for the assessment, I had made an overhead transparency of the problem.

"I'd like to learn more about what you understand about area and perimeter," I said to the class one morning, "so I have a problem for you to solve."

"I know a lot now!" announced Brandon.

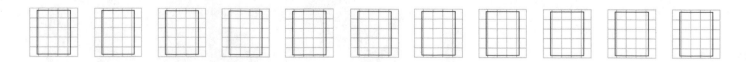

"Hold on, Brandon," I said. "After you solve the problem and write about your thinking, we'll discuss it. Then you can share what you know."

I turned on the overhead projector and read the problem aloud.

"I'm interested in knowing who you think is right," I told the class after I'd finished. "On a sheet of paper, explain your reasoning. Use sketches to help explain your answer. When you're finished, read over your paper to make sure that it reflects what you think and that you haven't left anything out. Also check for—"

I was again interrupted by Brandon. "Yeah, yeah, we know. Spelling, name, date, heading, that sort of stuff," he said and grinned.

"Exactly," I replied, returning his smile. "After you've handed in your paper, work on a menu activity until everyone is finished. Then we'll have a class discussion about the problem. Are there any questions?"

There were none, and the children started to work. The room became quiet as the students read the problem and thought about it. I circulated throughout the room to be available to answer questions or provide clarification, but today nobody asked for help. After about 25 minutes, all of the children had handed in their papers and were working on menu tasks.

I asked the class to put away their work and return to their seats for a discussion. When the students were seated and quiet, I asked, "What did you think about the problem about the garden? Talk about it with your neighbors." There was a lot of noise as the children compared reactions. After several minutes, I asked for the children's attention and called on Catheryne.

"This was hard, but I liked it because it really made you think," she said.

"How many of you agree with Catheryne?" I asked. Almost all the children raised their hand.

"I liked this problem," Rachel said. "It was just right. Not too hard and not too easy."

"I couldn't make up my mind," Erin said. "First I thought everyone was right, and then I decided Kathy was the most right. It was hard to know what to write."

I called on Alex next. "I thought it was really easy," he said. "It was obvious that Kathy was right."

The class erupted.

"No, she wasn't!"

"I thought she was right too!"

The children began to talk with one another again, clearly needing to share their thinking. I tried to insert some structure. "Talk at your tables about who you agreed with and why," I said. "Make sure that everybody has a chance to explain their thinking."

After seven or eight minutes conversation at most of the tables had stopped, so I asked the whole class, "Do you think we all agree who is right?"

"No," many children chorused.

"Why not?" I asked.

Mike, who was usually quiet during discussions, had a good point: "There are so many choices that make sense that I'm sure we don't all agree."

"Yeah, and this class hardly ever agrees about anything!" Sharnet added. Everyone laughed.

When the laughter died down I called on Rifka. She said, "I think Bill is right because let's say you wanted to increase the area a lot. You could buy more fencing to do that. But Kathy's idea is better because you could increase the area without buying more fence."

NOTE Sometimes the more assertive students tend to dominate conversations at the children's tables. Teachers need to try to prevent that from happening. It's helpful to remind the class regularly how important it is to hear everyone's point of view.

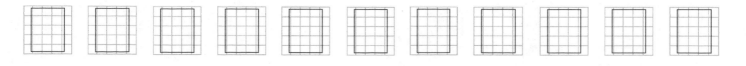

NOTE Some children are reluctant to participate in whole class discussions. Asking students to share their ideas with a small group respects their wish for not being singled out, yet provides you with needed information.

Kirsten said, "I agree with Rifka, because Kathy's method is easier to do. You save fence and you don't spend as much money."

Catheryne offered, "I think Bill is right that you could buy more, and Kathy's right too. So I collided their ideas. Bill buys more fence and they rearrange it the way Kathy suggests."

Rachel said, "I agree with Kirsten and Rifka."

Other students were waving their hand in the air, waiting their turn. I called on Kathleen.

"It was kind of a tie between Bill and Kathy for me, so I put both," she said. "It seemed like Bill knew that you could increase the perimeter to get more area and vice versa, so if you wanted to expand the garden I could see buying more fence. But if the original fence wasn't lying right next to the garden, let's say it was a foot or so back from the actual garden, then you could just expand into that foot without changing the area." I hadn't thought about that possibility and was reminded of how differently children can approach a problem.

Zak was insistently waving his hand. "I agree with Bill's way, because if you get more fencing you can make the garden longer and you'd have a bigger space."

I called on Eric next, who shyly shook his head. "I want Nathan to talk for me," he said. This was unlike Eric, but I didn't push him.

Nathan said, "We think Kathy's way is most logical, because you don't have to spend any more money. It's like the *Foot Stuff* problem, because like Kirsten discovered, you can have a bigger area with the same perimeter."

Erin added, "I agree with Kirsten's thinking too, because you could make the garden bigger with the same amount of perimeter, which is the most logical, like Nathan said. And obviously Bill's method will work, because you could buy lots of fence. But John's could also work too, which nobody has said so far. You could make a 3-by-2 rectangle and stick another tile on one of the sides, which would make the area bigger than what you started with and the perimeter smaller."

There was an immediate buzz of conversation.

"Some examples of what you mean would be helpful," I told the class. "Why don't we use the tiles on the overhead to explain?"

"Can I come to the overhead?" Eric asked.

"Sure," I responded, and turned on the machine.

Eric took six tiles and laid them on the overhead in a 1-by-6 rectangle. "Look," he said, "here's the 1-by-6 rectangle it said to start with. The area is 6 and the perimeter is 14, right?" He wrote $a = 6, p = 14$ next to the tiles.

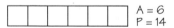

Many students nodded their agreement. "But what Erin, Nathan, and I saw is that you could make a 2-by-3 rectangle with the same six tiles. So the area is still 6, but the perimeter is only 10." Eric took six more tiles and arranged them into a 2-by-3 rectangle. He recorded the new area and perimeter.

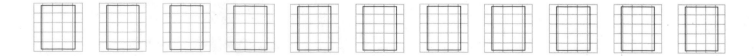

"So we made the perimeter smaller, but we didn't increase the area." Eric stopped, seemingly confused. He looked to Erin for help.

Erin jumped up and approached the overhead. She continued where Eric had left off. "Next we added a tile to the end of the 2-by-3 rectangle. What's the area?" she asked the class as she added the tile.

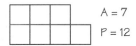

"Seven," several students called.

"Right. And the perimeter is 12, so here we made the original area go from 6 to 7 and the original perimeter go from 14 to 12. So this proves that John is right," Erin concluded.

She wrote $a = 7$, $p = 12$ and then she and Eric sat down. Again, the children all began talking at once.

"Hey, pretty amazing!"

"How did she figure that out?"

Rifka raised her hand and I nodded but signaled her to wait until the students were quiet.

"It might help people who don't get what Erin said to think like this," she said as she walked over to the overhead projector. I was pleased at how the students were taking charge of the conversation. I had spent a lot of time during the year teaching the children how to share their thinking in class discussions, and my hard work was paying off.

Rifka arranged the tiles into a 1-by-6 rectangle. "When you have a 1-by-6 rectangle, the area is 6 and the perimeter is 14, like Eric said. When you break it in half so you have two 1-by-3 rectangles, you can put them next to each other to make a 2-by-3. But when you do that, you lose the perimeter on the top and bottom." She drew an arrow to where the edges of the 2-by-3 rectangle met. "That makes the garden use less perimeter, even though the area is the same."

Many children applauded. However, I was still worried that some of the class might be having trouble following Erin's and Rifka's reasoning, so I said, "Talk at your tables about Erin's and Rifka's ideas. Do they make sense?"

A few minutes later I asked, "Does anyone have anything they'd like to say about Erin's and Rifka's ideas?"

Nathan said, "I've changed my mind about who's right. I never thought about it the way Erin said!"

Malkia had not contributed to the conversation yet today, and I was pleased that she now offered her idea. "Me neither! I agreed at first with Kathleen. I thought that if you just made the garden up to the border of the fence you'd get more area without using more fence. But now I think all three of them were right. Can I change my paper?"

"Sure," I said. "Anyone who wants to can. I'll give your papers back to you. Take some time to read them over. See if your thinking has changed. If it has, just draw a line under what you last wrote, and record your new ideas below it."

NOTE Children should feel free to share ideas and theories with their peers. A supportive learning environment is fostered when errors are seen as opportunities to learn rather than unfortunate mistakes.

The students' initial responses varied. Talon, Mike, Alex, Sharnet, Nathan, and Malkia initially agreed with Kathy, but Nathan and Malkia changed their mind after hearing their peers' ideas.

Talon's explanation was confused: *I agree with Kathy because you can use the same amount of fenceing if you want to change the area of the garden because I learned that if you change the perimeter of something, the area changes with it. That's why I agree with Kathy.* Underneath his written explanation he drew a 5-by-7 rectangle and figured the area correctly. Below this, he drew an irregular shape and wrote next to it: *Now the area of the square is about 44 squares when the perimeter/fenceing is changed.*

Mike's explanation, on the other hand, was clear and correct, though he didn't examine Bill's or John's ideas: *I think Kathy is right because I learned that you can change the area of something without changing the perimeter.* He drew two rectangles to explain his thinking:

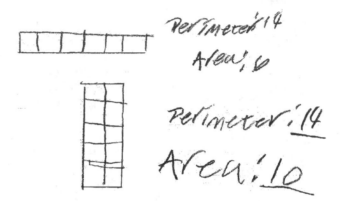

Sharnet wrote: *I think Kathy is right because I think that is away to make a garden larger by useing the same amount of fencing they have and move it to make the area of the garden larger. My other reson is if you do move some of the fence and make a bigger area it would work.*

Sharnet gave a partial explanation. Her sketch did little to explain her thinking.

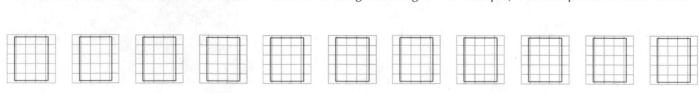

Malkia changed her mind but didn't explain why. She wrote: *I think Kathy is wright because you can [use the] same amount of fincing to make the area of the gordin larger. For example, You can put it as close to the*

edg as you can. Underneath a separating line, Malkia later wrote: *Now that we have had this deskution I think they are all right.*

Rifka changed her thinking after the class discussion.

> The Garden Problem
>
> I think that Kathy is right because if I make a 3x4 box,
>
> the perimeter will be 14, just like original garden, but the area will be 12, instead of 6, giving me more room to plant. I also agree with Bill, because if I make a 5x4 box,
>
> the perimeter will be 18, and the area

> 20. But if I use Kathy's way, it is not nessesary too buy more fencing. I do not agree with John because I do not think I can expand one thing while the other at the same time.
>
> Based on our discussion I think John is also right. I think this because if I have the original garden, I can make a smaller perimeter and bigger area by doing this: and adding one. The perimeter is 12 instead of 14, and the area is 7. The reason this happens is because when I put one part on top of the other, I lose the perimeter from the top of one part and bottom of the other.

Nathan was thorough in his first explanation and addressed Bill's, Kathy's, and John's methods, but he was not correct in all three cases. He wrote: *I think that Kathy's idea is right. These are the reasons I think that.*

Bill's idea which was to buy more fencing to make the area bigger is not true. You can widen the area but have the same perimeter just like we found out in The Foot Problem. *You can widen the area and make it larger but have the same perimeter.*

John's idea which was larger area less fence/perimeter is wrong. You can not make the area bigger with a perimeter less. The perimeter has to go around the whole garden.

Finally why Kathy's idea is true is because you can make the perimeter bigger but using the same perimeter there is the same space around the garden (the perimeter).

Nathan sketched a 1-by-6 rectangle and a 2-by-3 rectangle. He drew an arrow pointing to the 1-by-6 rectangle and wrote: *same perimeter less area.* Below that he drew a line and wrote: *After having a class discussion I realized that every single one of them is right. You can buy more if you want to but you don't have to. You can get bigger area with less fencing. I was very surprised when Erin showed the class that you could get a bigger area with less fence/perimeter.*

Rachel, Hilda, Catheryne, Rifka, and Eric initially agreed with both Bill's and Kathy's reasoning.

Hilda seemed to have no idea about the problem. She had joined our class in the middle of the unit and often seemed lost. I'm not sure how much I helped her. She wrote: *Well I think that Bill is right and Kathy because if they have less or a larger fens. because if you have less fens a you take biger steps and you will have a biger garden or buy a biger one.* She had drawn a 1-by-6 rectangle and written: *you have the regular fens*

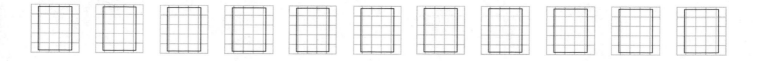

right hire. Below it she drew a 3-by-10 rectangle and she wrote: *Bill want a new fens like this one.*

I was surprised that Eric did not change his thinking after hearing what Erin said, since Erin was in his group. Eric had drawn a line under what he wrote initially and then written that he was going to "add a little about John," but changed his mind and erased it. What he first wrote was: *I think Bill and Kathy are right about the fence. But the only way Kathy can be right is if she expands the garden this way:*

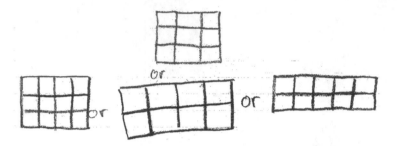

But with Bill all you need is money and you could make as big garden as you like.

I like Kathy's opinion better than Bills because I think anyone could have thought that up. But Kathy used her mind. Kathy's opinion was like The Perimeter Stays the same.

Four students—Neshey, Kathleen, David, and Zak—agreed with Bill. Neshey seemed to agree with John's reasoning as well, but she didn't explain why. She wrote: *I agree with Bill because if they have more fence place they can have more space to put the garden inside. But if they want to save money, they would have to go with John. But I still agree with Bill.*

Marcus agreed with John's idea but seemed confused: *I think John is right because if they wanted to increase the garden more they make it how long they wanted it then put fencing up. So I would go along with Johns idea.*

Erin and Kirsten both agreed that all three were correct, but Erin's paper did not reflect the careful thinking she revealed in her verbal explanation. She wrote: *I agree with all three of them because Kathy is right because you can do a 2 x 4 and that will have more area and the same perimeter.*

Luke was the only student to support both John's and Kathy's thinking. He wrote: *I think that John and Kathy are right. If you use the same amount of fencing you can make the garden the biggest it can be but if you don't use it all you can still increase the size of the garden. The original garden had an area of 6 square units and used 14 units of fence. If you do it this way it has an area of 8 square units but only uses 12 units of fence.*

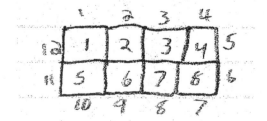

If you do it this way which also uses less fence like John said, you can get an area of 9 square units but also uses 12 units of fencing.

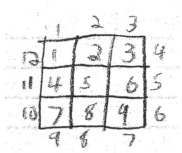

Now we move on to Cathy's idea of using all the fencing but increasing the area of the garden.

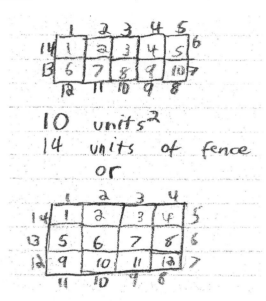

10 units^2
14 units of fence
or

which maximizes area to 12 square units but just uses the original 14 units of fence.

You could do Bill's way of buying more fence to increase the area but why? You could buy 2 more units of fence and make this garden but it has the same area as Kathy's, which doesn't require that you get more fence.

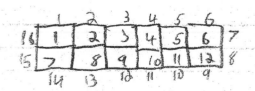

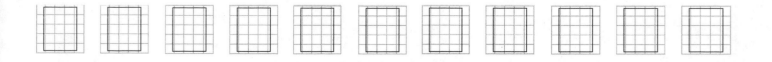

MENU ACTIVITY

The Perimeter Stays the Same, Part 2

Overview

The activity *The Perimeter Stays the Same, Part 2* extends the experience gained from *The Perimeter Stays the Same, Part 1* that different shapes with the same-length perimeter have different areas. It also challenges students to think about the properties of a shape with the maximum area and a shape with the minimum area, given the same perimeter. Students are led to the generalization that if a number of different shapes have the same perimeter, the ones that more closely resemble a square will have more area than those that are long and skinny. The activity relates to the whole class lessons *Spaghetti and Meatballs for All* (see page 54) and *Foot Stuff* (see page 41) and to the menu activity *The Banquet Table Problem* (see page 100).

Working in groups, students compare the three shapes they drew in *The Perimeter Stays the Same, Part 1*. Each group cuts out two shapes—the one with the greatest area and the one with the least area. All the cutout shapes are posted on a class chart, and the class then examines what is the same and what is different about them. They also think about what type of shape produces the maximum area and what type of shape produces the minimum area for the same-length perimeter.

193

The Perimeter Stays the Same, Part 2

You need: The other members of your group
The three shapes you created in
The Perimeter Stays the Same, Part 1

1. Exchange papers with someone in your group. Check your partner's shapes to be sure that each has a perimeter of 30 centimeters. Also check that the area of each shape is accurate.

2. With your group, examine the shapes and discuss what you notice about shapes with the same and different areas.

3. Cut out the shape from your group's papers that has the greatest area and the shape that has the least area. Post them on the class chart.

From *Math By All Means: Area and Perimeter, Grades 5–6* ©1997 Math Solutions Publications

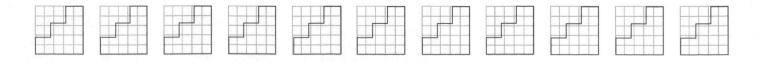

Before the lesson

Gather these materials:
- Student folders containing the work they completed in *The Perimeter Stays the Same, Part 1*
- Blackline master of menu activity for part 2, page 193
- One sheet of chart paper with a line drawn vertically to divide it in half, the left side labeled "Greatest Area," the right side labeled "Least Area"
- One sheet of chart paper for class discussion

Getting started

- Talk with the class about what they had to do in *The Perimeter Stays the Same, Part 1*.
- Tell the students to take out their work from part 1, show it to the others in their group, and see what they notice about the shapes.
- Hold a brief discussion about students' experiences with part 1. Ask the following question to guide the discussion:

  How did you make shapes with a perimeter of 30 centimeters?

  What problems did you run into while doing part 1?

- Present the menu directions.
- After the groups have posted their shapes with the greatest and least areas, hold a class discussion about the activity. First, ask the students to look for rectangular shapes on the class chart. Have students cut each of those rectangular shapes out and post them on a sheet of chart paper and record their dimensions, perimeter, and area. Post them in order, with a 1-by-14 first, then a 2-by-13, a 3-by-12, and so on. If any of these rectangles are not on the class chart, leave space so they can be added. Use the following questions to guide a discussion about the chart:

  What patterns do you notice?

  Why don't we need to add an 8-by-7 rectangle, a 9-by-6, and so on?

  How can you figure out the area of rectangles?

  What other menu activities are similar to this one?

- Ask the children to discuss what they notice about the areas of shapes that are not rectangles. Have them explain in their own words that the shorter, fatter shapes have greater areas and the longer, thinner shapes have lesser areas.
- Ask the children how this activity related to others they had done so far.

FROM THE CLASSROOM

I asked the students to take from their folder the work they completed for the menu activity *The Perimeter Stays the Same, Part 1*.

"Today I'm introducing the menu activity *The Perimeter Stays the Same, Part 2*," I told the class. "Can someone remind us what we needed to do in *The Perimeter Stays the Same, Part 1*?" Several students volunteered, and I called on Kathleen.

"Okay," she said. "You had to take a piece of graph paper with centimeters on it. And you had to draw three shapes that had a perimeter of 30 centimeters. You know, when you counted each little side there were 30 total."

"You forgot to say that you had to stay on the lines and that the shapes couldn't fall apart if you cut them out," Erin said.

"Oh, right," Kathleen agreed.

"And also, you had to write down the area inside each shape," Erin added. Then both she and Kathleen fell silent.

"Show your work to the others in your group and see what you notice about one another's shapes," I told the class. There was the sound of shuffling papers, and then the children began to comment on one another's work.

"That's cool!"

"Yours looks sort of like mine."

"Look at that one. It looks like a doghouse."

After a few moments I told the students to put their papers down. "How did you make shapes with a perimeter of 30 centimeters?" I asked. "What problems did you run into while doing part 1?" I knew that for many students doing this had been challenging.

Kathleen said, "When I was drawing, I started with a weird design. I'd count the perimeter and stop when it seemed close to 30. If it was more than 30, I'd erase some. I had problems with the first one. I kept stopping at 26, then I'd go over 30. I finally got it by biting into some of the corners." She used her hands to indicate cutting off a corner as the class laughed and several children mimicked Kathleen biting her paper.

"Who else 'bit' into their shape to adjust the perimeter?" I asked. Almost everyone had.

"It was hard, but I got help from my friends," Anfernee said.

"I liked playing around and seeing if I could get it," Catheryne added.

Marcus raised his hand: "Every time you had 25 squares inside, then the sides didn't have 30," he said.

The comment confused me. "Can you tell me a little more about that?" I asked.

"Well," Marcus said, "Every time I tried to make a shape with 25 I couldn't get 30 on the outside, you know, like you did when you showed us your shape." I realized that Marcus thought the assignment was to create shapes with a perimeter of 30 and an area of 25, like the example I had shown the class when I introduced part 1.

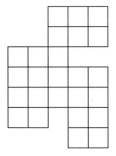

"Why'd you use the number 25?" Brandon interrupted brusquely. I realized I needed to speak privately with Brandon about pointing out errors tactfully, keeping others' feelings in mind.

"It was what Mrs. Rectanus used when she showed us that example. Hers had 30 on the outside and 25 on the inside," Marcus retorted defensively.

"Can someone clarify the activity for Marcus?" I asked the class.

David, who sat near Marcus, turned to him and said gently, "You needed to make shapes that had a perimeter of 30, you know, 30 on the outside. But the area—the inside—could be anything. It didn't have to be 25, like

NOTE Giving examples models possible approaches to a problem. However, examples sometimes limit children's thinking if they get the message that there's only one way to do something or if they think you're looking for a particular answer. Showing and modeling are helpful for many children, but be sure to check whether students interpret your examples correctly.

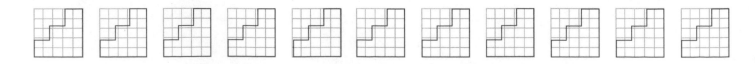

Mrs. Rectanus got." I was impressed that David connected the words *area* and *perimeter* to Marcus's concept of inside and outside. If David hadn't responded to Marcus as he did, I would have said something similar.

"Oh, I get it now," replied Marcus, smiling with embarrassment.

Marcus often needed one-on-one assistance completing tasks. Since he was among the least experienced students in the class as far as math went, I wasn't surprised by the difficulty he had understanding the activity directions. At the same time, contributing to a class discussion was unusual for him. He had taken a risk by sharing with his classmates what he had done, and I wanted to support him in that. I said, "Thanks for sharing your idea, Marcus. It was important to clarify what was expected, and I'm glad you brought up what you tried. Tell us more about what happened when you tried to make shapes with an area of 25 and a perimeter of 30."

"Well, I tried to make a shape like yours but just change it a little, so if I pushed in one side, I tried to pull out the other. But it didn't work," Marcus said.

I didn't want to penalize Marcus for misinterpreting the directions; I wanted him to work on the new activity. I felt that learning with his group was more important than redoing the previous activity correctly. "Listen to the directions for what to do for *The Perimeter Stays the Same, Part 2,*" I told the class. "Marcus, don't worry about drawing other shapes now. Share what you have with your group. If your group needs more examples, then you can draw another."

I posted an enlarged copy of the menu directions and presented them aloud. "In part 2, you need to work with your group," I began. "First, trade your sheet of shapes with someone else in your group. Count the area and perimeter of each other's shapes to make sure they are correct. Then, as a group, examine all of your shapes and discuss what you notice about shapes with the same and different areas. Finally, identify the shape with the greatest area and the shape with the least area. Cut them out and post them on the class chart under the appropriate heading." I pointed to the bulletin board where I had posted a sheet of chart paper. I had drawn a line vertically to divide the paper into two sections and labeled the left side "Greatest Area" and the right side "Least Area." "Any questions?"

Observing the Children

Hilda, Brandon, and Malkia ran into trouble trading papers. Brandon and Hilda traded while Malkia was intent on something going on in another group. When she turned back to her group, she demanded, "Hey—whose work am I going to check? Give me that!" and tried to snatch Hilda's paper out of Brandon's hands.

"Mrs. Rectanus, Malkia tried to take my paper," Brandon complained. I was sitting nearby and didn't respond, waiting to see how they would handle their conflict themselves. I didn't want to get involved if I could avoid it.

"Well, that's 'cause you weren't sharing it!" Malkia defended her actions.

"You were just staring out into space when I asked you where your paper was," Brandon replied angrily.

At this point Hilda interrupted. "Why don't you give Brandon your paper," she said to Malkia. "You look at mine, and I'll check Brandon's."

"Oh, all right," said Malkia grudgingly. I relaxed, and the three continued working.

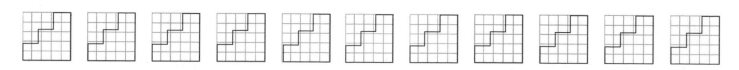

NOTE Malkia's confusion reminded me that children's initial understanding of a concept is often fragile. But confusion is a natural part of the learning process. It is important for children to have many opportunities to think about and verbalize ideas as they attempt to construct understanding.

"The area on this one is 20, not 25." Hilda had found an error.

"Let me see," Brandon said defensively, not quite believing Hilda could be right. He often didn't trust the reasoning and opinions of others.

Malkia interrupted. "Are we doing area or perimeter?" Her partners ignored her while Brandon carefully recounted the contested area.

"Oh," he said sheepishly when he realized Hilda was correct. He returned his paper to Hilda, and she changed the area on it. "We're checking both," he then told Malkia.

"Is perimeter on the inside or the outside?" Malkia asked, while Hilda pointed out another shape to Brandon for which he had miscounted the area.

"You're kidding me!" Brandon said, and again took the paper so he could recount.

"Is perimeter on the inside or outside?" Malkia repeated more insistently.

"Humph. Outside," replied Brandon, as he corrected the second area.

"Let's look at our shapes now to see which has the greatest area and which the least. Then we'll see what we notice," suggested Hilda. She, Brandon, and Malkia placed their papers in the middle of the table and began comparing them.

After Eric, Sharnet, Talon, and Nick's group exchanged papers, they reviewed the directions for the activity. Eric checked the area and perimeter of the single shape on Nick's paper.

"They're both right on this shape. Where are your other two shapes?" Eric asked as he handed the paper back to Nick.

"How many were we supposed to do?" Nick wanted to know.

"Three."

"Oh!" Nick said, and he quickly began making another shape.

Meanwhile, Sharnet told Talon, "Your perimeters are counted right, but you were supposed to make shapes with perimeters of 30, not 40."

Talon's paper reflected his difficulty in finding shapes with perimeters of 30 centimeters.

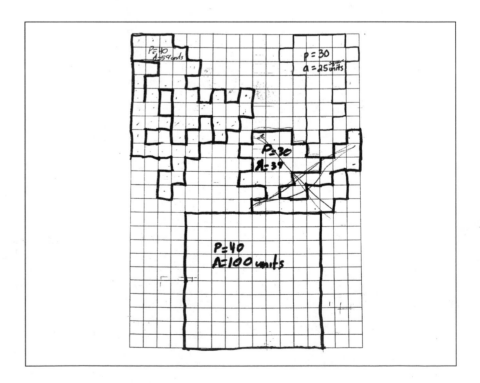

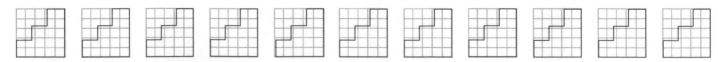

"Really?" said Talon. "No wonder it was so easy." He began drawing another shape on his paper. After a short time he said, "Got it!" and gave his paper back to Sharnet to check. In the middle of the shape he had written, *P = 30, A = 39.* Sharnet counted the perimeter.

"It's not 30 on the perimeter," she told Talon.

"Really? Let me see." Instead of counting the perimeter again, Talon randomly added a line to increase the perimeter.

"No, that won't work! You don't need to make it bigger, you need to make it smaller!" Sharnet cried.

"Humph," replied Talon, and he left his seat to get a new sheet of graph paper.

In another group, Nathan, Catheryne, Rifka, and Anfernee shared ways to keep track of the perimeter.

"Yours are right," said Catheryne to Nathan after they had exchanged papers.

"Yours are, too," replied Nathan. Both of them turned their attention to Anfernee, who was having difficulty keeping track of where he had started counting the perimeter of one of Rifka's shapes.

"I keep getting lost!" Anfernee said in frustration.

"Try this," said Nathan. "Use your pencil and put a little slash across each side that you count. Then you'll know where you started." Nathan took a pencil and slashed two sides on Rifka's shape to show Anfernee what he meant.

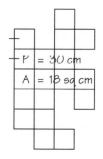

Anfernee visibly brightened and began counting with ease. Watching this interchange brought home again the value of having children work within a group. When someone has a question, someone else is usually able to answer it.

"Well," said Rifka when Anfernee had confirmed the accuracy of her shapes, "it looks like my long skinny shape has the least area, 14. Did anyone have a shape with less area?"

"No," replied Catheryne.

"Then let's cut it out for the class chart," Rifka said.

Nathan took out his scissors and began cutting carefully.

"What about the shape with the greatest area?" asked Catheryne. "I think the one that looks like a fat square is the biggest. What's the area of that shape?"

Anfernee had drawn the shape. He proudly replied, "Um … I think it was … yeah, it was 47."

"Is there another shape with an area more than 47?" Rifka asked.

After checking each shape, the group decided there wasn't, and Nathan cut out Anfernee's shape as well.

"It looks like long skinny rectangles give the least area and short fat ones have the greatest," Nathan observed.

Catheryne laughed, "I think they need to go on a diet," she said, sending her group into giggles.

In another group, Rachel looked at Luke's paper and commented, "You know, the ones with the biggest area are short and fat like a square."

Luke replied, "And the ones with the smallest area are tall and skinny."

"Yeah, like a twig!" Rachel replied and added this observation to her paper.

In his group, Luke found a shape with the greatest area.

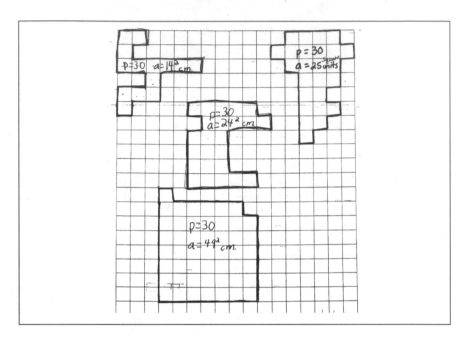

After looking at Luke's paper, Rachel wrote about the shapes that had the greatest and least areas.

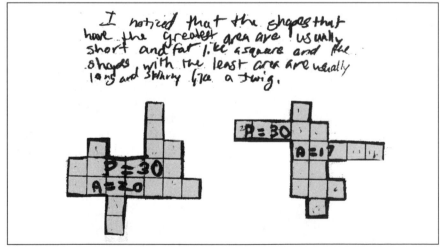

A Class Discussion Concentrating on Rectangles

A few days later, when all the groups had posted their shapes on the class chart, I gathered the students around the chart and began a discussion. I had placed several pairs of scissors, some tape, a marker, and a supply of centimeter-squared paper on a nearby table.

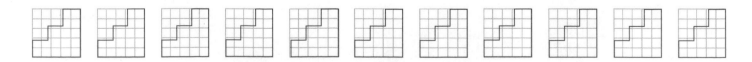

I thought it would be helpful for students to look initially at just the different-size rectangles that had perimeters of 30 centimeters to see how the area is greatest in the most squarelike rectangles and least in the longest, narrow rectangles.

"When I look at the class chart, I notice a variety of shapes, including several rectangles. Look at this one," I said, pointing to the 1-by-14 rectangle on the class chart.

David said, "I made that one. I got it by pushing in one side and pulling out the other to make it skinny."

"I got that one, too," several other children called.

"How many of you found the same rectangle as David?" I asked. About half the class had.

"The area of this rectangle is 14. I know that by counting the squares inside the shape. How do I know the perimeter is accurate?" I asked the class.

Brandon raised his hand. "You told us to check each other's shapes and we did," he pointed out. "But even if you didn't, you could just count around the outside. But I think it's faster just to count the long side and double it 'cause you have two sides, and then add on the ends."

"If we used your method, how would we count the perimeter of the 1-by-14 rectangle?" I asked.

"Easy," Brandon replied. "You go, 14 plus 14 is 28, then add one for each end—30."

"So we know that a 1-by-14 rectangle has a perimeter of 30 centimeters and an area of 14 square centimeters. Will someone volunteer to cut out that rectangle from a sheet of centimeter-squared paper? I'd like to begin a new chart of rectangles that have a perimeter of 30 centimeters, starting with the 1-by-14."

"I will," said Kirsten. She deftly cut the rectangle from the centimeter-squared paper and handed it to me. I taped it on a sheet of chart paper I had hung next to the class chart and labeled its dimensions and then recorded its area and perimeter.

"What other rectangles can be made with a perimeter of 30 centimeters?" I asked, sweeping my hand toward the class chart.

"The 3-by-12," Erin called, pointing to the rectangle on the Greatest Area side of the class chart. "I made that one."

"Would you cut another 3-by-12 out for us?" I asked Erin, who nodded and quickly began cutting. When she had finished I taped the rectangle to the chart paper underneath the first rectangle.

"What about the dimensions and area and perimeter of this rectangle?" I asked.

Many children raised their hand, and I called on Rachel.

"Well, it's a 3-by-12 because it's 3 cubes wide—oops, I mean squares, and 12 squares long. So the area is 36, since you have 36 little squares in it."

"And the perimeter?" I prompted.

"Use my method!" Brandon cried.

Looking at Brandon, Rachel grinned and said, "Okay. Twelve times 2 is 24, add the 3 on each end makes 6, and 6 plus 24 is 30." Brandon raised

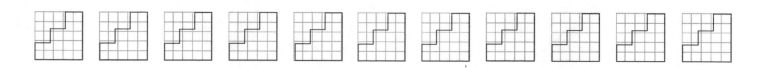

his arms in victory, and I recorded the dimensions and area and perimeter below the first rectangle, leaving a space for a 2-by-13 rectangle.

"Do you think we can make a 2-by-something rectangle with a perimeter of 30 centimeters?" I asked the children.

"Try a 2-by-13," Kirsten suggested.

"Why 13?" I asked her.

"Just a guess. The first one is something by 14, and the one we just did is something by 12, so I'm taking a guess and trying the number in the middle," she replied.

"Why not find out?" I said, handing her a sheet of centimeter-squared paper and a pencil. Kirsten took the pencil and confidently sketched and counted the perimeter of the rectangle.

"Yup! It works! Perimeter 30 and area 26," she said triumphantly. "Can I cut it out and post it?"

I nodded and handed her a pair of scissors and some tape. After Kirsten had taped it to the chart, I labeled the rectangle's dimensions and then recorded its area and perimeter. I wondered whether anyone had begun to see a pattern, so I asked, "Do you notice any patterns on our new chart that would help you predict what other rectangles will give us a perimeter of 30 centimeters?" Several children waved a hand in the air.

After waiting a few more moments I called on Luke, who excitedly said, "Look! It goes 1-by-14, 2-by-13, 3-by-12, and the next rectangle should be 4-by-11."

"What do you mean?" Talon asked.

"Look at the first number of each rectangle. It goes 1, then 2, then 3. So I bet the next will be 4. And if you look at the second number, it goes 14, then 13, then 12. I think it'll be 11 next," Luke replied.

David waved his hand and called, "Can I cut one out and see? A 4-by-11?" I handed him a pair of scissors and a sheet of centimeter-squared paper.

"I think I was right," Luke smiled, looking over David's shoulder.

"Does the pattern remind you of any other activities you've explored in this unit?" I asked.

"Oh, yeah! It's like the spaghetti-and-meatballs problem. It had a pattern, too," Luke said, handing me David's 4-by-11 rectangle. I taped it to the chart.

"Or the banquet table problem," added Rifka. "Remember how it went in a pattern? Anyways, if you count the perimeter of David's rectangle it's also 30. The area's 44."

I added the rectangle's dimensions and its area and perimeter to our lengthening chart.

"Let's take a look at the different rectangles we have so far," I told the class. "First is a 1-by-14. Then we have a 2-by-13. Kirsten made a 3-by-12, and David, a 4-by-11. What other rectangles would you predict will have a perimeter of 30, and do you see anything on the chart to help you? Talk to your neighbor." There was a buzz of conversation as the children discussed the question. After a minute or so I called for volunteers.

"If you follow the number pattern you started, you can tell which rectangle we still need," Erin said authoritatively. "Next is a 5-by-10, and so on from there."

"How will you know when to stop? At what point will we have found them all?" I asked. "Take a moment to think about that and discuss it with someone nearby." Again the room was filled with noise. After a few moments I called on Nick, who was waving his hand insistently.

"It's like that spaghetti-and-meatballs problem," he explained. "Remember how it started to repeat itself after awhile? I'm just not sure when it'll do that here. Can you continue the chart? Like, write down the dimensions of the next rectangles? Then I think I'll know."

I nodded. "Okay, everybody, what's next?"

"Five-by-10," several children called in unison, and I recorded it under the 4-by-11.

"Six-by-9."

I recorded it as well.

"Seven-by-8."

The chart was rapidly filling up.

Dimensions of rectangle	perimeter	area
1 x 14	30 cm.	14 cm²
2 x 13	30 cm.	26 cm²
3 x 12	30 cm.	36 cm²
4 x 11	30 cm	44 cm²
5 x 10	30 cm.	50 cm²
6 x 9	30 cm.	54 cm²
7 x 8	30 cm.	56 cm²

"Eight-by-7," several students called. I stopped before recording it on the chart.

"No, that's not right!" Rifka protested.

"It repeats!" This from Luke.

"You can't do that!" Erin added.

"Huh?" Marcus was confused.

"See," Erin explained. "we've already got a 7-by-8 rectangle. If we write 8-by-7, it's just the same. So we're done. They all repeat from there."

"A 7-by-8 rectangle is the same as an 8-by-7," Rachel reemphasized.

"Oh, yeah," Marcus said.

"So, do I need to add any other rectangles to the chart?" I asked the class. There was a chorus of nos.

"I'll cut out the ones we don't have yet," Rachel volunteered.

"I'll help," said Kirsten, and the two girls cut and taped the remaining rectangles to the chart. While they worked, I asked, "What is the area and perimeter of each of the rectangles the girls are cutting out?"

JT, who had been quiet during most of the discussion, jumped up. "The perimeters have to be 30. To get the areas, just multiply. Like 4 times 11 is 44. Five times 10 is 50. Six times 9 is … 54. Seven times 8 is …"

"Fifty-six." Mike supplied the answer for JT.

"Thanks," JT smiled

"What do you notice about the shapes of the rectangles and their areas?" I asked. "Think about that for a bit. Then talk about your ideas with a neighbor." There was much pointing and gesturing as students discussed their observations with one another. After two or three minutes I called for the students' attention.

"What do you notice?" I asked.

"The skinny rectangles have less area," Kathleen said.

"Yeah," Malkia agreed. "They look like they had the area squeezed out of them."

JT called, "They're like a string, long and narrow."

"There's hardly any area in the skinny ones," Eric agreed.

"Raise your hand if you found that skinny rectangles had a small area," I told the class, and about three-fourths of the class indicated they had.

"What can you say, then, about the rectangles with the greatest areas?" I asked.

Kirsten said, "The one that is almost a square has the most area, because you can fit the most inside it."

"Yeah."

"I agree."

Rifka noted, "I think it's interesting that when the sides of the rectangle are close to each other, like 7 is close to 8, you get close to a square number and you get the most area."

"This reminds me of the banquet table problem again," Eric said. "Remember the tables with the most tables inside them that you couldn't sit at? They were sort of like a square too."

NOTE Waiting before calling on a child gives all of the students a chance to think about the question. It also gives children the message that you want them to think carefully rather than respond quickly.

Talking About Shapes Other Than Rectangles

"Let's look at the results on your class chart again," I said to the class. "What do you notice about the shapes that aren't rectangles? Take a look at the chart and discuss with a neighbor what you see."

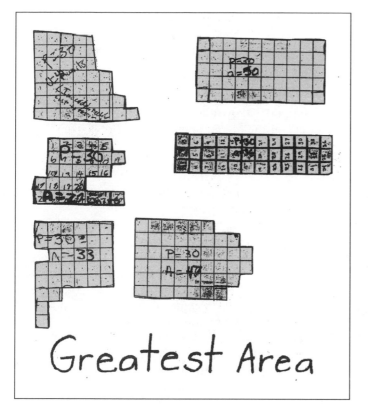

The class chart depicting the greatest and least areas.

I waited several minutes while the children looked over the chart and talked about what they noticed with each other. Finally I called on Catheryne.

"The shapes with the least area are long and skinny and weave in and out and the ones with the greatest area are big and fat and aren't very skinny," she said. Many other children indicated their agreement with Catheryne's assessment.

Malkia said, "The greatest-area side has one less shape than the side for the small areas."

"That's true," I said. "However, let's concentrate on what you notice about the shapes rather than how many there are." I didn't want Malkia's comment to deflect the children's attention from the mathematical ideas I wanted them to pursue.

Sharnet volunteered, "We're not really sure, but Hilda and I think that the greatest-area shapes are like more fatter and the least-area shapes are like more skinnier." Hilda nodded emphatically.

"Anfernee and I saw that the big shapes mostly have areas of under 30," Talon observed.

"And the little shapes are small and skinny and the largest are big inside," finished Anfernee.

Nick said, "The greatest-area shapes seem to be wide and the least-area shapes are longer." He used his arms to demonstrate.

"When you did this activity, the perimeter stayed the same for each shape. How is this activity like *Foot Stuff*?" I asked the class after everyone who wanted to had contributed their observations. "Talk with your neighbor." After a bit I called on Rachel.

NOTE By referring to other menu activities, I reinforce for the children that the activities and concepts in the unit relate to one another.

"In both activities the perimeter was always the same but the areas changed," she said.

"So the perimeter stayed constant in each activity?" I asked. Several students nodded.

I called on Nicole next.

"I think that the long skinny shapes in this activity look like our feet in the *Foot Stuff* activity," she said. "They're long and skinny too."

"And the square we made using the perimeter of our foot is like the big shapes in this activity," added Brandon.

"What do you remember about how the area of the foot compared with the area of the square?" I asked.

Many children raised their hand, and after a minute I called on Erin.

"The square was usually bigger than the foot," she said.

"You know," Rifka said, "I just thought about what Kirsten said when we were doing *Foot Stuff*. Here the ones with the least area are crammed in and long and narrow like our feet. And the shapes with the greatest areas are like the string perimeter squares from our feet." She stopped, struggling for words to express her thoughts. "They have a lot of space to come out. There's not much perimeter touching the squares on the inside of the big shapes. That's not quite right, but I don't know how else to say it."

Luke's hand shot up. "That gives me an idea," he exclaimed. "Look at the ones with the least areas. Look at the squares inside them. Can I come show something on the chart?" I nodded. Luke ran to the chart. His emotions were usually very apparent, and his enthusiasm for mathematics often enticed those students who might normally tune out to stay with him and pay attention. You never knew what Luke was going to say, and his comments often inspired interesting explorations.

Pointing to the 1-by-14 rectangle, Luke said, "Each square on the shape is taking up perimeter on *both* sides of the square. So when you make a long skinny shape, each square on it is taking up some of the perimeter, so you'll run out of perimeter faster."

"How does that help us with Rifka's idea?" I asked Luke.

"Well, she was talking something about how the bigger areas on the chart have more area inside them that's not touching the perimeter. What I'm saying is the opposite."

There was a hum of conversation when Luke finished, so I said, "Talk to your neighbor about Luke's idea. What do you think?" A moment or two later I called on Ann Maria.

"I think I follow what Luke is saying," she said. "It's like the narrow shapes have less area because some of that area is used on the perimeter."

"Exactly," said Luke. "And I figured out why the area is 14 when you make it skinny. Look." He took a piece of chalk and began drawing a row of 14 squares across the board. "The perimeter on this side is 14." Luke pointed to the top of the squares. "It's the same on the bottom. There are 14 squares there too. Fourteen plus 14 is 28, and if you add the two ends, the perimeter will be 30!" Luke was flushed with excitement.

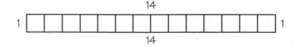

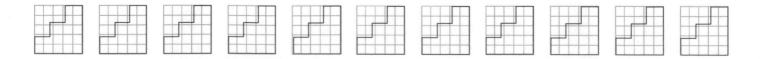

Nathan cried, "Hey, yeah! That's awesome! And it's got to be the least area you can get for a shape because it's the narrowest 1-times-something shape."

I got excited too. "Take a few minutes to think about the greatest area you can get with a perimeter of 30 centimeters," I said. "Talk to your neighbor after you think about it, and share your ideas." The class was silent for a few minutes, and then the student groups began talking.

A little while later I called on Erin, who came to the board.

"The shape with the greatest area, I think, will have an area of 50," Erin said. "See, I thought about our feet again in *Foot Stuff*. The greatest foot areas always looked like squares. So I thought next about square numbers. I knew that 7 times 7 is 49, which means the perimeter is 28." She sketched a 7-by-7 rectangle on the board, pointing out how she added the length of the four sides to get her answer. "If you add one square to the top row in the corner, you'll have an area of 50 and a perimeter of 30."

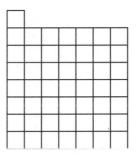

Eric's group were waving their hands frantically, and I called on Eric.

"We found a shape with a larger area, 56 square centimeters. All you have to do is go back and look at the 7-by-8 rectangle," he said. The rest of his group cheered.

I pointed to the 7-by-8 rectangle on the chart paper and said, "Come show us what you mean." Eric, Talon, and Nick approached the board.

"If you count the 7 squares on two of the sides, you get 14. Then count the 8 plus 8 and you get 16. Fourteen and 16 are 30, so this shape has a perimeter of 30 and an area of 56 square centimeters," Eric explained.

At this point, the students' interest appeared to be waning, and a change of direction seemed appropriate. "What did you think of *The Perimeter Stays the Same* as a menu activity?"

"Part 1 was hard," said Marcus, and the class laughed with sympathy.

Nicole offered, "It wasn't boring, and it was harder than it looked. Sometimes you used up too much perimeter and couldn't connect the ends, or sometimes you used too little."

During our discussion of the *Foot Stuff* activity, Kirsten had clearly explained that two figures (one regular and one irregular) with the same perimeter can have different areas. Now she said, "I thought it was too easy, because I had already learned that when you keep the perimeter the same you can change the area and vice versa. I knew right away that I'd be able to make shapes with a perimeter of 30 that had different areas."

Kirsten made shapes with areas of 27 sq. cm., 28 sq. cm., and 18 sq. cm.

"What did you do to challenge yourself?" I asked her, since Kirsten often pushes her own thinking. When she finds an assignment too easy, Kirsten sometimes asks me if she can change it in some way to make it more challenging for herself.

Kirsten thought for a moment, tilted her head, and shrugged. "Nothing, I guess," she replied with a smile.

Nathan also found the activity easy but nevertheless saw some positive aspects. "I think it was kind of easy but still challenged you, sort of like when you know you're going to be able to solve a puzzle. It's still fun to figure it out along the way."

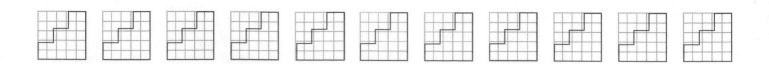

MENU ACTIVITY

Overview

Perimeter with Cuisenaire Rods

This menu activity gives students another opportunity to learn that shapes with the same area can have different perimeters and shapes that are more squarelike have shorter perimeters than shapes of the same area that are longer and thinner.

Working individually, with a partner, or in a group, students arrange four Cuisenaire rods—one red, two light green, and one purple—to create shapes on centimeter-squared paper. Children determine the perimeter of each shape they make and explore how to arrange the rods to get the longest perimeter possible and the shortest perimeter possible.

Before the lesson

Gather these materials:
- ■ An ample supply of Cuisenaire rods, enough so that each student, pair, or group can have a red rod, two light green rods, and one purple rod
- ■ An ample supply of centimeter-squared paper (see blackline master, page 195)

194

Perimeter with Cuisenaire Rods   I , P or G

You need: Cuisenaire rods
Centimeter-squared paper

1. Arrange one red rod, two light green rods, and one purple rod on centimeter-squared paper to make a shape that follows these rules:

   (a) When you trace around the shape, you draw only on the lines on the paper.

   (b) You must be able to cut out the outlined shape and have it remain in one piece. (Only corners touching is not allowed.)

2. Trace the shape and record its perimeter.

3. Do the same for at least four more shapes.

4. Experiment to find how to arrange the rods to make a shape with the longest possible perimeter and a shape with the shortest possible perimeter. Record these shapes and their perimeters.

5. Post your paper.

From *Math By All Means: Area and Perimeter, Grades 5–6* ©1997 Math Solutions Publications

---

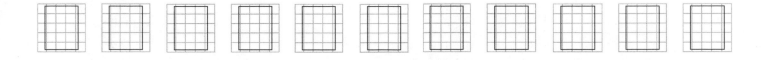

■ Blackline master of menu activity, page 194
■ An overhead projector, overhead Cuisenaire rods, and a transparency of centimeter-squared paper (optional)

Getting started

■ Give your students time to explore the Cuisenaire rods if they haven't used them before.
■ Present the menu directions. First, tell the students that they need four rods for this activity: one red, two light green, and one purple. They are to arrange these four rods into at least five different shapes and trace them onto centimeter-squared paper. Each shape must follow two rules: (a) when you trace around the shape, you draw only on the lines on the paper and (b) you must be able to cut out the outlined shape and have it remain in one piece (only corners touching is not allowed).
■ Demonstrate how to make and trace an arrangement, or ask a student to do so.
■ Tell the students that inside each shape they make they are to record its perimeter.
■ Ask students to experiment further to find the arrangement of rods that has the longest possible perimeter as well as the arrangement that has the shortest possible perimeter.
■ After the students have posted their papers, hold a class discussion. The following questions can help you guide the discussion:

What do you notice about the shapes posted?

How did you decide how to make different shapes?

How did different people record their shapes and measurements?

What other activities in the unit seem to relate to *Perimeter with Cuisenaire Rods?*

What was the shortest perimeter you found? the longest?

What do you notice about shapes with perimeters of 14 centimeters? with perimeters of 26 centimeters?

Why do all the shapes have even-length perimeters?

FROM THE CLASSROOM

"This activity is called *Perimeter with Cuisenaire Rods.* You may work on it alone, with a partner, or with a group," I told the class. "You'll arrange Cuisenaire rods into different shapes and figure out their perimeters. You'll post your paper so others can look at your results. Then we'll talk about the data."

I had posted an enlarged version of the menu directions on the board and put one overhead Cuisenaire rod of each color on the overhead projector. The children had worked with the rods before, but I had several new students whom I wanted to introduce to the manipulative.

"These are Cuisenaire rods," I said. "Tell us something you know about them." Almost everyone raised their hand, and I called on Ann Maria.

"They're different lengths," she said. "Some are long and some are short."

"Do you remember how long the rods are?" I asked.

She thought for a moment. "Oh, yeah. They go from 1 centimeter to 10 centimeters."

"Anything else?"

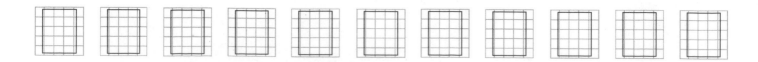

"Each color is a different length," said Luke. "The white one is 1 centimeter and the red one is 2 centimeters and it keeps on going like that. The orange one is 10 centimeters."

"They're really fun to play with!" added Catheryne enthusiastically. Other children nodded or murmured in agreement.

Kirsten offered, "You can use them for fractions. I remember when we used them to find fractions, like which rod was half of another, and a third of another, like that."

I removed the rods from the overhead, put down a transparency of centimeter-squared paper, and placed four overhead Cuisenaire rods on it: one red, two light green, and one purple.

"You need to use these four rods for the activity. That's one red rod, two light green rods, and one purple rod," I explained. "You'll arrange the rods on centimeter-squared paper to make shapes that follow two rules. One, when you trace around the shape, you have to be able to draw only on the lines on the paper. Two, you must be able to cut out the outlined shape and have it remain in one piece, so having only corners of centimeter squares touching is not allowed." I referred to the menu instructions I had posted. "Would someone like to try arranging the rods to follow these rules?"

Zak volunteered. He tried several arrangements as the students watched silently and finally decided on a J shape.

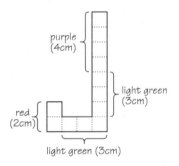

"How does Zak's arrangement fit the rules?" I asked the class. After a moment I called on Nathan.

"It fits on the lines, it's not hanging by a corner, and you could cut it out in one piece," he said.

I nodded. "After you arrange the shape, you need to trace around it," I said. Taking an overhead pen, I carefully traced around each rod in Zak's shape and removed the rods. "What's the perimeter of this arrangement?" I asked.

"Twenty-six," Erin announced confidently when I called on her.

"That's not right!" Nicole cried.

"Erin, why don't you come to the overhead and count the perimeter," I said. Erin carefully counted the units in the perimeter and confirmed her original total.

"Oops," said Nicole.

"That's okay, it's hard to count the small units from your seat," I reassured her. "For this activity, you have to make at least five different shapes that fit the rules, trace around each of them, and record the perimeter of each. After that you can experiment with arranging the rods to get the shape with the longest perimeter possible, given these rules, and the shortest perimeter possible. After you have recorded this information as well, post your paper on the bulletin board."

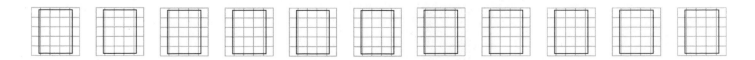

Observing the Children

Rachel, Catheryne, and Zak formed an unlikely group. The three sat together at a table but usually chose other partners when given a chance. Today, however, they worked well together. Rachel got a sheet of centimeter-squared paper for each person, while Catheryne got a supply of Cuisenaire rods, which she dumped onto the middle of the table. Zak read the directions to the activity aloud, and then they all began building a shape on their sheet of centimeter-squared paper.

"Can it be in a line?" Rachel asked. "I think the fatter or more bunched up it is, the less perimeter you'll get." Catheryne and Zak, engrossed in their own work, ignored Rachel. Rachel made a 4-by-3 rectangle with the rods and began counting. She recorded the perimeter inside the shape.

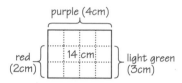

Rachel then rearranged the rods into a 1-by-12 rectangle and counted and recorded the perimeter.

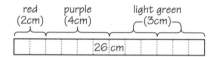

All of Zak's shapes but one had a perimeter of 26 centimeters.

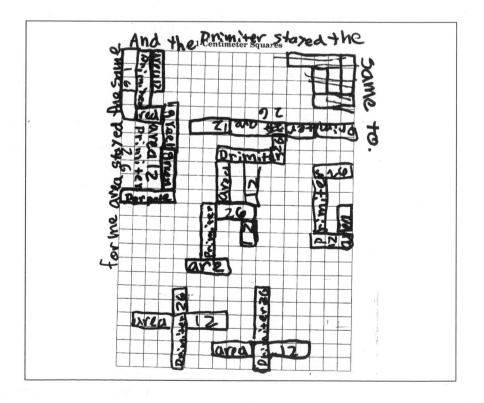

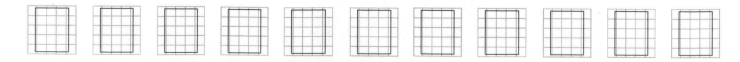

NOTE Sharing ideas with one another provides students opportunities both to cement their understanding of some ideas and to reconsider, extend, or revise their thinking.

"I think the long and skinny ones have more perimeter," Rachel commented. "Why?" Catheryne asked.

"Well, the first rectangle I made was a 4-by-3, and it isn't stretched out like this long one. The perimeter is smaller; it's only 14," Rachel responded. Catheryne leaned over and looked at Rachel's work.

"I agree that the biggest would be a big clump like this," Catheryne said as she duplicated Rachel's 4-by-3 rectangle, "But we have to experiment more."

Zak looked up from his work. "To me, all of them have a perimeter of 26," he said. On his paper Zak had written: *For me area stayed the same and the primiter stayed the same to.*

Rachel replied, "All of my shapes have an area of 12, except for one. Hmm." Rachel began recounting the area of that shape.

Zak said, "All mine have an area of 12."

"Aha! Counted wrong," Rachel announced. "Mine are all 12, too."

"Why do you suppose they all have the same area?" I asked the group.

"Easy," Rachel answered. "We're not cutting off the Cuisenaire rods, so the perimeter is changing but the area isn't."

"Not for me," Zak countered. "The perimeter is the same for all of them."

"Let me see!" cried Catheryne, as she took Zak's paper and began recounting the perimeters of each of his shapes. A few minutes later she said, "Not this one. It has a perimeter of 16." She pointed to a shape that resembled a stair step.

"Oh, yeah. You're right. I forgot about that one," Zak said.

Ann Maria and Kathleen approached the table where Zak, Catheryne, and Rachel were working. "Hey, guys," Kathleen announced, "our shapes always have a perimeter of 26!"

"Me, too!" said Zak. "Oops, I *thought* all of mine did."

"Not me," Rachel said. "I have a long skinny one that's got a perimeter of 28."

"Let me see that," Ann Maria said suspiciously. She recounted the perimeter of Rachel's 1-by-12 rectangle.

"No, it doesn't! Look, 12 plus 12 is 24 plus the two ends is 26," Ann Maria corrected.

"You're right," Rachel responded, laughing as she replaced 28 with 26.

"What's your shape with the smallest perimeter?" Ann Maria asked. "Mine's 16."

Catheryne, Rachel, and Zak immediately looked at their papers again.

"Sixteen," replied Zak. "I've got it, too."

"I have 14," said Rachel. She had written at the bottom of her paper, *The highest perimeter is 26 cm², the lowest perimeter is 14 cm².*

I noticed that Rachel had used an incorrect label. "Rachel," I said, "the notation you used, cm², is incorrect. Square centimeters measure area and centimeters measure length. Write centimeters instead, because perimeter is the length around the shape."

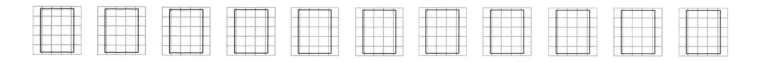

"Okay," said Rachel, and she corrected her paper.

"How'd you get 14?" Ann Maria demanded.

"Look," Rachel replied, "it's almost a square." She pointed to her 4-by-3 rectangle.

"Yeah," said Ann Maria. She immediately began sketching a 4-by-3 rectangle.

At another table, Rifka, Erin, and Kirsten were working intently. As I approached, Kirsten looked up and said, "We've found the smallest perimeter to be 14, and the largest is 26. We're trying to see if we can make every number between 14 and 26."

"How do you know that the shapes you've made are those with the shortest and longest perimeters?" I asked.

Erin replied, "You get the longest perimeter from making the longest skinniest rectangle you can, and that's a 1-by-12. And everybody knows that the more squarish a shape is, the shortest perimeter there is."

"How did you discover that?" I probed, ignoring her "everybody knows" comment.

"You can see it really easily in the *Area Stays the Same* shapes on the bulletin board," Erin answered.

Rifka joined in. "Since it was easy to see, we started wondering about the shapes in between 14 and 26," she said.

"What have you found out so far?" I asked.

Rifka replied, "We've found shapes with perimeters of 14, 15, 18, 20, 22, 24, and 26."

I knew 15 was wrong, because an odd perimeter was impossible. The perimeter of each rod is an even number since there are two of each length side. Also, when rods touch, an even number of sides is eliminated from the perimeter. However, I decided to allow the girls to continue with their investigation. Whether or not they discovered their error, I planned to address it when we discussed the activity at a later time. I moved on.

Rifka, Erin, and Kirsten tried to find a shape for each perimeter from 14 centimeters to 26 centimeters. They were unsuccessful. Later, they realized the perimeter of 15 was incorrect.

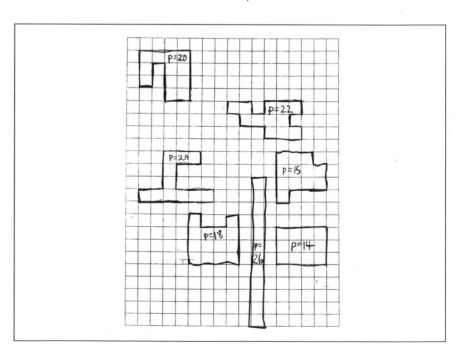

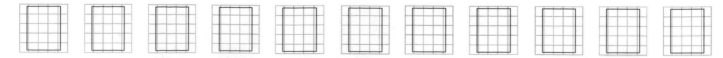

David and Mike found an efficient way to label the perimeter of each shape. They noticed that all of the perimeters were even numbers.

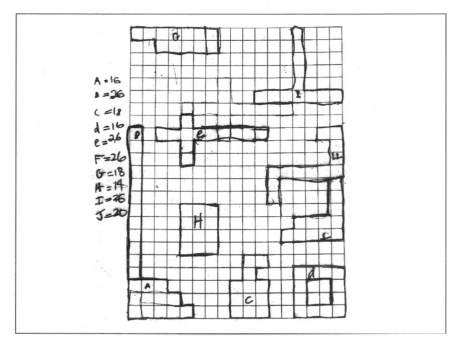

David and Mike had drawn a variety of shapes on their paper, labeled each shape with a letter, and made a key for each shape's perimeter.

"I don't get it. Every shape we've found has an even perimeter," Mike was saying to David as I approached their table.

"You might talk to Erin, Rifka, and Kirsten," I suggested. "They found an odd perimeter."

"Really?" said David. He and Mike looked at the girls with interest and then back at each other. Both started giggling.

"Uh, no thanks," replied Mike. "We'll just work on it ourselves."

To find the perimeter, Sharnet labeled and counted each unit.

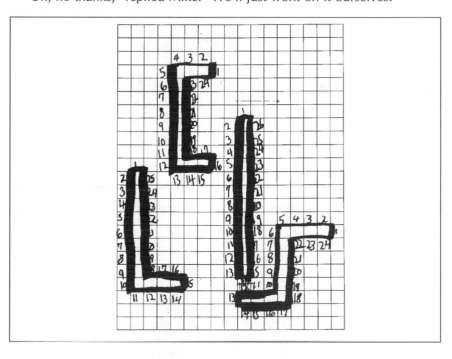

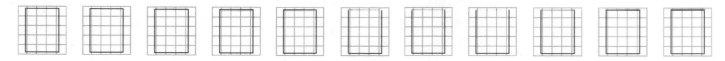

Sharnet was working alone today, to my surprise; she had never chosen to work alone in the past. (Later I learned the reason: Sharnet had had a fight with Kathleen, her best friend.)

"This is fun! I like this game," Sharnet remarked.

"What have you found out?" I asked her.

"I made four shapes so far. This one looks like an L, one is a C, this one looks like an I, and this is sort of like a Z," Sharnet answered.

I noticed that she had labeled every centimeter on the perimeters with a number. Sharnet had counted the perimeters in the banquet table problem the same way, and I was reminded that even though there are many ways to solve a problem, students often find one way that is most comfortable for them.

Brandon was working intently with the rods, using a ruler with inches marked on one edge and centimeters on the other.

"What are you doing?" I asked Brandon.

"This long skinny rectangle has the longest perimeter so far," he answered, grinning. "I'm using a ruler. Counting squares seemed really boring, so I decided to make it more interesting."

"How are you using the ruler?"

"I line it up, read what it measures, write it down, and go on to the next side. When I'm all done, I add all the sides together," he replied.

"Are you measuring in centimeters or inches?" I asked.

"Inches. I never thought about using the centimeter side," he answered.

"Give me an example of how you measure," I pressed. I was interested in his measurement skills.

Brandon said, "Take the long skinny rectangle. Measure one side." He laid the ruler along the 12-centimeter edge. "It's almost five inches long. Then measure the end." He used the ruler to measure one of the ends. "It's about a little less than half an inch. So 5 plus 5 plus a little less than half an inch two times for the two ends is 10 and three-fourths inches."

Brandon's answer reassured me. I knew that the units used don't matter as long as the student is consistent.

A Class Discussion

About a week later, I began a discussion about the problem. I had the children bring their chairs near the bulletin board so they could easily see the work they posted.

"What do you notice about the data we've collected?" I asked.

"Nicole's is pretty!" Sharnet cried. Nicole had used purple, green, and dark pink markers to color in each of the shapes she had found.

"There are a lot of shapes," JT noted.

"It looks like lots of people found the long narrow rectangle," observed Doug.

Nicole said, "Lots of the shapes look like letters. I see a G and an O and a J and an I."

"How did you make the shapes? Did you have a strategy in mind?" I asked. "Talk with your neighbor." I waited a bit, then called on Luke.

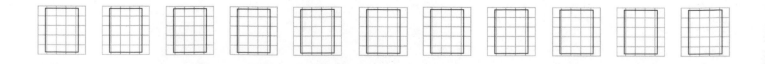

"I didn't really have a method in mind. I was working with Alex, and we just messed around and tried different things," he said.

"How many of you approached the problem the way Luke and Alex did?" I asked. Everyone but Nicole raised their hand.

Nicole offered, "I made a long narrow kind of shape, and then I changed it just a little bit, like turning the two-centimeter rod so it faced another direction."

"You mean you rotated it?" I asked, taking the opportunity to connect Nicole's description with standard mathematical terminology.

"Yeah. And then I kept changing the rods ever so slightly until my shapes got more and more squarelike," Nicole answered, pointing at her paper. The class seemed impressed.

"Did you plan to investigate the problem this way?" I asked Nicole.

"No, not really. After I did the first one, the idea just popped into my head."

"How did you decide to record what you found?" I asked the children. "There seem to be a variety of methods."

"Everyone had really different ways to record what they found," Nathan said appreciatively.

Nicole raised her hand and said, "Well, like Sharnet said, I used different-color markers to show where I put the Cuisenaire rods. I wanted it to be easy to see."

"It certainly is that. How did you keep track of the perimeters?" I asked.

"I wrote them on a separate sheet of paper," she replied.

Brandon asked, "Where is it?"

"I … uh, maybe it's in my menu folder. I guess I forgot to put it up," replied Nicole sheepishly.

"How else did you record?" I asked the class.

"Anfernee, Marcel, and I used a pencil to color in our shapes. Then we wrote the perimeter inside each little shape," Marcus said. He stood up and pointed at his group's work.

Neshey offered, "Hilda and I were working together. We outlined each shape and wrote the perimeter next to it. We also put the letter of the color of the rod inside each shape in the right position."

"I made a chart," said Catheryne proudly. "On one side I put 'Smallest' and I put the shape with the smallest perimeter. And on the other side I put the shapes with the largest perimeters." She had also miscounted several shape's perimeters, and labeled them in square centimeters.

Kathleen was sitting near Catheryne's paper. After looking at it for a moment she turned to Catheryne and quietly said, "That's a good idea. But I noticed that the shape in the 'Smallest' column isn't quite right. It's 16 centimeters, not 15."

"Okay, I'll fix it. Thanks," Catheryne said. She unpinned her paper from the board and headed to her table. I decided not to address the other errors Catheryne had made and made a note to myself to speak with her later privately about her work.

Kirsten said, "We put the number of the perimeter inside the shape. But then we discovered that this was going to be like the banquet table problem. There the perimeter changed too, depending on how you arranged the tiles. On this activity you had to arrange shapes too, but they were rods instead of tiles. The area was the same."

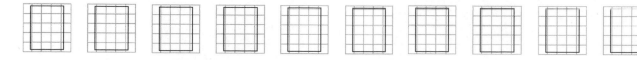

NOTE It is important to encourage students to make connections between activities and to give them opportunities to do so. Recognizing connections helps students carry over what they learned in one situation to other situations. When children consider how activities relate, they deepen their mathematical understanding.

"I agree."

"That's true."

"So the area stayed constant?" I asked, again modeling mathematical vocabulary.

"Yes," Kirsten replied.

"That's an interesting connection," I told Kirsten. Then addressing everyone, I asked, "What activities have we done that *Perimeter with Cuisenaire Rods* seems related to? Talk with your neighbor about this."

While the children were talking, I approached Catheryne, who was busy erasing the incorrect perimeter Kathleen had pointed out.

"I'm glad you're changing the perimeter," I said. "I noticed that some of your other perimeters need to be recounted also."

"Really? Like which ones?" Catheryne replied. I pointed out the shapes.

"Hmm," she said and began recounting the perimeter of one shape as I watched. "Oh! I miscounted, I guess." Catheryne wrote the correct number and *square centimeters* next to it.

"When you record the perimeter, you're not counting square centimeters but just centimeters, the length of one side of a square. So it's not accurate to write square centimeters," I explained. She smiled and erased the word *square*.

I called the class to attention and asked, "Which other activities does this relate to?"

"It reminds us of that *Area Stays the Same* activity, because you could get different perimeters there, too," JT offered. Several children applauded.

"What do you mean?" I pushed.

JT thought for a moment. "It was like when you cut the square, the string was either long or short depending on how you cut it," he replied.

"Can anyone think of any other related activities?" I asked, thinking specifically of the *Spaghetti and Meatballs for All* lesson and *The Banquet Table Problem*. The class was quiet.

"Let's look at something different then. When I count to three, softly say the number of the shortest perimeter," I said. "One, two three."

"Fourteen," the class chorused.

"How do you know?"

Rifka replied, "We knew that long narrow rectangles would give us the greatest perimeter and shapes that were more squarelike would give the least perimeter."

NOTE Having students explain how they figured something out tells them that you are interested in their thinking as well as the correct answer. After being asked to do this regularly in class, children begin routinely explaining their reasoning when they give an answer.

"And how did you know that?" I asked Rifka.

"From the *Area Stays the Same* activity. The squarish shapes always had the shortest string and the long skinny weird ones had the longest string," she replied.

"We noticed that too," added Eric. "The more smooshed the shape, like a ball or box, the less perimeter you get."

I wanted the children to focus on the data so I said, "Look at the work you did. Notice which shapes have a perimeter of 14 centimeters. What can you say about them?" The children began talking at once, with much pointing at shapes.

Brandon said, "They're all the same rectangle."

"Its dimensions are 3 by 4," Erin added.

Kirsten said, "See? Squarelike."

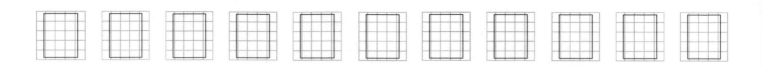

"All the area is inside, with not a lot touching the perimeter," Nathan observed.

"Let's look at something different, then. When I count to three, softly say the number of the longest perimeter," I said. "One, two, three."

"Twenty-six," the class chorused. Children immediately began looking at the shapes and pointing.

"What did you notice this time?" I asked. I called on Zak.

"The one with 26 is long and skinny," he replied.

Nathan offered, "It's a 1-by-12. The longest ones that are a 1-by-something will always give you the most perimeter because the area's all narrow, not fat like a square."

"There are others with 26 that aren't rectangles though," Rifka pointed out. "They're different shapes. They all have 1-by-something, but they go in different directions." She stopped, looking confused. "Did that make sense?"

"Yes," Kirsten responded to her friend. "It's like the ones whose perimeter is 26 have arms that stick out in different directions, but they still are made up of 1-by-something rectangles. That made this activity a little easy."

I wanted to draw the children's attention to how Rifka, Erin, and Kirsten had extended the problem. "Rifka, Erin, and Kirsten changed the problem a bit and investigated something different. Would you like to explain?" I asked the girls.

Erin said, "We decided to challenge ourselves and try to find all the perimeters possible between 14 and 26."

"What did you find out?" Brandon asked Erin.

She looked carefully at her group's paper and responded, "We found shapes with perimeters of 14, 15, 18, 20, 22, 24, and 26. We think because the shapes mostly have even perimeters, there has to be a way for 16, but we didn't have time to find one."

Kirsten had been looking at the papers hanging on the board while Erin was explaining what the girls had done. She blurted out, "Oh, Erin, there's one. Look at David and Mike's paper." She pointed excitedly to the shape they had labeled *d*.

"I knew there had to be one!" Erin replied.

"Yeah, but the shape doesn't fit the rules! It's got a hole in the middle of it!" Brandon exclaimed.

Nathan said, "But the menu instructions don't say that it has to be a solid rectangle like in the banquet table problem."

"But how would you count it? What's the perimeter?" Brandon quickly countered.

I hadn't anticipated this. As I often do when students disagree about a situation, I said, "Talk about this with your neighbor. How would you count the perimeter of that shape?" The noise level rose as the children argued passionately. After about five minutes I finally stopped the discussion. Some of the children had tuned out; others were staunchly restating their opinion.

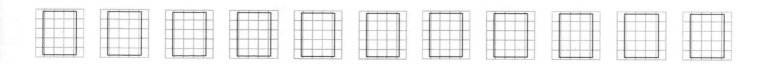

NOTE Being given in advance the order in which they will speak helps children listen to the conversation and reassures them that they will have a turn to share their thinking.

"One at a time now, let's hear what you're thinking," I said. "Remember to listen carefully to whoever is speaking and resist the urge to blurt out even if you disagree."

I looked at all those who had a hand raised and said, "Let's hear from you in this order: Nicole, David, Neshey, Luke, Ann Maria, Brandon, Nathan, and Rifka."

"I think it's okay to count that shape as 16. You're just counting the outside of it, and the 16 is the four sides of 4 on the outside," Nicole said.

David said, "I agree with Nicole."

"Me too. We made that shape and counted it as 16 also," Neshey agreed.

Luke said, "I disagree. If it was a building and you wanted to paint it, you'd have to count the sides in the middle so you'd know how much paint to buy." The children began talking about Luke's idea.

Ann Maria commented, "I was thinking about something else, but now I agree with what Luke said. That makes a lot of sense."

"Well, it sort of does make sense," Brandon conceded, "But it still seems unfair somehow."

Nathan replied, "I know what you mean, Brandon. It's like, we should have talked about this before we started the menu so we all agreed on the rules."

Rifka said, "What do you think, Mrs. Rectanus?"

"Actually, I hadn't thought about whether this might happen when I introduced the activity. But mathematicians consider the perimeter of a shape to be its outside boundary, and in that case the perimeter would be 16 centimeters. Also, usually we talk about perimeters of polygons, which are shapes made with only one solid inside region, without holes," I explained.

Mike had been listening quietly to the conversation. He raised his hand and said somewhat shyly, "I have a question for Erin. How did you get a perimeter of 15?"

"I counted it," Erin retorted.

"I think you should check it," Mike said, "because I think you made a small error."

Rifka counted quickly and blushed. "He's right, guys," she said. "It's 16."

"Then that proves our theory!" David cried. "We thought there was a way to make every even number from 14 to 26, and there is!" He and Mike raised their arms triumphantly.

"Why do you suppose all of the shapes you found have an even perimeter?" I asked the class. "Discuss this with your neighbor."

The children were getting restless and had few ideas to offer.

"The only thing I can think of is because the area is an even number," Nathan suggested.

Rifka said, "Maybe because the area is divisible by 2."

I asked the children to think about my question before tomorrow's math class and brought the discussion to a close.

In math the next day I reminded the students about the even-perimeter phenomenon.

"Every perimeter you found when you created shapes with the Cuisenaire rods was even, and I asked you to think about why that is. Take some time to share with your group how you thought about that question," I told the class.

The students talked animatedly for about five minutes.

"Well, what did you decide?" I asked.

Brandon began, "It has to be even because if you look at any Cuisenaire rod, it has four sides—"

"Six," Erin corrected him, thinking about the six faces of each rod.

"Okay, six when you're looking at all sides, but when you put it on the centimeter paper and trace it, you only see four sides, and four's divisible by two. And two's even. So that's why," Brandon concluded.

"I think it's because when you add up the areas of each of the little blocks you use for this, you get an even number," Luke explained.

"Tell us more about that," I said. I wasn't sure what he was thinking.

"Can I come up to the overhead?" Luke asked and I nodded.

Luke turned on the overhead projector and placed a red rod, two light green rods, and one purple rod in the center. Pointing to the red rod, Luke asked the class, "What's the area of this one?"

"Two," the class chorused. Luke wrote a 2 next to the rod.

"And this?" he asked, touching one of the light green rods.

"Three," many children called.

"So each of them is three," Luke repeated and wrote the numeral 3 next to each of the light green rods.

"Four," several students called, anticipating Luke's next question.

"And the area of the purple rod is four," Luke said, recording a 4 next to it.

"So 2 plus 3 plus 3 plus 4 is 12, which is even," Luke continued. "And no matter how you arrange the rods, the area of each individual rod doesn't change, so the area's always going to be 12."

"But so what? That's not even the question," Erin countered. "We're supposed to be figuring out why the perimeters are always even, not the areas."

"Right," Luke replied, unfazed by Erin's challenging tone. "Think about the ways you can put the rods together. They can go end to end, which will give you an even perimeter because you lose an even number of sides, two. If you lay them together the long way, you'll lose the side of the smallest rod times two, since it goes up next to one of the other rods." Luke pushed the red rod against a light green to demonstrate.

"See, you lose the longest side, two on the red rod and two of the light green sides. That's an even number of sides, four. So since the most perimeter you can get on a red is six and the most on a light green is eight, the difference is always going to be even," Luke finished.

"I get the taking-away-the-perimeter part," Rifka said, "But I don't see what that has to do with the area."

"Well, it doesn't really," Luke said. "But you see what I mean about the perimeters when you subtract them?"

Rifka nodded.

I wasn't convinced that Luke's classmates had followed his reasoning, judging by the looks of confusion and boredom on some children's faces, so I asked, "Who else has a way we might think about why the perimeters were even for this activity?"

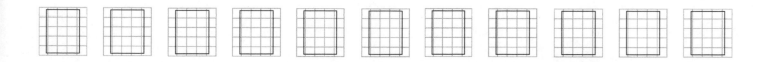

After a few moments of silence, Kirsten said, "I think it's because if you add up the perimeters for each of the blocks individually, they're all even. And whenever you connect them, you're always connecting one small side with another." She went up to the overhead and wrote the perimeter of each Cuisenaire rod next to where Luke had recorded its area.

"See, the red has a perimeter of 6, the light green is 8, and the purple is 10. They're all even numbers and when you connect them—" she pushed a red and light green rod together end to end "—you're losing two sides. So an even minus an even is even. Like 8 minus 6 is 2. All even," Kirsten finished to applause.

I ended the discussion here and had the children return to work on the menu.

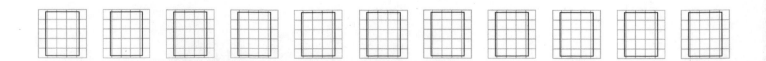

ASSESSMENT The Blob, Revisited

FROM THE CLASSROOM

In this assessment, children have the chance to revisit their thinking from an earlier assessment, *The Blob.* This assessment not only gives you insights into the children's progress, it also gives the students a way to reflect on their own learning.

To present the assessment, ask the students what they remember about the problem they did a while ago about the blob. Review the problem with them and then tell them that they will now have a chance to think again about the problem. Explain that as they are thinking, you'll pass back the papers they previously wrote. Then they are to reread their papers, see if they agree or disagree with what they wrote, and then write about what they think now.

When you review the students' papers, look not only at their current thinking but also at whether or not their ideas have changed. Keep in mind that learning happens over time and that partial understanding and confusion are natural to the learning process. This assessment can give you insights into the progress in children's thinking thus far in the unit.

"Who remembers anything about the problem we did a while ago about the blob?" I asked the class.

"Oh, I remember that," Ann Maria said. "It was this weird shape and it was a golf course or something and we were trying to find out how much sod it needed."

"That's close," I replied, turning on the overhead, on which I had placed a transparency of the problem. "We did talk about pretending the irregular figure was a golf course. You were asked to find the area of this 'blob.' Your friend suggested, 'Wrap a string around the perimeter of the blob. Then use the string to form a square, and find the area of the square. The area of the square will be the same as the area of the blob.' You had to decide if you agreed with your friend's reasoning, disagreed, or weren't sure. You wrote about your thinking, and many of you included a sketch."

There was a murmur of recognition.

"I'm curious about what you think now that you've experienced some activities to help you make sense of area and perimeter," I said. "First, think about how you would answer now. I'm going to pass back the paper that you wrote before about the problem. Reread it and see if you agree or disagree with what you wrote. Finally, write about this problem again and read it over to make sure it says what you mean." I wrote on the board:

1. Think about the problem
2. Reread your paper
3. Write

Then I continued, "Make any changes or corrections and then turn in both your old paper and your new one. You can work on any of the area and perimeter menu activities when you're finished. Are there any questions?"

"What if we totally agree with what we wrote the first time? Can't we just turn that paper in again?" asked Marcus, who avoided writing whenever possible.

"No," I replied. "If you find yourself agreeing with your original thinking, write what activities in the unit have more firmly convinced you that you are correct."

Marcus gave a resigned sigh and picked up his pencil, and he and the other children began to work.

The Results

In the initial assessment, 58 percent of students agreed with the method suggested for finding the area of the blob, 12 percent weren't sure about the soundness of the method, and 31 percent disagreed with it. At the end of the unit, after students had reread their first paper and wrote a second time, 33 percent of the class agreed, 8 percent were unsure, and 58 percent disagreed.

However, these statistics don't tell the entire story. A few children who were correct in their initial disagreement with the method reversed their position. Ann Maria was one. She wrote: *I agree with 'My friend' because if you do exactly what my friend said you will find out by yourself. It is correct because if you x's the length by width you will get area. How I know, well, if you do Bankquet table you will find out if you multiply length x's width you will under stand why my friend is right!*

Some students who had agreed with the method in the first assessment continued to agree. Talon was remarkably consistent in his approach. He wrote: *I agree with my friend's reasoning because I think that if you multiply the length times width you will be able to find the area of a shape. At the bottom is an example of my reasoning.*

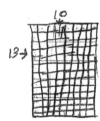

$$10 \times 13 = 103$$

Imagin that this rectangle is a paper filled with centimeter squares. The length is 13 centimeter squares and the width is 10 centimeter squares. 10 x 13 = 103, Now I just check to see if it is right. I was right it is 103 centimeter squares.

Kathleen firmly agreed with her original thinking.

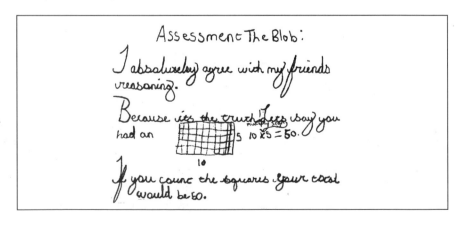

Neshey and Mike had both initially agreed with the reasonableness of the method suggested. When they revisited the assessment, both changed their mind and disagreed. Their reasoning, however, was erroneous.

Neshey wrote: *I disagree with my friend because, when she said to lay the string down around it to measure it and shape it to a rectangle and multiply length/width to find the area. First you don't make a rectangle you make a square.*

Mike contradicted himself: *I don't really agree with my friends reasoning (But it does work.) because it would be easier to make the string into a square because you only have to measure one part of the square to find out the dimensions.*

These results could have been disheartening. Yet I needed to remember that learning happens over time and with many experiences. I knew that some of these children were close to making sense of how the area and perimeter of irregular figures does and does not relate to the area and perimeter of regular figures.

However there were papers that showed that their writers had general new ideas about the situation. Kirsten referred to the activity *Foot Stuff: I disagree with my friend because when you keep the perimeter the same, the area changes. When you change the shape, keeping the same perimeter, into a shape that doesn't weave in and out or isn't long or skinny, but is bulky like a square or rectangle you get more area.*

These two shapes have the same perimeter but different areas.

Like in foot stuff, when you measured your foot and found the area in square centimeters, then puting the same perimeter into a square, they had different areas though same perimeter.

Another way to find the area would be to measure it in square centimeters, counting them all. That would be incredibly boring, but it's better than getting the wrong number.

After agreeing in the initial assessment, Malkia also referred to *Foot Stuff* as an activity that helped her understand the problem. She wrote: *I think it will work but I'm not shure. No because it would't work on our foot so it won't work on the blob. For example Emagin the blob as being the foot so of corse it won't work.*

For Luke, the menu activity *Perimeter Stays the Same* helped confirm his initial thinking: *I disagree with my friends reasoning because of perimeter stays the same, the menu item. In perimeter stays the same we figured out that long skinny shapes have more perimeter for the amount of*

area than squarish or rectangular shapes. The reason for that is that on long skinny shapes more of the area also uses the same perimeter. On big fat shapes lots of area is in the middle not using any perimeter. Therefor if you take the long skinny blob and make it squarish with the same perimeter it will have a larger area.

Erin commented on the difficulty of using square centimeters as a method for finding the area of an irregular shape. She was interested in finding an algebraic formula to make the process less tedious.

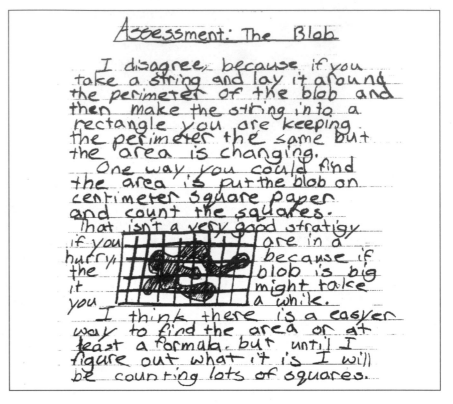

Assessment: The Blob

I disagree, because if you take a string and lay it around the perimeter of the blob and then make the string into a rectangle you are keeping the perimeter the same but the area is changing.

One way you could find the area is put the blob on centimeter square paper and count the squares. That isn't a very good stratigy if you are in a hurry, because if the blob is big it might take you a while.

I think there is a easyer way to find the area or at least a formula, but until I figure out what it is I will be counting lots of squares.

Catheryne's paper showed some understanding and some confusion. She might have understood that tracing the blob onto centimeter-squared paper and counting squares was one way to determine the area of the blob, but her paper did not give insight into that. She wrote: *I disigree because you need sqer sentem [centimeter] paper and add all the sqers. if you want you can thin yous the string for primitenr.*

I cheered Zak's response, although no one would say it was a wonderful piece of work. It did, however, show the change in his thinking since the initial assessment: *Im think that me friends are rong or right because if it is a blob it could also stretch on you and get the rong calcolations then other people. I'm not saying I'm right or wrong but that is the way I think.*

NOTE Experience has taught me that not every child will understand all that I want her to during the time I am her teacher. However, assessments such as this one help me see the progress that a student has made toward understanding concepts and ideas. I value learning about that growth. It informs me about my teaching practices as well as about my students' thinking.

ASSESSMENT

Area and Perimeter, Final Assessment

Too often the teacher or the answer book is the only evaluator of children's learning. Asking students to evaluate their own learning is a valuable way for students to reflect on their experiences and for teachers to learn how individual students responded to lessons and activities.

In this assessment, the children write down what they know about area and perimeter and tell how each activity helped them make sense of the ideas. They write about how area and perimeter are used in daily life and explain what they're still unsure about. Finally, students describe what they'd like to explore further.

Reflecting on what one has learned is abstract, and thus some children find it difficult to do. It requires them to synthesize their experiences and their learning. When students have a chance to talk about a topic before writing, they're generally more comfortable and have more to say. Holding a class discussion before this assessment serves as a helpful prompt. It's also important for this assessment to have the children's menu folders available for them, as well as the first *What Are Area and Perimeter?* assessment and any other work you might have collected.

Introduce the assessment by asking the class each of the following questions, one by one. Write the questions on the board or overhead as you ask and then discuss them.

1. What can you say about how the area and perimeter of different shapes relate?

2. What did you learn from the activities? Give examples.

3. When and where do people use area and perimeter in their daily lives?

4. What are you still unsure or confused about?

5. What would you like to explore further?

After you've discussed each question with the class, ask students to respond to them in writing. Encourage detailed explanations. Reinforce the purpose of the assessment by reminding the children that their responses will both help them think about what they have learned and help you understand their thinking. Tell the students that their writing will also be useful for you in preparing to teach the unit again.

FROM THE CLASSROOM

"It was close to the last day of school when we finished the area and perimeter unit. In preparation for the closing assessment, I had the children take out their menu folders containing all of their work for the unit, and I put on the overhead project the transparency on which I had recorded their initial ideas about area and perimeter.

"When we began this unit, I asked you what you thought area and perimeter were, and how they were used in real life. Here's what you had to say," I said as I turned on the overhead projector. "Take a minute to read what I recorded." The children read silently for a minute or so.

After most students were finished, Kirsten noted, "We didn't say a lot about how area and perimeter are used in real life."

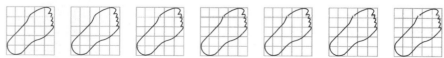

"That's true," Luke agreed.

Brandon said, "Wow. Our ideas seem so … babyish. Well, not exactly babyish, but I sure know a lot more now than I did then."

"I know," Rifka agreed. "It's like most everything up there is true, but I bet the list would be a lot different if we did it now."

"Do we each have to write a new list?" Marcus asked apprehensively. Marcus shied away from most things that required writing.

"No," I told him. "I have something else in mind. When we made this list, you explained what you thought area and perimeter are, but you didn't say much about how the area and perimeter of different shapes relate. What can you say about that? Take a few minutes to talk with your neighbor."

While the children talked with each other, I wrote on the board:

1. What can you say about how the area and perimeter of different shapes relate?

After several minutes I called the class to attention and said, "Who would like to start?" After a moment I called on Nathan.

"Simply put," he began, "area is inside an object and perimeter is around the object."

"Yeah, it's like area is the surface of something and perimeter is the length around it," added Nathan's tablemate Alex.

Nicole offered, "We decided that a relationship is that they can be used for the same reason. Like if you had a yard that was a certain dimension, say 9 feet by 12 feet, and you wanted to change the area of the yard without buying more fence, you'd need to understand about area and perimeter in order to know how to do it," she said.

"Yeah, it's kind of like when you use one of them you end up using the other!" Malkia said, pleased with her contribution.

"Tell us more about your idea," I prompted Malkia.

She hesitated. "Well, you can change them. Even if something has like the same perimeter, like two things or shapes, they might have different areas."

I called on Luke next.

"We have the scientific explanation," he began in a feigned serious voice. "I've prepared a statement." Luke picked up a piece of paper on which he had made some notes and stood up. "If you have a fixed number for one of them, you can manipulate the other to some degree by changing the shape." Luke bowed and sat down to applause.

"What do you mean?" I asked.

"If you have a shape and stretch it out, you can get a really long perimeter. And the opposite is true. We learned that in the *Area Stays the Same* activity," replied Luke, this time in his normal voice.

Kirsten said, "We think shapes that are more squarelike give you more area than shapes that are long and skinny like a line segment."

"Yeah," several children said. Others nodded in agreement.

"That's true when the perimeter stays constant or the same," I agreed. Then I said, "You really seem to have learned a lot about area and perimeter. What are some of the things you learned? Talk about that at your tables."

The room became noisy as children discussed my question. As they talked, I wrote on the board:

2. What did you learn from the activities? Give examples.

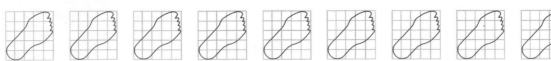

So far, the same children who contributed frequently to class discussions had been speaking up. Even though I knew students were talking with their table groups about the questions I asked, I wanted to encourage more children to share their thinking with the class.

After quieting the students I said, "What did you learn? Let's hear from someone who hasn't had a chance yet to contribute to the conversation." The usual hands were raised, but I called on JT.

"I learned new words," he said.

"Like?" I nudged.

"Circumference and diameter," JT replied.

"What did you learn about them?" I probed some more.

After a moment he said, "When we did *Round Things* I learned that circumference is the space around a circle and diameter is the distance between a circle."

Malkia said, "I just learned how to do it, you know, how to do area and perimeter. When we started this unit I didn't know anything!"

Malkia's willingness to say that she had been unsure at first seemed to give Marcus the courage to speak up.

"I learned how to play area and perimeter games," he said somewhat uncomfortably.

Mike raised his hand. "I learned that you can change the area without changing the perimeter," he said slowly.

"What helped you make sense of that idea?" I asked.

"It was when we made those shapes where the perimeter stayed the same," he replied.

This seemed to spark Rachel's thinking. She said, "I think that you can't have area without perimeter and you can't have perimeter without area. Sometimes when you change the area you change the perimeter and sometimes you don't, and vice versa."

Speaking in front of her classmates was always risky for Hilda, but she contributed also. "I learned that area and perimeter can change a lot, like a house can be different areas and different perimeters."

"Can you tell us a little more about that?" I asked her. Hilda shook her head no, and I didn't push her.

While Hilda was speaking, Luke was wiggling excitedly in his seat and waving his hand insistently.

"I learned that there are a lot of ways to make the same perimeter," Luke said when I called on him. "We did that in the spaghetti-and-meatballs problem."

Eric added, "Yeah, a lot of different rectangles fit 32 people."

"So shapes with different areas can have the same perimeter," I reaffirmed.

After several more students mentioned how certain activities had helped them, I said, "Let me ask a different question. Kirsten noticed that when we began the unit you didn't have much to say about who uses area and perimeter. Talk at your tables about how area and perimeter are used by people in their daily life." I wrote on the board:

3. When and where do people use area and perimeter in their daily lives?

"What did you come up with?" I asked after several minutes.

"Architects!" Nathan replied enthusiastically. "They need to know how big they can build a house and what shape each room can be."

"Rug companies too," said Erin. "You need to know about area and perimeter to know how much carpet to order."

"How about movers?" offered Kathleen tentatively.

"Explain how they might use area and perimeter," I prompted.

"Well, movers have to know how to arrange people's stuff in the moving trucks so it'll all fit," she answered.

"Good idea," said Sharnet.

Kirsten said, "I just thought of something. People who make garbage cans need to know about it. And people who make cups. Actually, anyone who makes anything round needs to know about area and perimeter."

Kirsten's comments were more about surface area and volume, making a leap to three dimensions. Indeed, the children seemed to be inspiring one another; their ideas were tumbling out.

Eric said excitedly, "Construction! Anyone in construction probably uses it all the time!"

Rifka offered, "If you wanted to put up a new fence, you'd have to know about perimeter."

"And area would help with a garden, and you'd need it too if you were laying tiles like in a kitchen or bathroom," Rachel commented.

Brandon added, "Sawmills. Workers cutting lumber need to know about area and perimeter." Brandon's father worked for a local paper mill.

After everyone who had wanted to had offered their ideas, I wrote on the board:

4. What are you still confused or unsure about?

5. What do you want to explore further?"

"Several of you have mentioned about how each activity helped you. I'm also curious about what you're still unsure about, and what you'd like to explore further. Take a minute to discuss these questions at your tables," I said. After a bit I called on Zak.

"I don't get it about pi at all," Zak confessed.

Talon raised his hand and said somewhat shyly, "I'm confused too. I know when you double the perimeter of a circle the area quadruples, but I still don't know why that happens."

Kirsten added, "I think I get that part, but I want to know more about pi. It's so interesting and there's so much I want to know about it."

Luke said, "I want to know about finding the formula for an oval. Counting squares seems like such a pain."

"I'm interested in learning what each of you got out of this unit," I told the class, "and in a moment you'll have a chance to write about it. Before you do, though, I'd like you to reread the work you did in the first assessment in this unit." I passed their papers back to them. "You should also refer to the work in your menu folders, and feel free to get up and read any of your work hanging on the bulletin boards," I continued, sweeping my arm around the room.

"Please address the questions I've listed on the board, and include as much detail as you can. I'm very interested in what you learned, and your comments will also help me when I teach the unit again in the future."

I was impressed with how seriously students took the assignment. The room was silent except for the sound of papers shuffling. "I can't believe how much my thinking has changed," Rachel whispered as I passed her table.

The children's papers gave me rich insight into their thinking.

Rachel wrote: *I can say that area and perimeter are like a team. The reason why I know this is because the area is inside a perimeter so without the perimeter there wouldn't be area and without area you couldn't have perimeter. Sometimes when you change the area you change the perimeter, but sometimes you don't and vise-versa.*

I learned that the shapes with more area are usually short and fat like a square (or a sandwich) and the shapes with less area are more long and skinny like a straw (or a carrot stick). I also learned that when you take a shape and change the perimeter into a different shape then you change the area. I learned about pi and how its 3.14 because we did a menu item and I found out that instead of quadrupling something it did it 3.14 times more. I also learned about what changes the area and perimeter and other things like that. I learned about circumeference and how the circumference is like the perimeter of something round.

Most of the activities helped me learn why the area changes the perimeter, what is the difference between perimeter and circumference, that circumference is different from reguliar perimeter because its for a circle not another shape + I learned about how when you double the circumference of something your almost quadrupling the area.

I still kinda don't understand some things about Pi like why it's 3.14 blah, blah, blah and stuff like that. The decimal I mean. Why its so long.

I think that people use area and perimeter in the real world doing stuff like figuring how much dirt they need for their garden, how many tiles builders need for a kitchen, or something like how much grass you need for a golf course.

JT wrote: *1. I learned how to use pi like when you do double the circumference you get four times as much area because when I did pi it looked like this*

this is the part that gives you four times as much. I am not so sure what the relationship is but I think it is pi because from what I heard it seems like it.

2. What I learned was how to get a better under standing of area and perimeter and I also learned that squares have a lot to do with it and I also learned a few new words like circumference is the space around a circle and diameter the distence in between a circle.

3. I think it helped me the most when I was doing banquet table problem because it should [showed] me that if youer table is just a line you will be able to seat more people and if yours is a square you will have less people seating.

4. I am a little unsure about what the relationship is and I want to dig depper in pi.

Eric noticed that each activity had the children actively engaged in doing mathematics rather than watching a teacher do it. He also noted overcoming his fear of exploring something he didn't understand.

5. I think they use it when making a house and making a car. I think house because you have to see how much area thers going to be and what will the permeter and when making a car they do almost the same thing.

> **Area and Perimeter**
> **Final Assessment**
>
> In my last years class we learned about Area and Perimeter. But I didn't learne as much as I did this year because we didn't have all the cool activeties like this year. I learned perimeter had a realy big relationship with area and I found that out in perimeter stays the same that perimeter was the out side of the area. Then I learned about circumference and how that's like a perimeter but aroud a **circle.**
>
> I learned what pi was it was real weird when I found out because every one I saw knew about pi. But then I learned that not every one knew and then someou told me that it was simple if you think about it. Like the diameter is always 3.4 of the circumference. I learned a whole bunch of stuff in this unit that it would take three pages. I used pi because it was the bigest discovery.
>
> The Activity help me in big ways — like instead of making us watch you do the work in a boring way you let us do ten activities. Each activity helped me by showing me area and perimeter in different ways.
>
> I'm not unsure about anything but I did want to explor pi but I didn't have the coureg to. I didn't think I was smart enough but now I know I am.
>
> There is area and perimeter in construcktion because people need to find the area of rooms and the hight os stuff. Carpenders use area so they can carpet a serten places in a room. They also need a perimeter because it can show them where to sfor carpeting. Reguler house hold people use it because what if the need to put in a dressor they will the area of that.

Alex commented on the value of persisting until something makes sense. He wrote: *I have lots to say about area and perimeter. Area is the sirfuce of something and perimeter is the length around it, however I have hardly anything to say about their realashship (I just found that out in case you were wondering).*

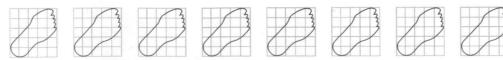

Each menu activity helped me by showing me what there is to see, for example in perimeter with cuisinare rods it was easy because I understood it and this activity let you measure area and perimeter.

There is nothing I am confused about or want to explore further.

People use area and perimater in their life. For example, when you go to the store you want the biggest watermelon, the biggest watermellon has the most area [I'm not sure whether Alex meant volume or surface area], another example when someone buys a house they want to know the area in square feet. One more example when you buy a plot of land for a garden you want to know the perimeter to make sure you are paying the right amount of money for the right amount of land.

Kirsten wrote about how each menu item contributed to various aspects of learning, including making conjectures and debating ideas: *Area and perimeter are connected by that they make up a shape. The outside of the shape is the perimeter and the inside is the area. Also, if you didn't have the perimeter, you couldn't get the area.*

When the perimeter stays the same, the area can change, so they have a big effect on each other. When the perimeter gets long and skinny the area goes down. But when you put the perimeter into a square like shape, the area grows. The area and the perimeter have a huge effect on themselves and what the shape looks like.

In Round Things I particapated in learning the "secrets" of π.

In Foot Stuff, I proved my theory that changing a shape into a square that had the same perimeter, the area would change. I learned there how to measure perimeter and how to explain your thinking to other people.

Double the Circumference helped me understand how to calculate the area and also how to think about why when the circumference doubles the area quadruples.

The Banquet Table Problem helped me understand that when you make the area long and skinny, the perimeter gets it's biggest. When you put the area into a rectangle, you can get the smallest perimeter.

Perimeter with Cuisenaire Rods showed me the same thing about area and perimeter, when I was trying to get the largest perimeter and the smallest perimeter.

I would like to explore π some more because there are so many things I don't know about it.

I'm not really sure who uses area and perimeter in their lives but I'll give it a shot. The people who make garbage cans need to know what size to make the circumference and the diameter. That also goes for people who make cups. When someone orders a chart of 15 x 11 paper, the people at the paper factory have to figure out what the perimeter would be to give the person the order. Area and perimeter are very important things in the real world and the mathematical world.

I had worried about Talon on and off throughout the year. His paper revealed what he understood about the area and perimeter of circles: *I think the relationship between area and perimeter is that both of them are together in a shape. Like square has a perimeter on the outside of it, and it has an area on the inside of it.*

I learned that if you try to double a shapes perimeter you end up quadrpleing it, and I learn a little bit about pi. I don't know what pi is.

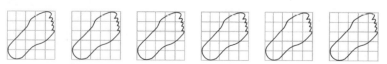

Doug used examples from science to explain his understanding of area and perimeter.

Each of the activitys help me understand the a circumference is the perimeter of a circle, and they helped me understand that if you try to double the circumference of a circle, you would quadruple the perimeter.

I think that I want to know more about pi. And I am still unsure of why if you try to double the circumference of a circle, it would of been quadrupled and not double like you wanted it to do.

I think that the people that use area and perimeter the most are carpenders and construction workers. Because carpenders would need to know how much area that their house that they are going to build would need and they would want to measure the perimeter to find out how much fenceing that they would need. And so do construction workers.

Area and Perimeter
Final Assessment

What can you say about the relationship between area and perimeter and how do you know?

Well, the relationship for the perimeter stays the same and/or root stuff works like a rubber band. To make it clear, I will give an example: Tie a strings end to it's other end, making a loop. Pretend the string is "perimeter" and the inside part of string (⊕) is "area". Now pull the string so it is skinny and the "area" gets smaller (⊖). This happens because you only have a limited amount of perimeter, and it isn't rubber, so it does not stretch. The "excess" string on the bottom gets "jerked" up, giving excess perimeter to be pulled, and the cycle goes all over again. This continues until the pressure cannot pull anymore, and the string is tight. The area slowly (or quickly) compresses, like air in a submarine tank. It has nowhere else to go, so it compresses until it has space to expand. And if you push two ends together it works in the opposite direction. It gets looser. But if you push too far, the area gets smaller.

What did you learn?
I learned a lot about pi, yet I haven't learned it all. I learned that pi the number is 3.14 159 26...... I also found that pi is found in any menu item involving circles. Pi will make math easier for me.

What are you unsure about?
Other than how to answer the first question, I am not stumped anywhere.

When/where do people use A/P in their life?
An example for when/where is when people get fake grass. They need to know the area to get the right amount of grass.

Nicole focused on how area and perimeter relate to each other.

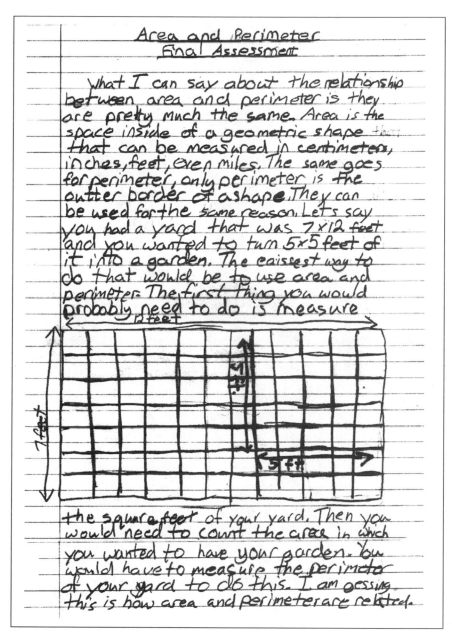

Area and Perimeter
Final Assessment

What I can say about the relationship between area and perimeter is they are pretty much the same. Area is the space inside of a geometric shape that can be measured in centimeters, inches, feet, even miles. The same goes for perimeter, only perimeter is the outter border of a shape. They can be used for the same reason. Let's say you had a yard that was 7×12 feet and you wanted to turn 5×5 feet of it into a garden. The eaissest way to do that would be to use area and perimeter. The first thing you would probably need to do is measure

the square feet of your yard. Then you would need to count the area in which you wanted to have your garden. You would have to measure the perimeter of your yard to do this. I am gessing this is how area and perimeter are related.

Luke was a student who craved challenges. He loved tinkering with math problems, and finding extensions for him as well as helping him learn how to extend his own thinking had been a focus of mine throughout the year. Luke wrote: *One of the relationships between area and perimeter is that if you have a fixed number for one of them you can manipulate the other to some degree by changing the shape. For example if the perimeter of a lawn has to be 10 feet you can make the lawn long and skinny with not as much area or you can make it more squarish and have a larger area. That is because if you make it long and skinny lots of the area inside is taking up perimeter, therefore making you run out of your 10 foot perimeter fast. If you make it fat and squarish then there is area inside that is not using up your limited amount of perimeter.*

I learned a whole lot about Pi during this unit. Pi is the relationship between a circle's circumference and its diameter. It is 3.1415925 so if you divide a circle's circumference by its diameter you will get 3.1415925.

Round Things helped me a lot because it first got me thinking about the relationship of a circles circumference and diameter which led to our very long and educational discussion about Pi.

Perimeter stays the same and spaghetti and meatballs also got me thinking about the concept I discussed earlier of long skinny shapes giving less area for more perimeter and bulky shapes giving more area for perimeter.

I want to explore finding a formula to get the area of an oval. I have a few theorys but I havn't had time to test them out yet.

I also want to find a way to get the area of an irregular shape with lots of bumps and curves.

Real Estate Agents would use area and perimeter a lot, I think, because they would want to find the area of a property to assess its value for a customer. They also would want to find the total floor area to assess value.

Painters would use area and perimeter to find out how much paint they need to paint a certain wall. They could also double or triple that number if they want to put on 2 or 3 coats of paint.

Floor refinishers would want to know how many new boards to get so they would find the area of the floor they were refinishing.

Last of all landscapers would find the perimeter of a yard to know how much fence to use on it.

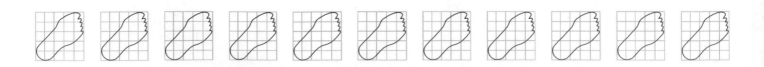

CONTENTS

HOMEWORK

The homework assignments have two purposes: (1) they give students additional learning experiences that can help them broaden and deepen their mathematical understanding and (2) they inform parents about the kinds of activities their child is doing in school.

There are five homework assignments, and each is presented in three parts:

Homework directions

The directions explain the assignment and include information, when needed, about what students should do in class to prepare for the assignment.

The next day

It's important for children to know that work they do at home contributes to their classroom learning. This section gives suggestions for incorporating the students' homework into classroom instruction.

To parents

A suggested note to parents explains the purpose of the homework and lets them know how they can participate. The mathematics instruction most parents had differs greatly from the learning experiences in this unit, and these assignments help parents understand what problem-solving mathematics instruction is and how it can help their child learn.

HOMEWORK

Hand Measurement

This homework should be assigned either after the whole class lesson *Foot Stuff* (see page 41) or after the menu activity *Double the Circumference* (see page 114).

Homework directions

Have students take home two sheets of centimeter-squared paper. On one sheet, they are to trace one of their hands, fingers together, and figure its area and perimeter. On a second sheet, they are to trace an adult's hand and figure its area and perimeter. Then they are to write about how these areas and perimeters compare. Students should bring the tracings and their writing back to class.

The next day

First, have students share their tracings in small groups, comparing methods and solutions. Then, in a class discussion, prompt the children to think about how this activity relates to *Foot Stuff* or *Double the Circumference.* Pose the following question: Does our hand area double between the time we are children and the time we are grown up?

Note: It's typical for children to look at two measurements and subtract the smaller from the larger as a way to measure the difference between them, which is different from seeing how many times larger or smaller one measurement is than the other. Encourage the students to think about these measurements as "twice as big" and "half as small."

Finally, ask students to predict whether the area of their hand will be the same if they trace their hand again, this time with fingers apart. Have them try this, and then have a class discussion about their results. While the area measurements should be about the same, the approximate nature of measurement will probably make for slight differences.

To parents

Dear Parent,

This homework assignment provides experience with figuring and comparing the area and perimeter of irregular shapes. In class, students decided on a method for finding the area in square centimeters of a tracing of their foot. On one sheet of the accompanying centimeter-squared paper, your child is to trace one of their hands, fingers together, and figure its area and perimeter. On another sheet, he or she is to trace an adult's hand and again figure its area and perimeter. Finally, your child should write about how the area and perimeter of the hands they measure compare. Please have your son or daughter take the tracings and their writing back to class.

In class tomorrow, we will compare methods for figuring these areas and perimeters, discuss how the area and perimeter of the hands compare, and talk about whether the area of our hand doubles as we go from childhood to adulthood.

As your child does this assignment, ask him or her to explain how he or she accounts for the bits and pieces of squares that are created by the irregular shape of the hands.

HOMEWORK

The Cost of Banquet Tables

This homework should be assigned after the discussion of the menu activity *The Banquet Table Problem* (see pages 100–113).

Homework directions

Assign students the following problem:

> If a banquet hall charges by the number of small square tables used, what's the least expensive way to seat 16 people at the same large rectangular table? 50 people? 60? 100? Any number?

The next day

Ask children to compare methods and solutions in small groups and then share their results with the class.

To parents

> Dear Parent,
>   This homework assignment extends the students' experience with the activity *The Banquet Table Problem*. Using inch-square tiles to represent square tables that fit together to make rectangular banquet tables, children investigated how many people can be seated at tables made from 12 and 24 tiles.
>   For homework, your child investigates how to seat 16, 50, 60, and 100 people at rectangular tables requiring the fewest number of small square tables and then thinks about what shape would use the fewest number of square tables for any number of people.

HOMEWORK

Results from Double the Circumference

This homework should be assigned after the discussion of the menu activity *Double the Circumference* (see pages 114-125).

Homework directions

Ask students to answer the following question in writing: What happens to the area of a circle when the circumference is doubled? Emphasize that they are to explain their reasoning.

The next day

Collect the assignments and read them to assess students' ideas. Because of their work in class on *Double the Circumference*, students should recognize that the area of a circle quadruples when the circumference doubles. However, they may not understand why. If one or more of the children's papers suggest ideas that would be helpful for others to hear, ask those students to share their thinking in a class discussion.

To parents

> Dear Parent,
>   In one of our recent math activities, students traced a circular object onto centimeter-squared paper and then found its area and circumference. The children then used string to form two new circles, one with a circumference half that of the original circle, the other with a circumference double the original circle's. They predicted the areas of these two new circles, measured the areas, and recorded their results on a class chart. As a class, we analyzed the measurements.
>   Your child's homework is to describe how the measurements of circles on the class chart compared and to tell why they think these differences occur.

HOMEWORK

Half the Square

This homework should be assigned after the students have had experience with several menu activities.

Homework directions

Assign students the following problem:

> On a sheet of centimeter-squared paper, draw two squares. One should measure 10 centimeters on a side, which means it has an area of 100 square centimeters and a perimeter that is 40 centimeters long. The second square should be about half as large, with an area of about 50 square centimeters. Measure its perimeter. Compare the perimeters of the two squares and write about what you notice.

> **Note:** There are several ways to draw a square with an area of about 50 square centimeters. One is to draw a 7-by-7 square, which gives an area of 49 square centimeters. Another is to connect the midpoints of each side of the 10-by-10 square to make a square that is half as large but rotated as shown.

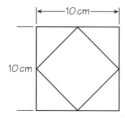

Don't tell students either of these ways; see what they discover.

The next day

Ask children to compare methods and solutions in small groups and then share their results with the class. If no one reports one or the other of the methods above, you may choose to show it. Whichever method is used to create the 50-square-centimeter square, the new perimeter measures about 28 centimeters. Although the area of the larger square has been halved, the perimeter of the smaller square is more than half the perimeter of the larger square—$^{28}/_{40}$ or $^{7}/_{10}$ or 70%.

To parents

> Dear Parent,
> In this homework assignment, your child explores what happens to the perimeter of a square when its area is halved. Your child is to follow these directions:
> 1. On a sheet of centimeter-squared paper, draw a square that measures 10 centimeters on a side. This square will have an area of 100 square centimeters and a perimeter that is 40 centimeters long.
> 2. Draw a second square that is about half as large and that has an area of about 50 square centimeters.
> 3. Measure the perimeter of the smaller square.
> 4. Compare the perimeters of the two squares and write about what you notice.
> In class tomorrow, your child will share his or her results.

HOMEWORK

Double the Perimeter

This homework should be assigned after the students have had experience with several menu activities

Homework directions

To introduce the homework assignment, draw a 1-by-1 square on the board or on squared paper on the overhead. Underneath the square, label its area and its perimeter: A = 1 square unit, P = 4 units.

A = 1 square unit
P = 4 units

Tell the students that you are going to draw a square with a perimeter that is twice as long; that is, with a perimeter that totals 8 units. Then draw a square with sides each 2 units long. Ask students what the area of this square is. Record underneath the square: A = 4 square units; P = 8 units. Point out that making the perimeter of the second square twice as long resulted in making the area four times as big.

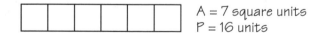

A = 4 square units
P = 8 units

Give each student a sheet of centimeter-squared paper to take home. Tell the students that for homework they are to investigate whether doubling the perimeter of a rectangle by doubling the length of each side always results in a new rectangle with an area four times as large. Ask them to test this for at least three rectangles, each one with different dimensions, by following these directions:

1. Draw a rectangle.

2. Record its perimeter and area.

3. Draw another rectangle in which the length of each side is twice as long as in the first rectangle.

4. Record the perimeter and area of the larger rectangle.

5. Write about how the areas of the two rectangles compare.

The next day

Have children report their experiences when they drew the rectangles and compared the areas. Any rectangle made by doubling the length of each side of another rectangle will have an area four times the size of the original. If this is not true for any student's work, have the class examine it. It may be that the student didn't double the length of each side. For example, a 1-by-3 rectangle has an area of 3 square units and a perimeter that is 8 units long.

A = 3 square units
P = 8 units

Doubling each side of the rectangle results in a 2-by-6 rectangle with a perimeter of 16 units and an area of 12 square units, which is four times larger.

A = 12 square units
P = 16 units

A 1-by-7 rectangle also has a perimeter of 16 units, which is double that of the original rectangle; its area, however, is only 7 square units.

A = 7 square units
P = 16 units

Relate this assignment to *Double the Circumference.* In that activity, doubling the circumference produced a new circle with an area that was four times as large, and halving the circumference produced a circle with an area that was four times smaller. Will halving the perimeter of a rectangle by halving each of its sides have a similar effect? Ask the class to investigate.

More for the next day

You may wish to pose the following conjecture for your students to consider:

> If you double the perimeter of any figure to make a larger figure of the same shape, the area of the larger figure will be four times the area of the smaller figure.

Then suggest that your students investigate this by experimenting with other shapes. The following illustrations show how this might be done for two different triangles:

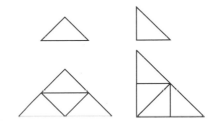

To parents

Dear Parent,

This homework assignment asks your child to investigate whether doubling the perimeter of a rectangle by doubling the length of each side always produces a rectangle with an area four times larger. Using the attached centimeter-squared paper, he or she is to do the following for at least three different-size rectangles:

1. Draw a rectangle.
2. Record its perimeter and area.
3. Draw another rectangle in which the length of each side is twice as long as in the first rectangle.
4. Record the perimeter and area of the larger rectangle.
5. Write about how the areas of the two rectangles compare.

In class tomorrow, students will present their results.

CONTENTS

BLACKLINE MASTERS

The blackline masters fall into several categories:

Area and Perimeter Menu

This blackline master lists the titles of all the menu activities suggested in the unit. You may want to enlarge and post this list as a class reference. There are a number of ways you can use it. For example, you can fill in the boxes in front of each title once you have introduced the activity and allow students to choose from among the marked activities during menu time. Alternatively, you can have students copy the list (or duplicate a copy for each child) and ask them to make check marks or tallies next to the tasks they work on each day. The possibilities are many.

Instruction Sheets

Two blackline masters provide instructions. One is for the whole class lesson *Foot Stuff*. The other is for the assessment *The Garden Problem*. You may enlarge and post these instructions or make copies for students to use.

Menu Activities

Six menu activities are included. (Reduced versions also appear in the "Overview" sections for the menu activities.) You may enlarge and post the menu tasks or make copies for students to use. (A prepackaged set of classroom posters of the menu activities is available from Cuisenaire Company of America.)

Recording Sheets

Blackline masters for centimeter- and inch-squared paper are included. Duplicate an ample supply of each of these and have them available for students.

Area and Perimeter Menu

☐ The Perimeter Stays the Same, Part 1

☐ Round Things

☐ The Banquet Table Problem

☐ Double the Circumference

☐ The Perimeter Stays the Same, Part 2

☐ Perimeter with Cuisenaire Rods

Foot Stuff

You need: String
          Centimeter-squared paper

1. Trace around your foot (with your shoe off) on a sheet of centimeter-squared paper.

2. Figure the area of your foot in square centimeters and record.

3. Cut a piece of string equal to the length of the perimeter of your foot. Tape your foot string, in the shape of a square, on the sheet of centimeter-squared paper.

4. Figure the area of the square and record the result.

From *Math By All Means: Area and Perimeter, Grades 5–6* ©1997 Math Solutions Publications

The Garden Problem

Bill, Kathy, and John are working together to make the following garden plot larger.

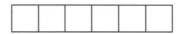

Bill says, "We have to buy more fencing, because if we increase the area of the garden, our current fence won't go all the way around."

Kathy doesn't think so. "That's not true," she says. "We don't need any more fencing. We can move the fence we have into a different position and still make the area of the garden larger."

John disagrees with both Bill and Kathy. "I know a way that we can make the garden larger," he says, "and use less fencing than we currently have."

Who do you think is right—Bill, Kathy, John, all of them, or some of them? Explain your reasoning. Include sketches to explain your answer.

The Perimeter Stays the Same, Part 1

You need: Centimeter-squared paper

1. Draw at least three different shapes on centimeter-squared paper, following three rules:

    (a) When you draw the shape, stay on the lines.

    (b) You must be able to cut out the shape and have it remain in one piece. (Only corners touching is not allowed.)

    (c) Each shape must have a perimeter of 30 centimeters.

2. Record the area of each shape you draw.

From *Math By All Means: Area and Perimeter, Grades 5–6*   ©1997 Math Solutions Publications

Round Things

You need: Something to measure with

1. With a partner or a group, find at least 10 circular objects. For each one, measure its diameter and its circumference.

2. Record your results on a chart.

Object	Diameter	Circumference
1.		
2.		
3.		
4.		
5.		
6.		
7.		
8.		
9.		
10.		

3. Look for a relationship between your diameter and circumference measurements that you could use to predict the circumference of a circle if you know its diameter. Write about what you notice.

From *Math By All Means: Area and Perimeter, Grades 5–6*   ©1997 Math Solutions Publications

The Banquet Table Problem

You need: Color Tiles
          Squared paper (1" or 1 cm)

A banquet table can be made by fitting together small square tables to make one larger rectangular table.

1. Arrange 12 square tiles into as many different-shape rectangular "tables" as you can. Draw your arrangements on squared paper and indicate the number of people each arrangement can seat.

2. Do the same for 24 tiles.

Extension:

The 100-Table Problem. If 100 small square tables are arranged into different-shape rectangular tables, what is the greatest number of people that can be seated? What is the fewest number?

From *Math By All Means: Area and Perimeter, Grades 5–6* ©1997 Math Solutions Publications

Double the Circumference

You need: A small circular object
Centimeter-squared paper
String
Tape
A partner or group

1. Trace the circular object onto centimeter-squared paper. Figure the area and record it inside the circle (___sq cm or ___ cm²).

2. Use string to measure the circumference of the circle you traced. Cut a piece of string that is twice the length of the circumference and use it to form a new circle on the paper. Tape the string in place. Predict the area of the new circle and then figure it. Record the area in the circle.

3. Discuss how you could describe the relationship between the circumference and area of each circle.

4. What do you think the area will be for a circle with a circumference that is half the length of the original circle? Predict first and then find out.

5. Record all of your data on the class chart.

From *Math By All Means: Area and Perimeter, Grades 5–6* ©1997 Math Solutions Publications

The Perimeter Stays the Same, Part 2

G

You need: The other members of your group
The three shapes you created in
The Perimeter Stays the Same, Part 1

1. Exchange papers with someone in your group. Check your partner's shapes to be sure that each has a perimeter of 30 centimeters. Also check that the area of each shape is accurate.

2. With your group, examine the shapes and discuss what you notice about shapes with the same and different areas.

3. Cut out the shape from your group's papers that has the greatest area and the shape that has the least area. Post them on the class chart.

Perimeter with Cuisenaire Rods

You need: Cuisenaire rods
　　　　　Centimeter-squared paper

1. Arrange one red rod, two light green rods, and one purple rod on centimeter-squared paper to make a shape that follows these rules:

    (a) When you trace around the shape, you draw only on the lines on the paper.

    (b) You must be able to cut out the outlined shape and have it remain in one piece. (Only corners touching is not allowed.)

2. Trace the shape and record its perimeter.

3. Do the same for at least four more shapes.

4. Experiment to find how to arrange the rods to make a shape with the longest possible perimeter and a shape with the shortest possible perimeter. Record these shapes and their perimeters.

5. Post your paper.

From *Math By All Means: Area and Perimeter, Grades 5–6*   ©1997 Math Solutions Publications

Centimeter-Squared Paper

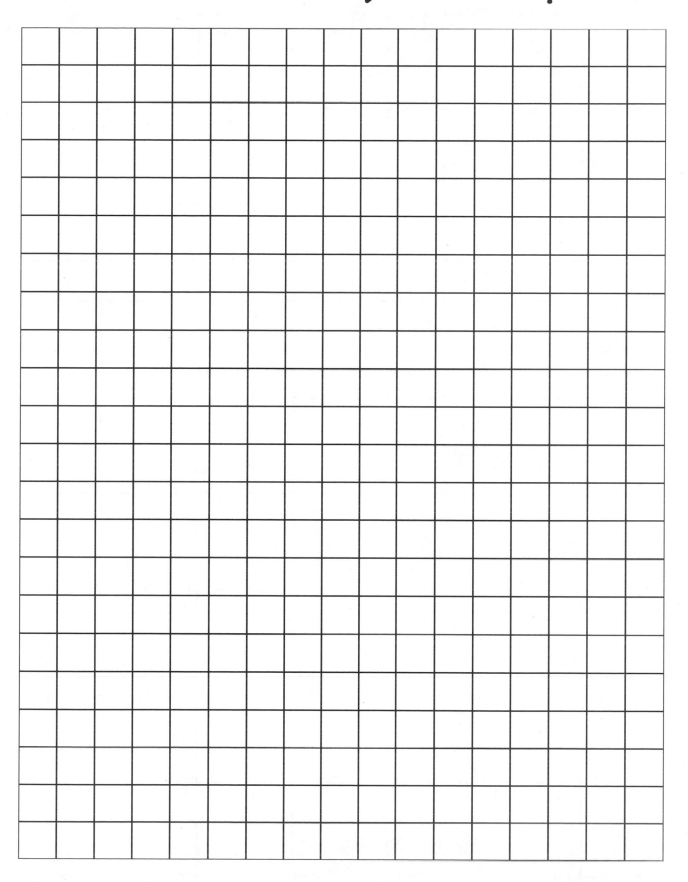

From *Math By All Means: Area and Perimeter, Grades 5–6* ©1997 Math Solutions Publications

Inch-Squared Paper

INDEX

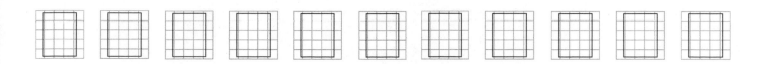

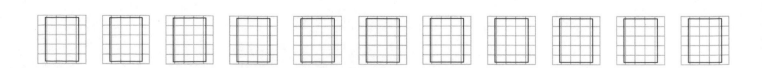